the **juicy** guide to
the city of
brighton & hove

juicy books limited

PO Box 3271, Brighton BN2 5AZ

▣ **gilly.juicy@virgin.net**

▣ **www.juicyguides.co.uk**

GW00586625

distributed by New Holland Publishers (UK) Ltd

Garfield House, 86 Edgware Road, London W2 2EA

▨ 020 7724 7773 ▣ 020 7724 6184 ▤ sales@nhpub.co.uk

credits

writen & compiled: Gilly Smith & Lucy Shuttleworth

edited: Jeremy Novick
sub editor: Jenni Moore

accommodation: Amanda Sangorski
clubs: John Chittenden & Lady Laverne
teenage & tweenage: Beatrice Warren & Hayley Sensicle
contributors: Barrie Alderton, Anna Arthur, Marina Baker, David Barrington,
Matt Blakestone, Phil Bodger, Dee and Paul Bonett, Simon Bradshaw,
Alexi Cawson, Rosie Davenport, Caraline Brown, Saul Dubow, Katy Gardner,
Gavin George, Joanne Good, Madeleine Gregory, Fred Hasson, John Hinchliff,
Julie Jennings, Emma Jowett, Andrew Kay, Philippa King, Jeff Mead,
Bryony Mortimer, Bill Parslow, Amanda Sangorski, Adrian Sensicle,
Hayley Sensicle, Peter Simmons, Paul Taggart, Louise Rennison, John Rowles,
Emma Shuttleworth, Mike and Gilly Webber, Clare Wilkinson, Sue Willett,
Lisa Wolfe, Kate Worth, Charles Wycherley.

cover photograph: Beatrice Haverich

colour map: ARKA Cartographics Ltd

design: Adrian Sensicle of moledesign   mole*design*@**cwcom.net**

dedication

for Jed, Elly and LouLou Novick, and Phil, Sofia and Lara Bodger

in memory of Martin Shuttleworth

publication details

First published in Great Britain in 2001 by
Juicy Books Ltd, PO Box 3271, Brighton BN2 5AZ

A catalogue record for this book is available from the British Library

ISBN 1-903320-01-1

cover, text & juicybooks logo designs © 2001 Adrian Sensicle / mole design

printed in England by zetacolour, East Sussex, UK

Gilly Smith is the author of "The Mediterranean Health Diet" (Headline), "Fibrenetics" (Fourth Estate), "Tantra and the Tao", (Robinson) and "Australia: New Food from the New World" (Andre Deutsch). Working with chefs such as Marco Pierre White, Jean-Christophe Novelli, and Pierre Koffman, on the Mediterranean Diet, and Australia's top 22 chefs in her last book, she has developed a critical edge to her love of good food. She left a career in TV and radio for publishing, and continues to write for the national press.

She moved to Brighton in December 1997 after 17 years in London. She lives in Kemp Town with author Jeremy Novick, their 2 small daughters and 2 dogs.

Lucy Shuttleworth worked in publishing as a press officer for Dorling Kindersley and as a publicity consultant and managing art editor for Simon and Schuster before becoming a script consultant for feature film production and distribution companies.

Lucy and her partner, Phil Bodger, moved to Brighton five years ago from London. Known as the local Yellow Pages, Lucy has come to know Brighton intimately in the five years she has been here. From the most obscure art shops to the best second hand bargains, the tastiest breakfasts to the coolest bars, Lucy is Brighton's local expert.

key to symbols used in text

📞 *telephone number*

📱 *mobile phone number*

📠 *fax number*

🖥 *internet access/web site/email address*

j *award winner/runner-up, latest juicy awards 2000*

introduction

The City of Brighton and Hove. How grand, how grown up, how typically Brighton to give itself a double barrelled name and parade its gold chain to the world, before nicking behind the bike shed to strip down to its latex bikini once the sun has gone down and the politicians have gone home. Will it change us, this city status? It might bring some more pennies into the coffers, and add a bit more kudos to the business community, but Brighton will still be the lounge lizard by day, and by night, the arty, tarty glamourpuss of a town that it always was. And whoever reckons that we'll start calling the place Brighton and Hove has probably been sitting too near to those nice spin doctors in Whitehall. Brighton might put a protective arm around its more pedestrian twin sister for the cameras, but only in that confident way that the shinier more beautiful sibling can afford to do. Hove doesn't care. Listen, if it wasn't separated by the beneficent Peace Statue, you think it would get city status? Have you been to Blatchington Road?

Meanwhile, the out of towners continue to make their way south, seduced by the architecture, the cafes, the people and the idea of ending their day watching the sun set across the English Channel. The celebrities are also packing their suitcases and scanning the property pages; Noel Gallagher and Posh and Becks have just bought into the city which never sleeps, probably because Brighton's and Hove's attitude of "vive la difference" is built into the bricks and mortar here. Zoë and Norman may live in a castle on their own private beach (in Hove actually) but if anyone bumped into them in Mothercare, they'd be more likely to discuss the merits of a three-wheeler than faint in star-struck heap. It's a live and let live kind of place which somehow makes people feel proud to call it their own. Endlessly accepting, always bursting with new ideas, ever evolving, life in Brighton - and Hove - just gets better and better.

It's this spirit that we've tried to pack into the pages of this updated version of the Juicy Guide. It's a guide for locals and anyone who wants to become one. You may be moving - or thinking of moving - into Brighton or Hove, and want to know how it lives and breathes when the beach is empty. You may have been living here for years and, for one reason or another - never find the time to wander around the shops or keep up with the frantic turn-over of bars, cafes, people and ideas. You may be new parents or parents to be, oblivious of the underbelly of baby groups, drops ins and endless kiddy activities. Whatever you want from Brighton and Hove, we're sure you'll find it in these pages. And if not, tell us what you need to know via the website (www.juicyguides.co.uk) or write to us at Juicy Books, PO Box 3271, Brighton BN2 5AZ so that we can make it even better next year.

An insider's guide, the Juicy Guide is a guide to life in a town by the people who live here. Everything in the book has been recommended by locals who've tried out the food and sat in the bars on a bad night as well as the good ones. They've put their friends in the hotels and B&B's, tried several homeopaths and plumbers before finding those they've recommended, and they've been to all the organic butchers. The schools we've listed are the ones we've heard good reports about from parents and pupils. There may be some omissions in the guide which we didn't come across, or which were born after we went to bed. Don't assume that because something is not here, it's not worth going to. Try it and tell us how it fared.

We've successfully plugged a gap in the market with our non advertising led critiques and as we spread across the country, Juicy will, we hope, become a name synonymous with integrity, with fresh, opinionated and independent reviews and recommendations to getting the best out of life. The new guides will still be written by locals, with a dynamic new website allowing them to submit reviews online. Tell your friends in Manchester, Glasgow, Bristol to visit www.juicyguides.co.uk and to tell the world about how great their own town can be. You can also tell us if you disagree with our restaurant, pub, club, bar and café reviews and we'll include the best in our monthly e-newsletter. Opinion is valuable, especially if is *not* for sale.

arrivals & departures

planes, trains & automobiles

In a year when we spent more time at home than we might have planned with trains and rain spoiling our commuting fun, we thanked God for e-mail. Face-to-face meetings suddenly seemed less important and the prospect of negotiating the A23 out of Brighton... no, sorry. Can't do that because Patcham's flooded. There goes that essential trip to Ikea. Meanwhile, the petrol strike made us take to our bikes and remember to share the school run - or maybe it had more to do with the fact that the sun was shining for the first time, or that the roads were emptied of fumes, or that cyclists took to doffing their helmets to each other in a spirit of camaraderie not seen since the launch of the City bid. So we vowed to stay on our saddles when it was all over, but then the rains came and soaked our enthusiasm. Still, it proved to more citizens of Brighton & Hove how easy it is to get around by bike, and put more pressure on the Council to complete its cycle routes around the centre of town.

The future of commuting depends largely on how we deal with global warming and how train operators Connex and Thameslink negotiate their franchises over the next year. Connex hopes to hand over to GoVia, which controls the Thameslink franchise, although it still officially holds the keys to the faster routes from Brighton to London until 2003. If it does, GoVia promises to make life easier for passengers, keep the crèche and rethink its ill-fated buffet service.

brighton bound

from london

Never ever (ever ever) take the A23 out of London unless you're coming from Croydon. And if you're coming from Croydon, then take the train.

The A23 is still the car park that its big brother once was - and in rush hour still is. Signs from Brixton and Holland Park may seduce you with the promise of a straight road south, but remember; if God had wanted us to drive through south London, He'd have made it possible. The M25 is there for a reason.

rat runs

from brighton to london

to south west london

A23, M23, M25 (Heathrow), junction 9 (Chessington World of Adventures). Third exit off first roundabout - A233 to Esher then A244 at next roundabout to Oxshott all the way to A3 into London, picking up signs for Fulham and Hammersmith or straight on for Wandsworth.

to west & north london

A23, M23, M25 (Heathrow) M40 - A40.

to N, NE, S & E london

M23-M25 to the Brands Hatch exit off the M25. Cut up through south east London into central London in about one hour 50 minutes.

A23 - M23 - M25 (Dartford) to junction 3 - A20 (Brands Hatch) to A2 for East London. Turn right into Kidbrooke Road (A2213) and Sun in Sands roundabout to Blackheath, right into Greenwich High St towards Surrey Quays and Rotherhithe and on to Tower Bridge and the City, or Blackfriars and Kings Cross.

For Dulwich, Brixton Clapham and routes off South Circular, take the A205 off the A20 at Eltham.

from london to brighton

from south west,

W or central london

A3 to A243 Chessington turn-off, M25 to Gatwick, M23.

from S & E london

A20 from New Cross and Blackheath, M25 - M23.

from NE london

Cross the river via the Blackwall Tunnel - A102(M). You'll see two signs for the M25; one directs you straight on down the A2 to the M25, while the other, shorter route takes you off the A2 via a right turn. Keep going straight through the lights until you see signs to the A20. Then M25, then Gatwick and the M23.

trains

National Rail Enquiries
☎ *08457 484950*
Connex customer service
☎ *0870 6 03 04 05*
Thameslink
customer service
☎ *020 7620 6333*

- Trains from Brighton to London run every 20 minutes.
- 50-minute trains leave Brighton for Victoria from 09.50 on a weekday and then at 20 and 50 minutes past the hour until 20.50.
- From Victoria, the 50-minute trains start at 09.08 and stop at 22.02.
- The Thameslink route travels to Bedford via London Bridge, Blackfriars, Kings Cross and Luton. It also runs plenty of fast trains, averaging just over an hour to Blackfriars.
- The last trains home are 01.00 from Victoria (unless you can deal with the milk train at 04.00), or the 23.04 from Blackfriars. Allow 10 minutes earlier from Kings Cross Thameslink and 10 minutes later from London Bridge. The last train to Victoria leaves Brighton at 23.02 and arrives in London at 00.39, while the milk train hobbles out at 04.00 arriving in Victoria at 05.52.
- If you don't want to cross London by Tube, jump on either line and change for the faster train at East Croydon or Gatwick. The same applies if you're coming from London and want to get home as soon as possible.
- Sunday trains are a nightmare, what with repairs to tracks and leaf sweeping and so forth, so avoid the headache and come on a Saturday.

Different rules again apply on Sundays. You might end up where you want to go, but then you might end up in Littlehampton, having visited every small seaside town between here and Bournemouth.

commuting

If the trains are running, commuting is an attitude; if you think of it as your daily meditation, opportunity for a nap, or the only part of the day when someone doesn't want a slice of you, it can be a delight. Compare it to sitting in a traffic jam or (heaven forfend) being in London and having to take the Tube, it's bliss. Starting the day sitting on the train with a coffee and croissant, staring out of the window, having a daydream or maybe reading the paper... it's the perfect way to start the day. Similarly, leaving London through south London and rolling into the green and pleasant land of Sussex before driving home along the seafront is a particularly welcome reminder of what life is all about. Of course, it's possible that maybe the trains aren't working, that maybe there's some air on the track or something... no, let's not go there.

Brighton is particularly well served by trains - you can go practically anywhere direct, from south west Wales to Scotland as well as the more obvious routes.

prices

- £14.80 day return with the condition that you arrive in London after 10am.
- A weekly ticket allows you to travel at any time of the day for £66 return, or £77 if you buy a ticket, which covers all Tube zones. A monthly costs £253.50, or £295.70 including the Tube pass. You won't have to queue and it works out cheaper than buying daily tickets.
- If you can leave after 10am, you can get a third off with a Network card that costs £20 a year; a £14-day return then becomes £6.60. There are also special deals to Victoria or London Bridge at £10 as long as you don't come back with the evening rush-hour crowd.
- If you're leaving your car at the station car park, it will cost you £3.50 for the day. Presumably someone will notice if it's been there a week, but it's still one of the best bargains in town.

coach

National Express (☎ **08705 808080**) has coaches leaving for London Victoria every hour from Pool Valley with stops at Stockwell and Streatham on the way. Day return tickets cost £8 and the journey takes two hours.

left luggage

- Travelite, 164-166 Kings Road

Arches, Brighton ☎ **01273 773776**.

planes

- Gatwick is 30 minutes away on the fast train, 50 minutes or so if you get the Hassocks hopper, and a taxi is also an affordable option.
- Long Distance Cars (☎ **01273 581581**) will pick you up from your terminal if you pre-book and give them your flight number. They charge between £40 and £50 depending on which airport you're going to and an extra £3 for an estate car. The M25/M23 route is extremely easy,
- Jetlink (☎ **08705 808080**) run bus services to and from Heathrow and Gatwick and take one hour and 50 minutes respectively. Allow for traffic jams on the M25 at busy times though. Also try One Stop Travel Shop (☎ **01273 700406**) or Brighton and Hove Buses (☎ **01273 886200**). The Council also runs a travel information line (☎ **01273 292480**).
- Luton is easy with the Thameslink service, but Stansted involves a train to Liverpool St and then a tube to Farringdon to connect with Thameslink. You can also try Jetlink (number above).
- TraveLine (☎ **0870 6082608**) for buses from Brighton across the country.
- Shoreham Airport (☎ **01273 296900**) offers a myriad of treats from

flying lessons to day or weekend trips, all pre-arranged.

taxis

- Brighton   📞 **01273 204060**
               📞 **747474;**
               📞 **205205**
- Hove   📞 **01273 202020**
- Portslade   📞 **01273 414141**

Proof that Brighton is a small city comes in the form of a cab receipt. From the end of Hove to the end of Kemp Town, any of the blue and white cabs will charge you around £7, with hops into town from either end at around £3 or £4.

You can now hail any Council-endorsed cab anywhere in Brighton and Hove as long as they've got Brighton, Hove or Brighton and Hove writ large upon their roof or side. Or pop along to one of the many cab ranks in town (ring **01273 202020; 747474; 204060**).

buses

Rumour has it that Brighton's bus service was used as the blueprint for Auckland's revamped transport system and is deemed to be the best in the world. Brighton must be the only place in the world where buses are named after its celebrated locals, as well as boasting the longest commitment to an environmental policy in the country. While the rest of the UK mutters about pollution and makes New Year resolutions to use the bus more, Brighton and Hove folk have changed their travel habits substantially. Bus usage here has gone up by 25 per cent in the past couple of years compared to a decline or static usage everywhere else in the country.

The environmental message is clear with pedestrians, cyclists and buses welcome in Brighton's fair city and cars barred from the city centre until 6pm. Car parks surround the main arteries, giving you little reason to clog up local lungs with carbon monoxide. And with asthma a serious concern in Brighton's basin, we need to do whatever we can to limit pollution.

The inequalities of the central fare system which penalised the less well-off have now been tackled with everyone from Newhaven to Shoreham now paying the flat fare of £1 (50p concessions). The inner cityers are not quite so happy since they too have to pay the £1 for their two stop trip, but hey, they can always walk. Apparently the rise will pay for the 23 new buggy/wheelchair-friendly, double-deckers, which will join the 5a and 5b route this year serving Hangleton, Hollingbury and Patcham.

tickets

- £12.50 pack of five-day passes; £13 for a weekly saver. Both are available from the Post Office, newsagents and One Stop Travel Shop at the Old Steine.
- £2.60 (£2.20 central area) all-day pass (available on board).

cars

Parking vouchers can be bought from shops displaying a green 'V' sign and come in books of £5 or more. A couple of 50p vouchers will enable you to park in the few bays around town while you drop back your library books, or get a couple of extra bits and bobs without going through the whole rigmarole of a multi-storey. To help visitors there are huge neon signs on the main routes, which tell you, how many spaces are available in the various car parks. There are a few available bays towards Hove where you can park for two hours as long as you don't return while the traffic warden has still got your number. From June 2001, the council is stepping up its enforcement of on-street parking.

bikes

This city loves to cycle and the cycle lanes (almost) allow cyclists to get around without fear for their lives. As a result, it's rare to see the face-down, flat-backed and helmeted cyclists that duck and dive through some of our other cities. Instead, if you're driving in Brighton and Hove, beware the head-in-the-clouds, hair-flowing-in-the-breeze-type of cyclist who doesn't notice when the cycle paths have run out into the main road because the sea looks just so lovely up ahead.

The Council has promised to extend the track that starts past Sainsbury's on the Lewes Road and leads down to the cycle tracks, which pick up at The Level. It also plans to extend the seafront cycle track east from Brighton Pier to the Marina and to continue the cycle lanes north from Preston Park along the A23. We hope that by 2002 Brighton and Hove will be a safer place for cyclists.

The cycle paths between Brighton Pier and Hove Lagoon can be cluttered with tourists, rollerbladers and children learning to ride their own bikes, but when the crowds have gone home, there's nothing finer than a ride beside the seaside on an out-of-season morning.

Do remember that Brighton & Hove is a city on a big hill, and if you've just moved into Hanover or Fiveways, and you're considering ditching the car in a bid to go green, you're going to get good and fit. The South Downs, too, is a curiously deceptive learning curve; most mountain-bikers can be seen pushing their multi-geared, techno cycles back from what seemed like a good idea at the time. The gentler slopes of the South Downs Way, a long-distance bridle track which runs along the back of Brighton and Hove, is a better bet. he number of cycling shops reflects Brighton's interest in this mode of transport. Prices vary enormously for repairs and maintenance, so shop around. One of the best finds is Baker Street Bikes (☎ *01273 675754*) where the price of a puncture repair is about half that of anywhere else in town and they can usually do it while you wait.

Contact Roger Simmons, the Council's walking and cycling officer (☎ *01273 292475*) for information on cycling and cycle routes.

limos

The stretch limos littering the seafront throughout the summer are more likely to be full of wedged-up holidaymakers than local glitterati, most of whom don't realise that you're not supposed to open the windows. Definitely for those hoping to impress their mates, a limousine service seating eight people costs about £100 for the evening; a turbo Bentley will set you back about £45 an hour.

ferry

Newhaven to Dieppe is a two-hour

hop on the Seacat. Phone Hoverspeed (☎ *08705 240241*), or check the Net or Teletext for special deals, or try its website: ▣ *www.hoverspeed.co.uk*

02

accommodation

This collection of hotels reflects the different moods, styles and personalities that are all part of today's Brighton and Hove. It's not a comprehensive guide; if you're looking for the cheapest deals, wander down the seafront to find the day's rates flagged up outside The Queens or Royal Albion. This chapter is about how different hoteliers see their Brighton and Hove: from the urbane, genteel Victorian city by the sea to the blatantly ostentatious sex kitten whose Regency and Georgian styles reflect the decadent and exotic character kick-started by the Prince Regent and his gang. The New Bohemians of The Pelirocco and Blanch House, with their pop-star designed rooms, may look like they are taking Brighton into a new chapter of arty indulgence, but plus ca change... Brighton (and less so, Hove) has always found a place for everyone to lay their head from sexy residents looking for a night away from the kids, to dirty weekenders searching for their fantasies.

budget

Even the most splendid of Brighton's old hotels offer mid-season, midweek cheapies and you can often find a room for £40 or even less. For instance, The Hilton will give you a seafront room for £50 if it needs to fill its rooms, so if the wind is up and Brighton's looking empty, haggle. All the prices quoted are per person, per night, unless otherwise stipulated.

Colson House

17 Upper Rock Gardens, Kemp Town

☎ *01273 694922*

🖷 *01273 626792*

✉ *info@colsonhouse.com*

The young owners of this immaculately decorated modern hotel have chucked out the chintz and it all looks fantastic. The rooms are bright and spacious, all with en-suite facilities, and everything is coordinated to perfection so there is no clutter, leaving more space for you to throw your clothes around. Prices between £18-£25 per person.

Cosmopolitan

29-31 New Steine, Brighton

📞 *01273 682461*

📠 *01273 622311*

📧 *cosmopolitan.hotel@lineone.net*

Not one for the style guru, but there are two very good reasons why The Cosmopolitan is listed: it offers one of the cheapest views of the sea and the Brighton Pier available, and it has a chintzy Sixties bar which often stays open all night. These more than make up for the décor - cable wallpaper and jungle carpet - as does the enthusiasm of the proprietor. If you want something special this ain't it, as the hotel itself readily admits, but it is clean and comfy with spacious bedrooms. And you can always take down the paintings of Don Quixote and Sancho Panza. Prices start from £55 for a double room with a £5 seaview supplement.

The Grapevine

29-30 North Road, Brighton

📞 *01273 703985*

📧 *www.grapevinewebsite.co.uk*

If you want to be in the heart of the heart of Brighton, you should look no further. The Grapevine is bang in the middle of the North Laine and if you want to hang out, not sleep much and meet other people who are doing the same kind of thing, this is for you. It's also clean and smart and friendly. Prices start from £30 for a double, but you can get in a dorm for £12.

Lichfield House

30 Waterloo Street, Hove

📞 *01273 777740*

Mobile: 07970 945464

📧 *feelgood@lichfieldhouse.freeserve.co.uk*

📧 *www.lichfieldhouse.freeserve.co.uk*

This small guest house caters for a clientele which wants modern, well furnished but individual style. Try the French Lavender room or the Mulberry Georgian room and book yourself an aromatherapy deep tissue massage or reflexology session in the on site treatment room. The service is friendly and efficient and there is a communal breakfast room, which houses a fabulous old jukebox - which you can check out on their website. Although not situated in the heart of Brighton (it's about 15 minutes walk from the centre), there are plenty of bars and restaurants nearby, and parking is much easier. Prices start from £20 per person.

Penny Lanes Hotel

11 Charlotte Street, Brighton

📞 *01273 603197/684041*

📠 *01273 689408*

✉ *pennylanes@pcscience.net*

The first room you enter in this Victorian house is the lounge with its modern art adorning the walls, books lining the shelves and thick and luscious rugs. The resident cat rubs against your leg... What do you mean I can't stay here forever? The breakfast room is just as impressive, and if you can wrench yourself away from the ground floor you'll see the rooms maintain all the design sense exhibited downstairs; they're light, airy and all en-suite. The proprietor (the one with the good taste) is helpful and friendly with the good sense to equip the rooms with duvets. Prices start from £20 per person, children half-price.

Premier Lodge

144 North Street, Brighton

📞 *0870 7001334*

£49.95 for a room slap-bang in the centre of Brighton? That's what you'll get from this national chain of top value, stylish business hotels. Ignore the concrete exterior; the décor is urban minimalist with sub-Rothkos adorning the walls and Swedish homestore furnishings in the comfortable if generic rooms. The food reflects the interior design so expect reasonably priced continental fare. If you can't get into The Oriental

and can't afford the seafront rooms at The Grand, this is a good place to stay, particularly if you need the hotel's business services.

Sea Spray

25 New Steine, Marine Parade, Brighton

📞 *01273 680332; Fax: 01273 684966*

✉ *seaspray@brighton.co.uk*

🖥 *www.brighton.co.uk/hotels/seaspray*

Newly refurbished with shiny, happy en-suites, new carpets, brightly coloured walls and duvets and remote control colour TVs, with a couple of deluxe rooms sporting four poster beds. A five-minute walk from the hippest joints in town, it offers sumptuous vegan and vegetarian breakfasts. Prices start from £25 per person (for shared rooms) including breakfast. Check out the best website in town too.

Valentine House

38 Russell Square, Brighton

📞 *01273 700800*

📠 *01273 707606*

✉ *stay@valentinehousehotel.com*

🖥 *www.valentinehousehotel.com*

A quaint, recently refurbished Georgian terrace house retaining most of the original features. Fortunately one concession to modernisation is en-suite bathrooms, always preferable to having the privy in the garden.

Stylish friezes and delicate floral designs line the stairwells and the bedrooms. Georgian décor was very plain and in the updating it has become a bit twee - old-style Laura Ashley as opposed to Duchess of Duke Street, but the owners know a lot about local history and the whole atmosphere is deeply historic. Prices start from £20 per person sharing a double room.

Walkabout Inn

79-81 West Street, Brighton

☎ *01273 719364*

Central place to stay until you move on or get your own place. It can be noisy but the atmosphere is friendly and it's cheap. Doubles cost £70 per person per week, triples and quads are £60 and dorm beds are £55 per week. All the rooms have individually controlled radiators, wash basins and lockers, although the word is that sometimes the hot water can run out. The kitchen is too small and the TV is temperamental, but it's a good place if you are new in town and your budget is tight.

affordable treats

The Beach Hotel

2-4 Regency Square, Brighton

☎ *01273 323776*

Three Georgian houses knocked together to house 30 sea-facing rooms

with balconies. Aimed at the slightly older market, the hotel has a no laddy-youngsters' policy; any that turn up are advised to try The Pelirocco around the corner. A double room will cost £75 in mid-summer.

Brighton Pavilions

7 Charlotte Street, Kemp Town

☎ *01273 621750*

🖷 *01273 622477*

📧 *sanchez-crespo@lineone.net*

This previously comfortable but modest guest house has undergone a major refurbishment and transformed itself from The Chester Court to Brighton Pavilions. The good-sized, light rooms now boast Roman busts and statues, ochre and Indian Red décor and classic design features more associated with the Regency Pavilion than a traditional guest house. Who says Brighton is a touch camp and theatrical? Prices vary greatly depending on season, but expect to pay from £30 per person. The themed rooms such as Royal Pavilion with its gold fabric draped four poster bed and Titanic Pavilion with its antique brass bedstead are all en-suite and prices start from £36 per person.

Cavalaire Hotel

34 Upper Rock Gardens, Brighton

☎ *01273 696899*

🖷 *01273 600504*

B&Bs may occupy every other address in this street, a 10-minute walk from the town centre, but the Cavalaire is... how can we say it? The Pavilion to their garden sheds. The owner is passionate about Brighton and this is reflected in his local knowledge and the many pictures, which cover the downstairs walls. If you live in a beautifully decorated house with light airy rooms that contain trendy furniture and four-poster beds, then staying here will genuinely be a home from home. See the rooms on the website then book online. All rooms are non-smoking. Prices range between £38 single en-suite) and £80 (superior double en-suite) per room.

Dove Waldorf Hotel

18 Regency Square, Brighton

📞 *01273 779222*

📠 *01273 746912*

This Polish-owned, family-run hotel is an oasis of calm, which you probably won't ever want to leave. The double beds are huge - and happily, so are the rooms. Most can convert into family-size rooms and the front-facing ones also have a sea view. The minimalist and cosmopolitan décor is in neutral and light colours, complimented by wooden furniture and palms, while the plush pile carpets will ensure you'll return home vowing to redecorate. The owner is charming and helpful and has created a genteel guest house, which is a real treat. Prices vary according to size, but expect to pay between £40-£60.

Granville Hotel

124 Kings Road, Brighton

📞 *01273 326302*

📠 *01273 728294*

📧 *granville@brighton.co.uk*

🖥 *www.granvillehotel.co.uk*

Runner up in last years Juicy Awards for hotel of the year. Allow Charlie and Joadi, the resident cat and dog, to guide you around this stylish and individualistic seafront hotel. Sigh as they show off the stylish Brighton Rock Room, opulent and romantic... Gasp at the stunning views from the sophisticated and ornate Palace Pier Room... And gaze at the unique Art Deco bathroom in the Noel Coward Room. All rooms are en-suite, some even have jacuzzis - it will all make you feel awfully bohemian, darling. The hotel's food has a reputation for being organic, free range and delicious. Prices range from £37.50 (single) – £67.50 (double) per person.

The Lanes

70/72 Marine Parade, Brighton

📞 *01273 674231 or 01273 670973*

📧 *thelanes@mistral.co.uk*

Forget for a minute that The Lanes hasn't been refurbished since the Seventies. The rooms are good-sized and airy and even some of the 'back-facing' rooms have full views of the sea and Brighton Pier. The Lanes may fall unintentionally into the kitsch department with its velvet wallpaper and chintzy carpet, but the rooms themselves are fairly plain. And the décor is not so important when you have a late residents' bar on offer. If you really want to get into the seaside bit, check out the squishy waterbed in room 118 (£66 during the week, £110 at the weekend). B&B per person £25 to £65. Prices are lower during the week, and the sea-facing rooms are generally £10 more in price.

Paskins Town House

19 Charlotte Street, Brighton

☎ *01273 601203*

🖷 *01273 621973*

✉ *welcome@paskins.co.uk*

An organic breakfast menu with vegetarian options far outweighing the usual beans on toast or veggie sausages was the appeal of this small, but perfectly-formed guest house. The whole building conveys a sense of calm, from the breakfast room and lounge bar to the cosy pastel bedrooms; no embossed flowery wallpaper here. If it gets too calm, don't fret: the bustle of Brighton's

town centre is a mere 10-minute walk away. Four-poster rooms start from £35 per person per night with four posters at £40.

Strawberry Fields

6-7 New Steine, Brighton

☎ *01273 681576*

🖷 *01273 693397*

✉ *strawberryfields@pavilion.co.uk*

🖥 *www.brighton.co.uk/hotels/*
strawberryfields

This hotel stands out for its family-friendly attitude. Children are offered reduced rates, under-twos are free and they even have a play area and toys in the lounge. The hotel also offers a baby listening service with NNEB qualified supervision - so you can hit the town knowing your little darlings are in good hands. The rooms are average size and standard décor, velveteen wallpaper is evident in some, but all are clean and bright. Prices start from £28 per person, with family rooms from £75 per night.

Sussex Arts Club

7 Ship Street, The Lanes, Brighton

☎ *01273 727371*

The five double bedrooms (£80), one single (£50) and the Arts Club suite (£100) with its four-poster bed make this one of the best small hotels in central Brighton. Mary and her staff care not a jot for a famous face, which is probably why Julie Burchill made it her home for a year before she moved to Hove. Residents can mingle with Sussex's Bohemian set in the late bar.

indulgent

The Belgrave

64 Kings Road, Brighton

📞 *01273 323221*

📠 *01273 321485*

🖥 *www.infinitihotels.com*

This light and airy modern hotel has a picture of the Prince Regent in the foyer, which is its only concession to Brighton's history. Everything else is downright modern, including a very Star Trek procedure for turning on the lights in your room. A downstairs bar and restaurant provide good international cuisine and the rooms are spacious, comfy and clean with ornate marble bathrooms. The front-facing rooms also have views of both piers. Prices vary greatly and deals are always available. Expect to pay from £70 (single) and £90 (double).

Blanch House

17 Atlingworth Street,

Kemp Town

📞 *01273 603504*

Deeply glamorous, boutique hotel, which has a 'boudoir' to satisfy everyone's deepest fantasy, including Noel Gallagher, who stayed here when he was househunting. Choose

between the exquisite Moroccan, Indian and Rose rooms, the fluffy fairytale snowstorm room, or the piece de resistance, the Perrier Jouet suite with its Art Deco lights, six-foot double bed, free-standing bath in the middle of the room and complimentary bottle of PJ. As we write, proprietors Chris and Amanda are waiting to hear if their mate Damien Hurst will design the top room. Chris is a master cocktail mixologist and the lounge lizards residents' bar must be the coolest place to hang out in town - unfortunately it's only open to residents and those eating at the sublime C Restaurant. Prices start at £90 per night for the Rose and Indian rooms and rise to £190 for the Perrier Jouet suite. All the rooms have CD players and power showers.

The Grand

Kings Road, Brighton

📞 *01273 321188*

📠 *01273 224321*

What can I say? Every film or TV series that is worth watching has a chase scene, a balcony-dangling scene or just a 'bus going past the front of the building' scene that involves The Grand. It is an impressively ornate building, which has housed more presidents than the White House, more Prime Ministers than Number 10, and more celebrities than The

Priory. It's worth saving up just to pop in for a drink if you can't stretch to an overnight stay. The staircases, which run through the building, are bigger than most people's houses and the bedrooms are equally spacious and indulgent. Prices start from £250 per room for a sea-facing double; deluxe doubles, which offer access to a balcony, start from £250. But if you fancy the Presidential Suite, expect to pay upwards of £1,300.

Hilton West Pier

Kings Road, Hove

☎ 01273 329744

Corporate twin of Brighton favourite, The Metropole. While other chain hotels in town will insist on inflicting their appalling taste on their guests, the Hilton's more subdued style is much appreciated. The ylang ylang body lotion and lavender-scented 'relaxing water' is another nice touch, and displays an understanding of what a night in a hotel should all be about. The balconies overlooking the English Channel could do with a lick of paint though and the much-hyped Hilton health club is a rainsoaked dash down the road to the Metropole. A twin is £170, double £190 and the really swish suite is £395. Prices come down according to demand though and you can get a room here for £50.

Hilton Metropole

Kings Road, Brighton

☎ 01273 775432 *free* ☎ 0990 515151

🖷 01273 207764

Situated on the seafront next to the Grand Hotel and although lacking its neighbours' history or grandeur, is more than a match for many of the other big hotels on the front. There is a bar and restaurant with a covered conservatory looking over the Channel, and a downstairs nightclub for those of you with the stamina and stilettos required. Obviously it lacks the character of the smaller guest houses, but who needs character when you have a sauna, steamroom, spa and on-site beauty consultant? Prices vary greatly and deals are always available. Expect to pay from £90 per person for a seaview room.

Montpelier Hall

Montpelier Terrace, Brighton

☎ 01273 203599

🖷 01273 706030

Montpelier Hall boasts a beautifully landscaped walled garden which offers exotic greenery and some of the rarest, most exotic plants in Brighton including peony trees and a pond containing fish - Koi Carp, apparently, but don't think about that net - they don't taste so great. The house dates from 1846 and retains an ambience from that a bygone era with its grand rooms and calm elegance. The staff maintain a discrete distance and that combined with the lived-in feel of the lounge and dining room, lull you into the false sense that this is actually your house and that Queen Victoria is still on the throne... The hotel offers evening meals and cream teas at an additional price to the B&B rate, and non-residents can eat here as well. Prices between £50-£80 (double) per night, £300-£480 (double) per week.

Old Ship Hotel

Kings Road, Brighton

☎ *01273 329001*

🖷 *01273 820718*

A beautiful listed building with a sense of times past, boasting the title of being the oldest hotel in the city, right on the seafront with a sea-facing bar and restaurant? Couldn't go wrong, could it? Well... some regulars may swear by it, but the Old Ship's multimillion make over can't hide the terrible food (we got food poisoning), the cold rooms, and howling gales which blow the curtains inside out. Double sea-facing rooms start at £130 per room but go up depending on the season. The glorious regency Paganini ballroom, scene of the Latest Juicy Awards last year, is still resplendent in its original charm though and is available for weddings, divorces, barmitzvahs...

The Oriental

9 Oriental Place, Brighton

☎ *01273 205050*

🖷 *01273 821096*

📧 *info@orientalhotel.co.uk*

🖥 *www.orientalhotel.co.uk*

The Juicy award winning Oriental with its individually designed rooms, ornate furnishings and moody lighting has become the place to hang out for Brighton's creative and artistic types. All the rooms are equipped with oil burners, hanging plant baskets and candles and decorated in different colours. The doubles are en-suite, though the singles aren't, but if you bump into a famous DJ or poet on your way to the loo at 3am, who cares? Downstairs there is a bar and breakfast room, and in the basement is a dining area stuffed with ferns, wooden furniture, a mellow vibe and a lovely skylight. It's really very cool indeed. Prices between £25 and £35 per person. Dining area available, prices on request.

Hotel Pelirocco

10 Regency Square, Brighton

☎ *01273 327055*

🖷 *01273 733845*

📧 *info@hotelpelirocco.co.uk*

Rock & roll! The Pelirocco is the kind of hotel where happening young musicians hang out. The downstairs bar, pop culture art and available PlayStations have attracted the attention of virtually every lifestyle magazine in the country. Bedrooms have been personally designed by celebs including Primal Scream's Bobby Gillespie, cabaret artist Lenny Beige and local Brighton artists Sugarglider, so expect pop art chic, beige and surreal, respectively. Shock your mother when she rings for you and has to ask for 'The Pussy Room', which was been designed by the owner of Pussy, a kitsch gift shop in the North Laine. There really is nothing else like it in Brighton, so if you want to pretend to be a pop star for a night - and at these prices you can - book early. Singles from £45, doubles from £70, per room.

Prince Regent

29 Regency Square, Brighton

📞 *01273 329962*

📠 *01273 748162*

free 📞 *0800 0199332*

📧 *reservations@princeregent.com*

📄 *www.princeregenthotel.co.uk*

Brighton is many things including refined, genteel, understated and urbane, but the Prince Regent is none of these. Located in a Regency mansion opposite the West Pier, the hotel is opulent, utopian, baroque and overstated. Gold leaf edging, thick velvet drapes and Hepplewhite furniture contribute to its baronial atmosphere. Ensure you book one of

the sea-facing rooms for the maximum effect and lay back in your four-poster bed, barking orders at the servants. Plainer rooms are available if theatricality ain't your thing. Rooms described here start from £95 (£125.00 for a Four Poster Bed) but others are available from £45.

The Regency

28 Regency Square, Brighton

📞 *01273 202690*

📠 *01273 220438*

If Joan Collins ran a guest house, this would be it. Unashamedly exploiting Brighton's heritage this hotel offers the Regency Suite, an ostentatious, canopied four-poster room with all the trimmings - gold brocade, velvet tassels, heavy rococo drapes and a view of the Square and the West Pier. Although this room is the piece de resistance, there are other comfy doubles and singles available. The bar and lounge are decorated in a similarly ornate fashion, and the one careful lady owner is herself a vegetarian so all breakfast tastes are catered for. Regency Suite costs around £110; other rooms between £40 and £80 depending on time of year.

The Royal Albion Hotel

35 Old Steine, Brighton

📞 *01273 329202*

Burnt down last year - reputedly a

chip pan disaster - the Albion has been restored to its former glory -that is its Regency glory rather than its paint-chipped, mid-Seventies faded splendour. Sea-facing rooms start from £145 per person.

gay

The following hotels are predominantly gay and lesbian - most are aimed at gay men, but I guess you'll find out what's what soon enough. Those looking for accommodation in gay-friendly households should make Freddie's noticeboard in the Scene 22 café in St James's Street their first port of call.

Alpha Lodge

19 New Steine, Brighton

📞 *01273 609632*

Ashley Court Guest House

33 Montpelier Road, Brighton

📞 *01273 739916*

Court Craven Hotel

2 Atlingworth Street, Brighton

📞 *01273 607710*

Cowards Guest House

12 Upper Rock Gardens, Brighton

📞 *01273 692677*

Hudsons Guest House

22 Devonshire Place, Brighton

📞 *01273 683642*

📧 *hudsons@brighton.co.uk*

New Europe Hotel

31-32 Marine Parade, Brighton

📞 *01273 624462*

Shalimar Hotel

23 Broad Street, Brighton

📞 *01273 605316*

White House Hotel

6 Bedford Street, Brighton

📞 *01273 626266*

self-catering

Best of Brighton and Sussex Cottages

Windmill Lodge, Vicarage Lane, Rottingdean, Brighton, BN2 7HD

📞 *01273 308779*

📠 *01273 300266*

📧 *brightoncottages@pavilion.co.uk*

📧 *www.brighton.co.uk/cottages*

contact Susannah or Heather

This company owns many properties in Brighton and the surrounding area and is continually adding to its list, so phoning for a brochure is recommended. Try the following cottages for the best of what is on offer and expect the prices to rise in the summer and supplements for extra people. Prices include electricity, gas, linen and cleaning.

accommodation indulgent • gay

Horseshoe Cottage in the village of Rottingdean sleeps four in one double and two single rooms. The village is on the seafront about six miles from Brighton and has maintained its olde worlde charm, although it does now boast a Co-op which opens late(ish) on some nights. The cottage is very old and its size and steep staircases reflect its grand old age, but it is mod in all its cons and only a 10-minute bus ride from town. Costs £320 per week.

Seapoint Cottage is situated next to Roedean School overlooking Brighton Marina. About five minutes' drive from Brighton, it has direct access to some rural walks and is peacefully set back from the main coast road. It sleeps seven, with two doubles, one twin and a single and costs £320 per week.

Also available is a penthouse in fashionable Brunswick Square which sleeps 10, a town house in Kemp Town, other cottages in villages further from Brighton, and a Tudor Manor House in East Sussex which sleeps 18 people... the list goes on.

Brighton Holiday Flats

50 Kings Road, Brighton, BN1 1NA

📞 *01273 260100*

📧 *bookings@brighton flats.co.uk*

📧 *www.brightonflats.co.uk*

You can't get more Brighton than these 22 self-catering apartments, situated on the seafront in the heart of all the rock and souvenir shops. They have all been recently refurbished and the larger flats have a panoramic view of Brighton's beach nightlife - so when you are sitting in your spacious lounge with a G&T you can watch your friend queuing for a nightclub. The flats are booked up very quickly in the summer so be warned! Prices for a studio which sleeps two are between £180 and £280 per week; four-person apartments start from £210 per week, and the larger apartments with sea views and the ability to sleep five start from £320 per week. Prices rise in peak season.

Brighton Lanes

14a Ship Street, Brighton, BN1 1AD

📞 *01273 325315*

📠 *01273 323882*

📧 *intermkt@pavilion.co.uk*

contact Gordon House

This company owns two adjoining fisherman's cottages built in 1562, which are situated in Brighton's Lanes. They are furnished with original oak and pine furniture and retain the old stairwells and doorframes. Ideal for families, the cottages comprise a lounge, kitchen, double bedroom on the first floor and two small bedrooms on the top floor. People were smaller in the 16th century, so unless you're

Ronnie Corbett or Lulu it's going to be a tight squeeze, but the history of the houses makes it worthwhile. Two modern apartments are also available in Ship Street which sleep four. Spacious and comfy they may be, but these lack the character that the cottages have. Cottages cost between £400-£500 per week depending on season. Apartments cost £220-£350 per week. Day rates available.

Metropole Court and Cliff Edge Cottage

Cliff Edge, 28 Marine Drive,

Rottingdean

📞 *01273 302431 contact Harold/Valerie*

📠 *01273 307744*

The Metropole Court apartments are situated above the Metropole Hotel on Brighton seafront. Part of the accommodation deal is the free use of the Metropole's health club facilities and entry to the Metro nightclub. One-bedroom flats, most have twin beds in the bedroom and a sofa bed in the lounge. Recently refurbished, two of them also have a glorious seaview. More expensive, the penthouse sleeps three people and also has a seaview. All the apartments have a kitchen, dining area, lounge and bathroom. The furnishings are rather pink and frilly (think Laura Ashley meets Barbara Cartland), but if you're just using it as a base to sightsee and enjoy the view,

it's not too distressing.

Also available during the summer season is Cliff Edge Cottage which, as its name suggests, is on the edge of a cliff. Situated in the village of Rottingdean, about six miles along the coast from Brighton, the cottage sleeps two people and offers amazing views over the Channel. Off-season prices for Metropole apartments from £260 per week, Penthouse suites from £300 per week, rising to £420 in summer. Cliff Edge Cottage costs between £260-£330 per week and is not available for single nights.

backpackers

Baggie Backpackers

33 Oriental Place, Brighton

📞 *01273 733740*

Brighton Backpackers

75-76 Middle St, Brighton

📞 *01273 777717*

Friese Green Backpackers Rest

20 Middle St, Brighton

📞 *01273 747551*

camping

Sheepcote Valley

Off Wilsons Avenue,

east of Kemp Town

📞 *01273 626546*

03

history

Brighton has always lent an identity for the various and disparate people who flocked here, from the original "Bright-helmstone", meaning 'stony valley' to "Dr Brighton" given by William Thackeray in praise of its famous medicinal properties. Locals began to call their town "Brighton" in the 1660's but it did not receive official status until 1810 when the town's commissioners officially sanctioned the name. The aristocrats and socialites who followed the Prince Regent in search of laudanum and sea water called it 'London by the Sea', and dubbed it 'The Queen of Watering Places' in the days when spa visiting was de rigeur. These days, Brighton is the perfect tag to give a town that revels in its ability to dazzle and shine.

at the beginning

It is a widely considered assumption that Brighton's history began with the Prince Regent and his colourful entourage. But the story begins way before that. High on Whitehawk Hill are the remains of a Neolithic encampment that dates back further than the Egyptian pyramids. The Saxons too were early Brightonians and the town's first fishermen. By the time the Normans invaded, Brighton had established itself as a flourishing fishing community and by mediaeval times had become the largest fishing village in Sussex.

Due to its location on poor soil and a cliff top, Brighton never developed as a 'squirearchy', opening its arms instead to outsiders, particularly to dispossessed rural folk who flocked to the town to gain employment. Brighton's famous free thinking character developed because it was an open community, owned by many rather than a few.

By the beginning of the 16th century, Brighton had become a service town, and flourished through its trade and industry. Ships transported fish to the north and returned with coal. But in the great storms of 1703 and 1705, disaster struck; the lower town and most of the shore were destroyed, inspiring Daniel Defoe to describe Brighton "as an old and poor fishing town in imminent danger of being

Brighton's resources were stretched even further in the 1880's with the arrival of the railway which allowed the less well off to travel from London for the day.

Two of Brighton's most visible landmarks, the Palace Pier and the West Pier, were both built in the latter half of the 19th century, the West Pier in 1866 and the Palace Pier in 1889. The West Pier was designed by renowned pier engineer, Eugenius Birch, and in its prime had its own theatre. Between the wars, it was used by day-trippers going to and from France. Now in elegant decline, there are plans to restore the Pier to its former glory, but it is still a magnificent sight and must be one of Brighton's most enduring and haunting images. The Palace Pier's fortunes have been very different; built in 1889, it is still an unadulterated pleasure zone for Brighton's growing number of visitors. A Grade II listed building, it still draws the crowds in their millions.

The Prince Regent's legacy lives on, and Brighton has cultivated its hedonistic and theatrical character through the centuries. A favourite location for illicit trysts, the town embraces its romantic reputation. Lilly Langtrey, the famous Edwardian actress and Edward VII's mistress, lived in Brunswick Square. Lewis Carrol wrote *Alice in Wonderland* when he was living in Sussex Square, and it is said that he was inspired by the vision of his protégé, Alice, wandering in its beautiful gardens and disappearing into the secret tunnel that runs from the lower gardens directly to the sea. Rudyard Kipling, lived in nearby Rottingdean and his house is now open to the public. Oscar Wilde, and his beloved Bosey frolicked on the seafront. Max Wall was born in Kemp Town and there are whispers that a statue in his honour will soon be erected. Laurence Olivier lived in Royal Crescent. Other famous names include Ivor Novello and Noel Coward who composed their music whilst staying at the Lanes Hotel in Kemp Town.

In the 1960's, Brighton became the setting for the clashes between the mods and rockers, glorified in Franc Roddam's film, *Quadrophenia*. In the last two decades, Brighton has become the home of the Party Political Conference, and scene of the attempted assassination of Margaret Thatcher at the Grand Hotel during the 1984 Conservative conference when a bomb exploded, killing five people and injuring 34.

Modern Brighton is as much a hybrid as it ever was. It continues to act as a magnet for tourists and emigrés who want to submerge themselves in its singular culture. The dispossessed love it too and Brighton has a chronic homeless problem that shows no sign of abating. Film folk and new technology types are moving here in droves attracted by the town's arty and vibrant reputation as home of British cinema; Hove's early film pioneers, George Albert Smith and James Williamson invented both the close up and the editing process here. In Kemp Town alone, the high concentration of media people persuaded the council to transform the ailing local comprehensive into a media college, but only time will tell if the experiment will work. Today, Brighton continues to thrive, and as ever its denizens revel in their town's diversity.

further reading

Encyclopaedia of Brighton
Hove Pioneers and the art of Cinema

seaside brighton

As soon as the sun shines, the South East packs its buckets and spades and heads to Brighton, looking for espressos and candyfloss in the place they call London-by-the-sea. From the newly restored station, Queens Road leads right down to the seafront via the centre of Brighton's least interesting part of town, the shopping mall Churchill Square. Stop off at Borders for a good book, then head for the sea. Turn left for the Pier and the candyfloss, or right for the coffee and calm.

The peeling balustrades stretching back from the Brighton Pier against the shimmering whiteness of the Regency squares on Marine Parade, the Volks railway, deckchairs, pebbles and naturist beach give off the mixed signal of decadence and decay which is Brighton's charm. The fish and chip bars on Madeira Drive are a glitch in the Council's plan to create a San Francisco in Sussex, but somehow a perfect reminder of what British seaside towns should all be about. In a city where the best summer clubbers tips straight out on to the beach at dawn, fish and chip caffs like The Madeira Café provide an important service: breakfast starts from 3am. It even does a vegetarian breakfast in this veggie capital of the UK.

brighton pier

The Pier with its palm readers (invariably out to lunch) and dolphin derbies has mercifully enclosed its brain-shattering arcade in a noise-proof bubble, leaving promenaders free to wander out to sea, or take a quick ride on the Waltzer or the trampoline that can be found in a cage on the edge of the pier. A stop for lunch at the fish and chip restaurant standing grandly in the middle of the Pier is also a must, with its offer of a glass of champagne accompanying your mushy peas.

The new Aquarium Terraces are still waiting to play their part in Brighton's busy social life. Cream, the Liverpool superclub is supposed to be coming to town and a feast of cafés promise to spill out on to the mid-level prom.

the west pier

Along the promenade towards Hove is the 130-year-old, grade one-listed West Pier, floating like a ghost ship as the starlings mass above at sunset. Its decline began after the Second World War from lack of investment and it closed in 1975 when it finally became unsafe for the public. But its shell remains unchanged since 1916, and its concert hall and theatre are the best surviving Victorian and Edwardian entertainment buildings in Britain.

Celebrities have fought for its renovation, with Chris Eubank in the red corner, but investment perched like the pennies on the shoveha'penny machines on the Brighton Pier and remained just out of reach... until the Lottery came to its aid in 1998. A restoration programme is due to start, and the West Pier Trust plans to restore the spirit of its Twenties heyday. A consortium is poised to rent space and aims to fill it with restaurants, conference facilities and performance space by 2003. Hard hat tours still run every day at 2pm (3pm in summer) and last an hour and a half for anyone over 16. Ring **01273 207610** to book.

between the piers

Lottery money has also reached the shores of the beach between the piers. A flurry of activity has transformed what was a rather tacky line of fish and chip booths into an alfresco pleasure dome. From the Mary Poppins Carousel to the giant sandpit to the new children's playground beyond the West Pier, the seafront has enough to keep the kids happy, while a new stretch of cafés serves the grown-ups. Shame the paddling pool had to go though. The sandy volleyball court gives the girls something to watch as the sun goes down, and the town's best clubs, The Beach, The Zap and the Honey Club entertain sun-drunk, pre-clubbers on a new terrace leading out to the sea. Even the hippies have got wise and in high summer the beach towards Hove is littered with Thai trousers, sarongs, ankle bracelets and fruit stalls. If the beach were sandy, we could be in Goa.

the peace statue

Above the bartering and the basking, the evening rollerbladers glide towards the manicured lawns that separate Brighton and Hove. It is here you'll find the peace statue of the angel, as it smiles down at the mini-shorts and crop tops which make The Ellipse more Venice Beach than hippy India. Hire your rollerblades from Pulse at 23-25 Kings Road Arches (📞 *01273 720788*) to the right of Alfresco's as you look out to sea. Pulse have got new blades, long boards and the extremely cool three-wheeler kick boards, which they hire out throughout the year at £3.50 per hour, £5 for two hours, or £10 a day, including all protective gear. Take your passport or proof of ID if you don't want to leave a credit card or £50 deposit.

the fishing museum

The Fishing Museum (📞 *01273 723064*) celebrates what Brighton used to be (and still is to the tiny minority of fishermen pushed out of town to Moulsecoomb's housing estates). The museum strews its fishing nets and boats across the beach in a bid to catch the tourist trade even if the local cod is less willing. The fish shop next door sells fish straight off the boats (Rick Stein swears by it), while another sells smoked fish which it will sandwich up for you if you fancy eating it right then and there. The availability of fish depends on the catch, but the museum is open throughout the year. Look out for the Blessing of the Nets as part of the Brighton Festival in May (see The Season chapter) when the first mackerel catch is barbecued and sold to a salivating crowd. If you fancy hiring a fishing boat, ask at the museum for a list of skippers who are willing to take you out. It says much about Brighton that Andy Durr, whose passion drives much of the fishing museum's activities, is currently mayor of Brighton and Hove.

from brighton pier to the marina

Beyond the buzz of the beaches between the piers the mood changes. Things are a lot less glitzy and ritzy and the peeling balustrades seem to peel that little bit more. On that side of the Pier there's a shiny Mary Poppins carousel, this side there's a sad little caterpillar rollercoastering its way through a giant apple. It might not be awash with cash, but there's a quaint old world charm to this part of town and it's curiously refreshing to find a part of the world that doesn't know what a cappucino is.

Black Rock originally marked the boundary of Brighton, although the Marina now lies beyond it and calls itself part of town. Back in the Thirties there was an open air swimming pool built on the site of a terrace garden, but it closed in 1978 and the area is now pretty much disused, apart from as a car and coach park for tourists who can take the Volks train up to the Pier. Word has it that the Council is looking for a suitable property magnate to take it in hand and develop this whole area into the paradise Kemp Towners deserve. Plans to extend the Volks Railway into the Marina have to be included in any proposal, so expect a watersports, café-lined pleasure fest to take Kemp Town into a new era.

Concorde 2 has risen from the ashes of the original Concorde - once the coolest and hippest of all Brighton's clubs - and is now Kemp Town's home to weekend gigging and drinking. Apart from the very fine Volks Tavern (see Clubs for details), it's the only reason why anyone would go down to Black Rock by night unless you're going to sit on the beach and look at the stars. By day, Planet Cycle and various kayaking shops hire out bikes and boats, and in summertime the caterpillar emerges from its winter hibernation to take screaming four-year-olds through its giant apple. The pitch and putt, Peter Pan's playground and an new assortment of other low tech rides provide a quieter amusement away from the Pier and is largely aimed at younger children. In the summer, the little train runs every 15 minutes and is a particular treat for younger kids.

the naturist beach

The Naturist Beach at Kemp Town is awash with naked bodies (mostly men) throughout the year. As soon as the sun shines, they're out, making a stroll on a balmy February afternoon a surreal experience. Actually forget that. They're there all the time, it's just that when it's very cold you sometimes have to look twice to see them. Brightonians turn the other cheek as naked men parade their wares, sometimes a little too close for comfort, but those of a nervous disposition should stay well away. The built-up shingle is a thoughtful gesture by the Council to shelter the naturists from the stares. Brighton Belle (Hove, actually), Julie Burchill refers to it as "Ghost Brighton, the one part of Brighton that could happily have played host to one of those arch-miserabilist Eighties videos by The Smiths or Pet Shop Boys". Behind the beach is Duke's Mound, a dirty scrubland that tries to keep itself respectable with its climbing plants and bushes, but is more of a cruising haven for the local gay community. Each to their own, but it's not a place to visit after dark.

the marina

Beyond the meditative fishermen lined up on the sea wall, lies the extraordinary expanse of Brighton's Marina, a world unto itself with million-pound Princess yachts moored outside box flats, a floating Chinese restaurant with roof tiles shipped from China, Fatty Arbuckle's, McDonalds, an enormous bowling alley, a swanky David Lloyd health club with café/bar looking out to sea, an eight-screen Virgin cinema complex and brand new casino. The locals get as far as the gym, bowlplex, cinema and the huge Asda superstore, while visitors head for the collection of factory outlet shops that make up the town square. The pubs and restaurants perch seductively on the water's edge, but fail to persuade Brightonians to call it their own.

As we went to press, the Marina was having a bit of a facelift. Its fortunes have changed since the Brent Walker Group bought it in 1985 and then backed off a massive investment plan leaving it a cold, soulless kind of place. As the rich kids moved in, the moneybags finally noticed its potential and a 100-room hotel, oyster bar, theme bars and cafés is about to serve its growing community. Holidaymakers Neilsens are building an office on the new waterfront that can accommodate its 100 new staff, and it's still a buzzing place for the foreign postings attached to giant employers such as American Express. Word has it that the bijou residences and super-smart facilities are even attracting the boys from Montpelier.

For seagoing folk, it offers much more (Marina enquiries ☎ **01273 819919**). For those popping in from Barbados en route to France, there's a boatyard (☎ **01273 609235**), with a 60-ton travel hoist and separate crane to deal with those essential repairs, as well as storage facilities, direct sea access and berthing for 1,300 craft. There's also a launderette, showers and washrooms for berth-holders and 24-hour security, which covers the Barrett complex. Apparently in its 20-year history there's never been a single burglary.

The Marina's very friendly yacht club bends over backwards not to be 'snotty yachty' (☎ **01273 818711** for membership details). The club offers sailing courses to newcomers in its Club Class in an attempt to lure new folk into the sailing fraternity, in which Club members take novices out in their own yachts on six Saturdays in spring and another six in autumn. Its Cruising and Motor Boat sections also take non boat-owning members out on trips. There's also a Diving section which meets every Tuesday for training.

RYA recognised sailing lessons for children and adults are also available at the Marina from Neilsens (☎ **01273 626284**), whose fleet of identical Sigma 8ms sits on the West Jetty. Neilsens also do pre-flotilla training courses on a Moody 31.

If you want to charter a boat for anything from a stag or hen party to a wedding, corporate do or ash scattering, Mike Snelling (☎ **0973 386379** or **01273 693400**) is a local skipper who will put you in touch with charter-licensed boat owners. Some of the boats are wheelchair-friendly too. He's also the man to call if it's a beautiful evening and you fancy a trip out to sea to watch the sun set. Nick Light, the skipper of The Aquamanda (☎ *01483 417782*), a twin, 6.3litre-engined Aquastar, is also available if you want to book his boat for a corporate venture or sightseeing trip. During the festival, you can take a trip from the West Quay at 6pm every night (6pm and 7.15pm on weekends) for a tenner. Book at the Dome Box Office (☎ *01273 709709*) If you pop down to the Marina, you'll spot some other water tours, but why go out with a load of tourists when you can hire your own?

The average price of hiring a boat is £40 per hour, but as it's just a matter of chatting to the boat owners, it's all open to negotiation. Each boat can take up to 12 people, and some skippers are happy to do a last-minute, four-hour trip up and down the coast on a nice evening for about £150, provided they haven't got anything on. Mike warns that if you want to book a boat for the day in mid-July, you'll have to book six months ahead, but if you fancy a sunset trip in February, five minutes notice will probably be enough! Of course, you can always splash out on your own Princess Yacht, or pop down to the harbour to dream; the Marina is home to the largest sales office in the UK (☎ *01273 686368*). Prices range from £140,000 to more than £1million.

Mike Snelling will also organise fishing trips and anglers will be pleased to know that there are several wrecks in the area where a host of specimen cod, pollack and conger gather. Ground fishing offers more in the line of cod and whiting in the winter; and tope, dogfish, bass, black bream and skate in the summer. The Marina's fleet can take up to 120 people out at one time which has encouraged Brighton to become a popular venue for angling competitions.

hove lagoon

If you're a complete beginner in seagoing activities, it's probably best to learn the ropes at Hove Lagoon (☎ *01273 424842* ✉ *windsurf@hovelagoon.co.uk*) which - and this the reassuring bit - is only four feet deep. Their fully-trained staff teach RYA courses in sailing, windsurfing, canoeing and just about any other watersport you can think of. Local schools make good use of the facilities for their older kids. Varndean School spends the last week of its summer term down at the Lagoon, Thomas A Beckett teaches its kids to build rafts there and St Christopher's puts it's pupils through sailing courses. This summer, there are multi-activity week breaks on offer to kids and parents will be able to leave their children with trained staff from 9am-5pm. Hove Lagoon is open to anyone over the age of six, and it's a good opportunity for holidaying parents with older kids to get some time to themselves.

diving

Sport divers report that the diving in the area is for the hardy, but visibility can get up to ten metres; seven metres is the average though, and if you lose sight of your buddy, you're on your own. There are a good deal of wrecks to explore, although they tend to be quite deep, and plenty of fish - even if they are the grey, edible kind. The English Channel is not the Red Sea, but if you want to keep your diving up in this country, it's not as bad as you might think. From July, the sea can be quite warm (17 celsius last year), and a 5mm suit will do you just fine. Beware the strong currents and join a dive club; the following have been recommended by our diving chums. Sunstar (☎ *01903 767224*); Newhaven Scuba Centre (☎ *01273 612012*) and Scuba Diving GB (☎ *01273 383444*). If you don't want to go with a club, the Marina can offer you a boat and skipper.

surfing

Throughout the year, the sea is awash with surfers; that Surfers Against Sewage has opened its only branch outside Cornwall tells you how popular it is here. To the uninitiated, the waves don't look enticing enough to get your kit off for in the middle of winter, but there are enough bottoms being hauled into wetsuits on the beaches east of the Marina, around the West Pier and at Hotpipes behind the Old Power Station at Shoreham to prove us wrong. Fanatics report that it's only because it's the nearest surf to London - and because the apres-surf is suitably cool. According to the papers, the waves can get up to 12ft, but on an average surfing day, they don't get higher than your chin. Surfing around the West Pier is probably the most laid-back, with the longer established East Marina surfies least likely to share their breaks. For a tide timetable, ring the Marina (☎ *01273 819919*). A useful website to use for Brighton surfing conditions is 🖵 *www.sharkbait.co.uk* and 🖵 *www.scip.org.uk/surfers* for Brighton & Hove surfers against sewage.

the undercliff

The landslide of the cliff between Asda and the Marina beaches has meant that one of Brighton's best-loved walks is in jeopardy this year. As we write, the undercliff walk is still closed, but hopefully it will be open by the time the sun shines - which could be anytime really. Once upon a time, the swell of the surf would hit you in the face as you donned your Kagoul and braved the winter gales on this solitary walk from the Marina to Rottingdean, and many are still willing to chance it. But the landslide was so unexpected that it could happen again - and anywhere along the cliff - if we continue to have as much rain.

In the summer, this is where you'll find the locals playing in the rock pools with their kids, swarming around the café in the cliff wall at Ovingdean Gap, and cycling or jogging along the neat little groynes which partition off the stretches of sandier beach. They also serve the purpose of encouraging a more secluded, private kind of sunbathing in summer, away from the overwhelming activity of the beaches between the piers.

the season

Most towns and cities just meander through the year, maybe stopping off for a few fireworks, or to pick up a bit of wrapping paper, but that's about it. Brighton - and now Hove, by default - is different. If you were ever in any doubt that Brighton was unlike anywhere else in the UK, just take a look at the festivities and activities that take place during its social season. Maybe the word 'season' is a bit of a misnomer. Certainly it gives the wrong impression - what we're talking about has nothing to do with social class or periods of time. What we're talking about here is a loosely-linked series of events that spans just about the entire year, a collection of some of the most extraordinary, eclectic festivities to come out of one town. Long established events like the London to Brighton bike rides and vintage car rallies, you probably know all about. But Brighton is also an arty, tarty glamourpuss of a city and if you think it's going to be content with a few old bangers, forget it. From the month-long May Festival to the explosive Guy Fawkes night in Lewes and the gloriously irreverent Burning The Clocks ceremony at the Winter Solstice, Brighton rocks. And it feels like the party rarely stops.

the brighton festival

A carnival to match the likes of the Edinburgh Festival, Brighton Festival starts on May 5th when the city's 45 schools parade along the seafront into town decked out in fancy dress. Now in its 35th year, the Festival runs through to May 27th with more than 800 performances, including free ceilidhs on the beach, high-tech multi-media performances in dance and theatre and live world music and jazz, pull in the crowds from in and out of town, while the local cafes and restaurants go alfresco to accommodate all the extra punters.

This year the spectacular Drummers of Burundi, who topped the bill at Womads' Spirit of Africa Tour, join Bare by Toa Fraser which was a runaway hit at last year's Edinburgh Festival. The Minwaza Company of Tokyo, one of Japan's leading shadow puppet and magic lantern companies, arrives with stories of adventure and fantasy within the splendour of the Royal Pavilion's Music Room. And for opera buffs, The Classical Opera Company brings Mozart's Il Re Pastore to the Theatre Royal. Kim Itoh returns from Japan with more ideas to knock modern ballet off balance and if it's anything like the kind of stuff he did here in 1999, unmissable.

The middle weekend is traditionally the time when the streets fill with acrobats and mime artists for The Streets of Brighton festival. This year, the artists are getting a little more community minded with events in pubs and clubs from Whitehawk to Moulsecoomb, while Red Earth continue to build their reputation with stunning live art installations. Last year, most people were wandering around working out where to find the performances, but for information check out the programme which should be available from Komedia, as well as cafes around town for some of the most progressive street art you're likely to see.

The following Sunday (20 May), Dieppe's best food producers sell their wares in Bartholomews at the Dieppe Market. Brighton, meanwhile, goes back to its roots as the first mackerel catch of the season is paraded on the beach for a massive lunchtime barbecue outside the fishing museum. The blessing of the nets, an old Pagan custom, is little more than an excuse for a party for the local fishermen and their families, but this year will again revive the Christian interpretation with a blessing of the catch by Brighton's community vicar, Canon Michael Butler. Brighton's and Dieppe's mayors join in with the sea shanties, hymns and readings, and as the mackerel is thrown on to the barbecue, a Punch and Judy show reminds us of what the seaside is all about.

For information about the Festival, phone the Brochure line 📞 *01271 336023* or check the website 🖥 *www.brighton-festival.org.uk*. Events at the Dome can be booked via the box office 📞 *01273 709709* or e-mail 📧 *tickets@brighton-dome.org.uk*

glyndebourne

For opera fans, Glyndebourne offers its theatre space for the Festival line-up. Glyndebourne itself is only open during the summer, with its own festival running from May to August, so it's a fabulous sight to see the succession of DJs, evening dresses and picnic hampers all heading through the gates of the Glyndebourne Estate on a hot summer's day. The information line 📞 *01273 815000* is open all year.

open houses

If you're one of those people who feel stifled and put off by the oppressive silence of art galleries, but still like to gaze wistfully at other people's creations, this is for you. The Open House season is a unique idea peculiar to Brighton, and something which has grown and grown over the past 19 years. Local artist Ned Hoskins had the original bright idea to exhibit what his work looked like in the real world - in his own home. The aim was that visitors could have a chat while they gazed, or a glass of wine, and the chance to be a sociable human in a warm home rather than some isolated being in a cold gallery.

Across town, other groups copied Ned's idea and it has now become the biggest show of contemporary art in the South East, attracting 15,000 visitors a year and a wealth of international art collectors and critics. This year, more than 200 homes across Brighton and Hove will be exhibiting paintings, stained glass, sculptures, ceramics, photography and furniture. Everything is for sale and it's great fun, whether you want to buy, chat, or just have the opportunity to nose around other people's homes.

The Fiveways Group of artists is one of the most organised among the participants, with Ned Hoskins now taking a back seat to new chairperson, Lucy Parker, the proud owner of the most glamorous garage in Cleveland Road. Some of the Open Houses even welcome you into their gardens - or in most cases, their backyards, which have become famous for displaying amazing creativity in such confined spaces. Make a date to nose around Chesham Street in Kemp Town and Upper North Street in Montpelier. Both streets open up their gardens and homes during Festival weekends, and the idea is simply to walk in and look around.

To join the house or garden artist's scheme, either contact one of the groups or approach the Festival office ☎ *01273 700747*. The benefits of being in a group come down to cost. The Fiveways, Beyond the Level, Kemp Town and Seven Dials groups are well established, can attract sponsorship, and have mailing lists which will save a fortune in postage if you're serious about selling your work. Newer groups include Rottingdean, Hove and Montpelier.

charleston

The Charleston Literary Festival rounds off the springtime feast of culture with a host of luvvies discussing their respective oeuvres in the grounds where Vanessa Bell hung out with her sister Virginia Woolf and their Bloomsbury chums. Charleston is a treat of a literary festival, not least because of its extraordinary setting. The garden is one of the gems that studs the Sussex landscape and much of the festival takes place in a marquee on its lawns. Visitors are encouraged to take tea in the grounds and breathe in the spirit of an era that still lives on in the farmhouse's museum. A recent successful exhibition of Bloomsbury art at the Tate and other galleries has given Vanessa a posthumous stamp of approval, so Charleston's literary festival should be awash with new fans this year.

Open from April to October, Charleston itself houses the astonishing collection of artworks that Vanessa Bell and Duncan Grant, her lifelong partner, amassed throughout their lives. Look out for Gouache table tops, experimental painting on the backs of doors and picnic plates, Picassos and Matisses abandoned in dark halls, and some of the first post-Impressionist work casually scattered throughout the house, illustrating the spontaneous creativity which characterised their lives.

The Bohemian complexity of the relationships within Charleston's walls, and the creativity that spun from them, is almost tangible. When Vanessa and Duncan first moved into the rented farmhouse in 1916 as conscientious objectors working the land instead of fighting for their country, David "Bunny" Garnett (Duncan's friend who was later to marry Duncan and Vanessa's daughter, Angelica), moved in too. While Vanessa's brief affair with Roger Fry, apostle of Cezanne and the Post-Impressionists, also earned him a room in the house until his death. Angelica had grown up believing that her real father was Clive Bell, father of Quentin and Julian. At that time, Clive was living with the flamboyant patroness of the arts, Lady Otteline Morrell, and would often visit with his long-term love, the socialite, Mary Hutchinson. He moved in during the Second World War and lived happily in the unconventional family unit, staying on to live alone with Duncan after Vanessa's death in 1961.

Virginia Nicholson, Quentin's daughter, remembers Charleston as a place where "messy creativity was a way of life". In her sumptuous coffee-table book, Charleston: A Bloomsbury House And Garden, Virginia describes "the wonderfully uninhibited, irreverent quality to the decoration of the house which is that of a child let loose to experiment".

meanwhile, back in brighton...

party in the park 2001

Southern FM's pop extravaganza is on June 24th this year from 12noon to 4pm. Last year more than 60,000 fans turned out to watch Craig David, Billie, Five and Louise, among others, entertain the crowds - free.

the season charleston • meanwhile, back in brighton...

the peace festival

7th July on Hove Lawns from 11am 'til late

A cross between Womad and Glastonbury and all in our own front yard, with enough tents full of kids activities, live bands and things to do to keep you thinking about Peace all day long.

the essential festival

Stanmer Park, Brighton

Last year's Essential Fest was a top weekend and this year promises to be even bigger. Again, like last year, Saturday will be Dance Day and Sunday will be Roots Day - a perfect combination. Dance yourself silly and then chill out. Set for the weekend of 14/15th July, there will be seven arenas featuring the cutting edge of dance and roots music. Tickets go on sale on April 1st. There is limited car parking but extra buses and trains will be laid on to ferry festival goers to and from the centre of Brighton. This is a non-camping event. Check local and national press for line-up details.

pride 2001

On July 28 Brighton and Hove celebrates its title as Britain's Pink Capital as 10,000 of the town's most flamboyant residents parade from the seafront through the town centre to Preston Park. Pink In The Park is where the floats come to rest, offering seven hours of dance, champagne, performances, funfairs and market stalls.

rallies

Every weekend sees some sort of rally along Brighton's popular Madeira Drive, from time trials for exciting sports cars to Beetle maniacs and Mini obsessives parading their motors, through to the simply odd, like the rally for coach-spotters!

heritage

Mid-September sees one of the largest heritage events held under the European Heritage Days umbrella as Europe celebrates its historical architecture by teaching the public some of the tricks of a bygone trade. On the boundary of Brighton and Hove, The Regency Town opens huge marquees on the lawns of Brunswick Square and fills them with demonstrations of the traditional skills, crafts and materials which built Brighton and Hove's Regency architecture. Adults and children can try their hand at brick-making, stone carving, bodging, decorative painting, gilding,

the season meanwhile, back in brighton....

lead casting, spinning and weaving. Meanwhile, organic pigs roast on spits and the real ale flows. It's an enormous event with around 15,000 visitors over the weekend and, once again, it's absolutely free.

lewes fireworks

It must be something in the Sussex air, but the wild party spirit spreads even to the gentle suburban town of Lewes - once a year anyway. On November 5th, unhealed memories of religious persecution are ripped open to fuel a fire which burns throughout the town in a terrifying display of tar barrel races and pyrotechnics and effigies are erected and burnt at the stake. Be warned, though. everyone goes to Lewes on Bonfire night so if big crowds in small spaces make you feel uncomfortable, steer clear.

Street crime - bag-snatching, pick-pocketing... - is also a problem, so we recommend a picnic high on the hill above the town where you can watch the entire proceedings in safety, or wait until the following weekend and take the kids to see the tamed-down version of the same procession in the neighbouring East Hoadley.

new year's eve

The Old Steine becomes the focus for Brighton and Hove to get truly soppy about how lovely life is down here. Early evening sees an enormous family-friendly crowd gather to watch bands on the stages at the Old Steine and Victoria Gardens, as fire-eaters, jugglers and a wild variety of street artists crank up the euphoria gauge before the fireworks welcome in the New Year. Last year, the festivities kicked-off with Burning The Clocks, a kind of Burning Man Festival of Brighton. It's a mix of Pagan celebration and pyromania in which lantern clocks representing the old year are cast on to a sculptural bonfire to bid the year goodbye. Normally celebrating the winter solstice, Burning The Clocks was moved to New Year's Eve last year when a storm meant that of the 75,000 expected visitors, only the (fool)hardy and drunk actually made it. But while the fireworks fizzled and the limp lanterns drifted off, Brighton dusted itself down and got on with the party. It's a seaside thing.

For a full events listing, call the Council ☎ *01273 292711/292712*, or obtain an information leaflet from the Tourist Information centre at Bartholomew Square.

restaurants

It's 8.30pm on a warm summery midweek evening, the sun is taking its time to set behind the West Pier, and Brighton is out for the night. Silhouetted groups of people are gathered on the beach, drumming, chatting, gazing. Lovers stroll on the vast sandy stretch the tide has left behind, and dogs chase sticks into limp waves. We wander into Alfresco, with its glass dome and sea view pizzas, and ask for a table. An hour's wait, we're told. Fair enough; it does have the best view in town. We have a drink on their terrace instead, munch olives and feta cheese and realise that we need more to eat. So we wander down the beach towards Brighton Pier, past the drummers and the lovers and look for food. Nothing. We get to El Taco Way. Closed. Last food served at 8pm. Finally we reach The Beach, a typically Jeckyll and Hyde-ish beach-front zone — by night one of Brighton's best clubs, and a chromefest of a café-bar by day and evening. So we sit down. There's a menu, some (stressy) service and a table. We order a pizza and a lager and have to pay upfront, but we're chilled and happy to have found some food at last. The only problem, our Uni student waitress tells us, is that there's been a run on cutlery. And napkins. And most of the pizzas are off because they didn't expect so much business.

"Excuse me. Have you got any black pepper?"

"Sorry", she smiles. "It's the heatwave. Nobody anticipated it".

This is an old story about Brighton and even more so, Hove. One of Britain's favourite holiday destinations, the City attracts more than five million holiday makers, weekend clubbers and day-trippers every year, yet most restaurants - on the seafront in particular - carry on as if they haven't even noticed. The Boardwalk, a welcome arrival in the dearth of eateries on the beach, looks so promising with its decked terrace and designer interiors, but if more than two people order at the same time… Let's just say it's advisable to take a good book to read while you're waiting.

Only a few streets back into the Lanes and into Kemp Town, things are beginning to change. The place is bustling with new restaurants chasing the cool

Brightonian's over-stuffed wallet and the London refugee's more modest budget (what's left after spending all their hard-earned on their interiors). The thousands of students from Sussex and Brighton who spend their year off travelling and tasting some of the world's finest cuisine, come home to demand it in their own town. Zel and C-Side have joined Ha! Ha!, The Greys, The Pub With No Name and others in providing great pub grub in just about every nook and cranny in town, while those who try to get away with bad service and passable food find that their punters are finding somewhere else to spend their pennies, somewhere where food comes in flavours other than cheese and onion.

Moshi Moshi, the new conveyor belt sushi bar in Bartholomews, serves some of the best Japanese this side of Tokyo without costing an arm and a leg. And with its mirror and glass ceiling cleverly reflecting the worst of Bartholomews' hideous architecture outside into its urban lantern, Moshi reminds us that that we food lovers have other senses which are begging for attention. It's this, more than anything, that has changed in Brighton over the past year. And, we're sorry but we have to exclude Hove from this story. There's the odd new place, but really, as far as food is concerned, in Hove it's still yesterday.

South East Asians believe that a great chef appeals to all five senses when preparing a meal, paying attention to the look, the smell and the taste of the food as well as the conviviality of the service and the surroundings. Terre a Terre has built its success on this, with lessons learnt from the best of Australia's Asian inspired restaurants, and now that some great new restaurants in town are also following the golden rule of the East, the complacent old school might find things getting a little uncomfortable around here.

For years One Paston Place was the only place to take your bank manager or your rich auntie - despite the sour taste that the snobby service often left in the mouth. Since the sublime C Restaurant moved in a few streets away, its former fans are leaving in their droves and opting for the richer experience that eating fabulous food in beautiful surroundings, served by lovely people can provide for the same amount of money. The Gingerman, Victors, Whytes, even Havana with its new menu and new décor, are also pushing up the standards all over town, proving that there are plenty of places now to get some of the best food in the country, And they're all within ten minutes of each other.

But we need to let our chefs know that we love them if they're to stay around. Take Victor's; tucked away in the little cobbled streets behind Bartholomews, Rosario is the chef, the host and the winner of two Michelin forks ("Ah done wun to go for ay star - Ah'd av to get a pestree chef"). With hours between courses, bespoke menus as well as a la carte and set menus, and a tarte tatin to rival Marco's, Victor's is much more than a restaurant. Once Rosario has cooked for you, he'll come and sit with you, regaling you with tales of food and wine. But even if booking is essential and the place is full every night, Rosario is frustrated. "People know me all over the world, but not in Brighton." His clientele are the regulars who go the distance to taste his exquisite food, but it's only when he promotes his £21 for three course menu that the Brightonians flock in. It's a cheapskate mentality which hurts Rosario's Gallic soul, but it's not greed that causes the angst. He wants more from his punters. He wants to get to know people, to show them that he knows what they like, to give them the kind of experience that will make them come back again and again, to do what Brighton's most famous DJs do - to take his people higher. And it doesn't have to be expensive; we gave him a budget of £15 per head (without wine) and purred all the way home.

Meanwhile, on the seafront the restaurants are still piling up the chairs at 8pm on a summer evening, while the Kings Road restaurants shut up shop at 10pm, despite the beach opposite being packed with (potentially hungry) people watching Priscilla, Queen of the Dessert on the Stella Screen on the Beach. "When we close depends on the weather" the waiter at El Taco Way tells us as the crowds head into town in search of some good food. "8, maybe 9 at the latest". And that's for a plate of tacos. Good food as you gaze out to sea, a table on the beach, a waiter who's enjoying the night as much as you are; it's not so much to ask, but ask, you have to. While the smart restaurants are cleaning up in Brighton, the future of eating on the beach, in the side streets and in Hove, is in your hands. Help us make a difference by telling us what you think on our opinion page on *www.juicyguides.co.uk*.

reviews

restaurants

Okay, so we got it wrong in the last edition. We thought you'd want to know which places suited your pocket, but it appears that your palate is much more important. So this year, we've done both. Italian, Chinese and African cuisine are now found under their own headings, but in wallet order from bites to eat to the pure indulgent.

african

The Nile House

17 Preston Street, Brighton

📞 *01273 326003*

Sudanese cuisine in Food Street. The delectable Hanni serves up arm wrestling and Jeb Khaled sing-alongs with the Sudanese spiced chicken, cod or lamb in this friendly little BYO. Sudan may not be well known for its culinary excellence - and the Nile House doesn't even attempt to take you there - but the aroma of cardamom is almost enough to give you a whiff of Africa.

asian

Bali Brasserie

Kingsway Court, First Avenue, Hove

📞 *01273 323810*

Bizarre eating experience in the ground floor of a block of flats in Hove with a Saturday night clientele stuck in the Seventies and foreign exchange students posing in Balinese saris. The bar is mirrored and nobody's going to tell the management that there's a new century outside. But the food is excellent and authentically Indonesian; the three-course rice table at £15.95 is the most popular with a buffet main course, but a mee goreng and Tiger beer will still give you change from £10.

The Coach House

59 Middle Street, The Lanes

📞 *01273 719000*

A brightly coloured little joint, serving a mixture of tasty Mediterranean and Thai influenced food (Thai green chicken curry; chilli prawns at around £6.95). Popular with cyber types from the nearby media centre. The bar heaves in the evening, but they have been known to run out of food by 9pm. Averages £20 per head.

The Fish Bowl

74 East Street, The Lanes

📞 *01273 777505*

Nice little find at the seafront end of East Street where the fish and the music are mellow by day and hopping at night (see bars). Almost always empty at lunchtime, it's a surprisingly easy place to get great fusion food for kids (fishbowl basket of mixed seafood bites with a sweet and sour plum sauce at £4.95) while gorging yourself on poached smoked haddock on bed of chive mash and spinach (£6.45). The kitchen closes at 7.00pm, and the music cranks up to turn it into one of the nicest bars in town.

Jim Thompsons

Unit 1, The Terrace, Madeira Drive, Kemp Town

📞 *01273 666920*

As we went to press, they were still advertising for staff so we have yet to taste the south east Asian treats they promise. They're already doing a roaring trade in Cambridge and London and with Indonesian artefacts for sale, JT looks like it might provide

some welcome quality food on the seafront.

Krakatoa

7 Pool Valley, The Lanes

📞 *01273 719009*

On the site of the original Terre a Terre, this Indonesian restaurant is tucked next to the bus station, but near enough the seafront to feed a more chilled-out club crowd. Upstairs the Japanese/Balinese-style low tables with floor cushions encourage you to take your shoes off, assume your best lotus position and idle the night away over a nasi goreng and a Tiger beer. The menu takes the best from the Orient with sushi preceding Gado Gado and sake an alternative to Tsing Tao. A breath of Bali in the heart of Brighton. Averages £15 per head.

Wok Wok

34 Duke Street, The Lanes

📞 *01273 735712*

Indonesian noodles (specially sweetened on the kids menu) and delicious Chinese dishes at reasonable prices (around £6). The red banquettes make you feel like you're on the set of Happy Days and the staff are particularly friendly; on Sundays one of them turns into a face painter and balloon blower as Wok Wok pitches itself as the place for a family lunch. Avoid the buffet and save up for the nasi goreng for the outrageous price of £7.25, but have a mango champagne cocktail and forget the bill for a while.

caribbean

The Tamarind Tree

48 Queens Road,
Brighton

📞 *01273 298816*

Gentle vibe and Jamaican fare from brothers Mike and Kush who came to Brighton University from south London and stayed to build a little slice of Jamaica in Queens Road. Fish roun de road, jerk chicken, akee, rice and peas (£6-£8), the ingredients come fresh from Brixton market to Kush's kitchen where he paints his plates with mangoes and avocados, flau flau and roti to the low throb of dub reggae. By the weekend, the music cranks up and the birthday parties turn it into another country, but try it on a rainy Wednesday evening to get a taste of a West Indian summer. Remember it's a BYO.

chinese

China China

74 Preston Street, Brighton

📞 *01273 328028*

Straight out of the back streets of Kowloon, this is about as earthy (but authentic) as Chinese food gets. £4.50 for a set meal.

China Garden

88-91 Preston Street, Brighton

📞 *01273 325065*

The most opulent Chinese restaurant in town. A piano player playing smoochy jazz accompanies your meal adding to the sophisticated ambience that permeates the atmosphere. The food is superb but pricey: set dinners range from £16.50 per person to £32 per person. The drunken fish fillets (£7.95) are sublime and their crispy duck Cantonese style (£6.95) is unbeatable. The staff are efficient but not over-friendly and the wine list is extensive.

Gar's

19 Prince Albert Street, The Lanes

📞 *01273 321321*

Popular Chinese restaurant that bustles at night with post-cinema and theatre diners. The food is standard Chinese fare but the atmosphere buzzes. Lemon chicken (£5.50) fresh asparagus, mange tout and beanshoots in garlic (£4.50). Half price food for the theatre goers and early eaters if you're in before 7.30, but you can stay all night.

Gourmet Palace

48 St James Street, Kemp Town

📞 *01273 604060*

Great new Chinese with a take-away fit for a banquet - and plenty of Kemp

Town folk do sneak it home and pass it off as their own. Try the scallops with asparagus (£5.50) or the chicken with honey bean (£4.00).

Lee Cottage

6b Queens Road, Brighton

📞 *01273 327643*

Inhabiting the spot where the lovely Cheungs once was, this is a very different experience to the family run affair to which Chinese people gravitated and which was part of Brighton history for aeons. But hey, things move on, and this is reasonable Chinese fodder with an "eat all you like for £15" policy which gives you licence to pig out. Problem is there's only so much seaweed, aromatic duck, chicken in black bean, Singapore noodles, banana fritters and ice-cream that you can eat, and you probably wouldn't spend as much as £15 given the choice - which you're not.

The Pagoda

Pontoon 5, North Wall, Brighton Marina

📞 *01273 819053*

Floating Pagoda in the Marina where the tiles come all the way from China and the food doesn't - that the Pagoda is stuck in a time before we knew what Chinese food without the MSG tastes like, won't put its clientele off. It's smart and courteous, it rocks with the waves - but not enough to put you off

your food - and serves the requisite duck and pancake deal. Steer clear of the blander veggie and chicken dishes and you could even enjoy the food too. Averages £20-£25 per head.

Sunbo Seng

70 East Street, The Lanes

📞 *01273 323108*

The elegant interiors of this Chinese restaurant might look lovely, but it doesn't really compensate. The sea bass with ginger and spring onions (£12 per lb) and four heavenly vegetables is gorgeous, but the place lacks atmosphere on most nights, and the MSG and soggy noodles let it down badly. When Zen finally realises that most of north London has moved to Brighton and sets up some serious competition, it might encourage Sunbo Seng to pull up its socks.

Yum Yum

22 Sydney Street, North Laine

📞 *01273 683323*

Authentically sparse noodle bar above a fine Chinese supermarket in the heart of the North Laine. A team of Chinese women toss their nasi gorengs in a line of woks next to the counter, but this is far from the stylish noodle bars of Soho. More Penang night market meets Camden on a Saturday afternoon, it's a great place to grab a plate of mee before heading back into the buzz of Brighton's best shopping area. Cheap, cheap, cheap.

Bankers

116 Western Road, Montpelier

📞 *01273 328267*

One of the best fish and chips shops in town. As much a restaurant as a takeaway, and you've also got the option to have your fish cooked in matzo meal (a light, non-greasy Jewish alternative to batter) which makes all the difference. Under £10 per head.

Bardsley

22-23a Baker Street, Preston Circus

📞 *01273 681256*

Said by *The Independent* to be one of the four best fish and chip restaurants in the UK, the tables are Formica, but the fish is line-caught (so no bruises) and fried in palm oil. Roy and the Bardsley family have been doing it for 30 years and don't seem in the least bit tired of their trade. In fact, they've just opened on Saturday evenings because they love it and people love them so much. They close early (8.30pm) and do takeaways. Bring your own wine and enjoy. Under a £10 per head.

The Beach

Kings Road Arches, Brighton

📞 *01273 722272*

With a sun terrace and the only food on the beach after El Taco Way has packed its bags at 8pm, how could it fail? But fail it does, if you're looking for something to write home about. The pizzas are all right, and the lager is suitably cold, but this is simply somewhere to fill your boots when you can't be bothered to cross the road. Service is friendly enough, with students doing the honours, but someone should tell The Beach it's missing out on a golden opportunity. Pizzas are around £5.

Bennetts

32 Egremont Place, Queen's Park

📞 *01273 674456*

Cheerful, unpretentious, wine bar that serves an extensive and eclectic menu: Thai-style mussels (£6.95) deep fried onion rings (£2.65), Cajun vegetables en croute (£7.85) and traditional English breakfast (£3.95). The staff are lovely and the cocktails are fab - Bennetts specialise in Brighton's favourite drink, Sea Breeze, a double vodka, cranberry and grapefruit juice (£3.90).

The Boardwalk

250 Kings Road Arches, Brighton

📞 *01273 746067*

New, and much needed wholefood café just to the west of Brighton Pier with a decked terrace leading out on to the beach. Inside, the two tiers are always packed on a sunny day, although the service is typical of Brighton's beachside fooderies; by 1.15pm on a bright wintry Sunday lunchtime, the food which was very so-so had already run out. Skip the lunch and sip a hot chocolate before a long promenade down to the West Pier, or hang out and watch the sun set on a summer evening.

Brighton Pier Fish and Chip Shop

Brighton Pier, Brighton

The one eaterie in this guide that - odds-on - everyone will go to. Come down for the weekend as a tourist and you'll end up there. Live here? Then have your friends visit and take them there - it's worth it. Expect change from a tenner.

Browns

3-4 Duke Street,

The Lanes

01273 323501

Part of the Oxford/Bristol/Cambridge/London/Edinburgh chain, this is the seaside sister where you know you'll get good latte, good food and trendy service. Always busy for lunch, but not so hot on dinner. Don't bank on Browns bar next door for a sandwich; a bar is a bar, and bless, they can't do everything well. Average per head for lunch is £10.

Bushby's Brasserie

24 Ship Street, The Lanes

01273 321233

Modern English cuisine served in a warm and cosy environment by relaxed and friendly staff. Bushby's is a showcase for English cooking and each beautifully presented dish has been created using a delicate fusion of flavours. Salmon fishcakes on a bed of mixed leaves with a fresh Thai dressing (£4.65), pan roasted breast of duck, served pink dressed with a plum sauce, garnished with game chips (£10.95). But if just want to snack, try one of their baguettes: goat's cheese and chargrilled vegetables (£3.85).

The Curve Bar

45 Gardner Street, North Laine

01273 603031

In the heart of the funky North Laine, The Curve Bar attached to the Komedia Theatre is a bright spacious bistro, designed to attract a sophisticated pre-theatre crowd. The mosaic entrance, stainless steel bar, soft moving light show and mezzanine dining area add a classy edge to Brighton's counter culture ghetto. Breakfast is a wash-out with white toast offered when the croissants are off, but by dinner they hit their stride; avocado feta and caramelised smoky bacon salad, Jamaican chicken, griddled fish of the day, stir fry organic tofu, roast crispy duck at an average price of £9. Beware the wide open doors on a summer evening unless you bring you've remembered to bring your fleece.

First Floor Restaurant

25-26 New Road, Brighton

📞 *01273 682401*

Perched above Mrs Fitzherbert's, The First Floor is a revamped attempt to claw back the pub's customers who loved its once fine kitchen. Setting itself apart from the rabble beneath, the food is fab modern British, with fish not only dominating the menu but providing much of the decor too in the gorgeous and huge aquarium from Aquatech across the road. Try the terrine of chicken and duck with mushrooms and foie gras with homemade walnut or sundried tomato bread (£5.95), pan fried John Dory served with chard, tomatoes and wild mushrooms and truffle vinaigrette (£14.95), followed by creme brulee with mixed wild berries and lemon schnapps (£4.95).

Food For Friends

17-18 Prince Albert Street,

The Lanes

📞 *01273 202310*

Recently revamped with pale green walls and Scandinavian tables, the trendy interior belies the old-fashioned type of veggie food with its emphasis on raw and crunch. Staff are as kind and reconstructed as you would expect, and the pinboards are stuffed with ways to help you to similar enlightenment. Newspapers, water and empathy are free. Under £10 per head.

Fudge's of Brighton

127 Kings Road, Brighton

📞 *01273 205852*

A traditional eatery on the seafront where the staff show how it should be done, with plenty of personality mixed with a real understanding of what people want from a restaurant. The menu is excellent, with a wide variety from both table d'hôte and a la carte options. Two courses for £13.95 and three for £17.95 mean that you won't get through half of the Spanish-style, slow-roasted lamb or chicken stuffed with bacon and wild mushrooms, but the desserts are too tempting to ignore. The music is lounge, the food is large, and the service makes it the perfect place to take your parents for a special meal.

The Golden Girl

10 Manchester Street,

Kemp Town

📞 *01273 603147*

Traditional English cafe food at its best, served in cosy, homely surroundings. One of the oldest buildings in Brighton, it boasts charming waitresses who will go out of their way to accommodate children, but be warned, it can get smoky. The chips are perfectly cooked: fillet of plaice and chips (£4.50), egg, sausage chips and peas (£3.90). Or go for a blow out and have a three-course meal for (£6.99). If you want comfort food, they specialise in steam puddings drowned in custard (£1.85).

Ha! Ha!

Pavilion Buildings,

Brighton

📞 *01273 737080*

Bang opposite The Pavilion, this is yet another of Brighton's missed opportunities. The stripped pine minimalism and spacious, canteen-style seating and bar area, the hot chilli onion rings or bruschetta (£3.50) and chargrilled tuna (£9) look promising enough, and the kitchen certainly delivers. The Warhol-type glass wall cabinets displaying Ha! Ha!'s own products, and the waiters' brown leather aprons and matching upholstery are dead chic, but try taking a child with you and you won't get in. With no families in for lunch or early dinner, the place is almost empty except for weekend evenings when it rocks its socks off.

Hanrahan's

Village Square, The Marina

📞 *01273 819800*

Brighton's answer to the Sistine Chapel, Hanrahan's is worth a visit for the ceiling alone. Frescos and Arabian silks billowing over your Tex Mex is a weird enough experience, but the camel and swordfish on the balcony? Still on a beautiful summer evening, you can join them and watch what happens on those posh yachts after the sun has set. The new manager has done a spring clean and whisked out most of the menu that used to have people waiting for an hour or more on a Saturday night, and replaced it with good solid fodder from steaks and lamb shanks to smoked salmon and Chicken Caesar salads (all around £6).

Indigo Café

52 Lansdowne Place, Hove

📞 *01273 775565*

Indigo buzzes at lunchtime, but by the evening it has lost its fizz with George Michael's greatest hits droning incessantly against a backdrop of its modern interior. But it is a treat for children. Go for the tasty lunch menu offering gourmet sausage and mash smothered with gravy (£6.95), or garlic baked red pepper served with tomato, anchovy, onion, and garlic (5.95). Puddings include creme brulee served with mixed berries (£3.50), sticky toffee pudding (£3.25) and tart au citron (£2.95).

Jackson's Wharf

The Marina

📞 *01273 675365*

The church pews and monastic thrones lend a solid theme to this Scottish and Newcastle hostelry where you can grab a bite before or after a film at the UGC if a Big Mac isn't your thing. The bar food is something you'd expect from an M&S chiller cabinet, but there's nothing wrong with that unless they boast otherwise. And they don't. The restaurant upstairs looks like it might offer more (wild boar sausages with mash and rosemary and redcurrant sauce - £7.45) but doesn't. The kids' food includes real vegetables though, which is a rarity around here. Get a good chef in and this place, with its lunchtime views over the harbour, could be rocking.

Lucy's

26 Kings Road Arches,

Brighton

📞 *01273 220222*

This beachside restaurant tucked into the Arches serving whatever you need according to the time of day was just the job when it opened last year. Breakfast was delicious, lunch light and dinner suitably proper (calves liver and pan fried salmon), but only open from Easter to early Autumn. An occasional treat when the sun shines.

The Regency

131 Kings Road,

Brighton

📞 *01273 325014*

Fish, Scottish steaks and meaty grills - a British seaside treat with a bit of Italian know-how. Children-friendly restaurant on the seafront which heaves with happy campers on a summer's evening. The tourist love it, the locals reckon it has the best fish and chips in its price range, and the kids get a kiss and a lolly from its very own Italian mama. Try the seafood platter for £5.95 or any of the fish from hake to cod, served with proper seaside chips for £4.10.

Richards

102 Western Road,

Hove

📞 *01273 720058*

Spacious wine bar with a good menu, but too many people have reported the poor delivery and sketchy service, so forget dinner; there's plenty more fish on the seafront. A great breakfast bar to enjoy one of the best cups of coffee in town over the (free) newspapers before heading out on to the Western Road, it's also big enough to accommodate the evening crowd.

restaurants english

Room 101

101 Trafalgar Street, North Laine

📞 *01273 704000*

Trafalgar Street, the northernmost fringe of the North Laine, has been enjoying a bit of a renaissance over the last year or two, and Room 101 provides some much-needed trendy drinking and eating space. Lamentably, as with so many refurbished spaces in Brighton, attention has been lavished on the aesthetics and interior fittings to the detriment of service and quality of what's on offer. The food is 100% vegetarian and although well prepared and put together, was pricey given the location and service. Cold too; a Post-it note stuck over the designer radiators read 'Please do not remove the radiator covers' suggesting that previous occupants of our table had taken decisive action against the chill.

Saucy

8 Church Road, Hove

📞 *01273 324080*

Said to be Julie Burchill's restaurant if you're into star spotting, and beginning to attract some modest food awards, Saucy is Modern British with interiors to make your grandchildren laugh in years to come, but lacks what it tries to boast about most. The orange, red and purple banquettes are probably more interesting than the red onion tarte tartin (£4.25) and smoked haddock fish stack with bubble and squeak (£8), but the honey baked figs (£4.25) are truly divine.

The Station

100 Goldstone Villas, Hove

📞 *01273 733660*

Looking like Ha! Ha! but with little of the culinary charm, this is the pub which gets up more Hoveites noses than any other we heard about. It may be good looking but remember that beauty is only skin deep. The food is a shocker, the welcome is lacking and most locals prefer the smoky old gin palace which it replaced. At least the old pub had Sky and allowed children in during the day. Still, bang next to Hove Station, it's somewhere for travellers to wait while someone clears the rain off the track and at weekends, there are enough gorgeous young things to distract you from its inadequacies.

The Strand

6 Little East Street, The Lanes

📞 *01273 747096*

Tucked behind Bartholomews away from the traffic of The Lanes' tourists, The Strand is one of Brighton's more interesting restaurants. The waiters are trendy, friendly and if they don't know which wine would go best with your seared salmon, celeriac and butter bean fritter (£13.25), they'll find out. The food could be better and the prices lower, but this is a delightfully relaxed little bistro with Dusty Springfield albums aiding digestion (and you may need her help to digest the vegan Californian rolls).

Tiger Bar

98 Trafalgar Street, North Laine

📞 *01273 693377*

What it doesn't quite deliver after dark when the North Laine traffic has gone home, the Tiger does surprisingly well at lunchtime. The service is a little dazed and confused, but the Jamaican Jerk Chicken (£7.95) is actually quite good. It's one of the few places where you can take a carnivore who likes a drink in the North Laine. Beware the house red; it's powerful stuff.

Tootsies

Meeting House Lane, The Lanes

📞 *01273 726777*

Part of the London chain, this has got all the hamburgers you'd expect as well as (expensive) salads. The Caesar is around £6, more if you add chicken, the large chargrilled chicken with a choice of seven toppings is £7.95) but in the summer, the terrace outside is perfect for a long sunny lunch. They're also particularly kiddy friendly and there's enough space

inside (up and down) and outside to get away from the little monsters if you're not that way inclined.

Troggs Café Bar

124 Kings Road, Brighton

📞 *01273 204655*

If you've ever considered veggie food to be dull, visit Troggs for a serious eye opener, thanks to the imaginative and beautifully presented vegetarian and vegan cuisine. There is a relaxed and friendly atmosphere with informative waiters happy to discuss the menu - none of that 'why ask me' attitude. We took an out of town vegan friend there for dinner, who was adamant that it was one of the best vegan restaurants experiences she'd ever had. Equally telling (from the point of view of a confirmed carnivore) Troggs is a number choice for eating out because the food is always so reliably delicious. The food in the café next door isn't quite so hot, but the cool blue is a treat on a baking summer lunchtime, and the basement courtyard is a suntrap for those looking for something to eat near the beach.

french

Café de Paris/ La Parisienne

40 St James Street, Kemp Town

📞 *01273 603740*

During the week, this French bistro

looks more like a tribute to Toulouse Lautrech or a bottle of Perrier Jouet. On Saturday though, the place hops with the kind of hedonism the French haven't seen since the days of Lautrech himself with local raconteurs such as Victor Spinetti sending the invited crowds into a whooping, table top frenzy. The set menu means that you'll still have to pay at least £10.95 even if you can't find room for the moules, pork Dijonnais and tiramisu (tiramisu?) The two names refer to the weekday split in focus from the down-stairs venue to the street level bistro.

Café Rouge

24 Prince Albert Street, The Lanes
📞 01273 774422

One of the good things about being a chain is that it gives you time to sort yourself out and, like Pizza Express, Cafe Rouge has sorted itself out just fine. Consistent quality and service is the key to success - and that's what they provide. Newspapers for non-rush hour types, areas for the smokers and a great stress-free attitude towards kids. Also at 10 Victoria Grove, Hove (01273 776789). Ave. lunch - £10.

Crepe Dentelle

65 Preston Street, Brighton
📞 01273 323224

Maud and Philippe have created a warm little bistro with reasonably-priced galettes and crepes. The atmosphere is a little cliched - piped Piaf, an exhibition of Breton Marionettes, Philippe's cocked chef's hat - but the welcome is genuine and the food good. You'd never find a place like this in London these days, or even in France, but it's a happy little reminder of how things used to be. Average per head is £10-£15.

Cripes

7 Victoria Road, Montpelier
📞 01273 327878

Established cosy restaurant offering some delicious formula and make-up-your-own fillings in crepes and galettes (a Brittany speciality made with wholemeal buckwheat flour). Fillings are varied with something for everyone including children, who have a special menu. On-the-board specials change throughout the week. Small cocktail menu is supplemented by excellent beer and cider choices. Average per head is £18.

La Fourchette

101 Western Road, Montpelier
📞 01273 722556

Tastefully and stylishly decorated in warm, primary colours, La Fourchette opened to gasps from the broadsheets last year and could barely cope with its popularity. Early devotees reported overbooking and rushed service with

Pascal, the chef, assuming Basil Fawlty theatrics in the midst of the chaos. Since then, things have quietened somewhat and it's all the better for it. The wine list may be limited but the haute cuisine menu offers a mouth-watering range of delicacies from locally caught fish to moules marinieres and scallops (£10.95), ragout of chicken with wild mushrooms (£11) and roast Mediterranean vegetables with basil pesto (£10). For pudding, try the assiette de gourmet, the chef's selection of the best in the house.

Le Gastronome

3 Hampton Place,

Montpelier

☎ 01273 777399

Surprisingly unpretentious French restaurant just off the main drag of the Western Road with a sumptuous, but inexpensive menu, considering the quality of the fare. Of the five menu options, try the menu gastronomique for three courses of the chef's favourites at £17.95, or £19.95 for four courses. The breast of duck with green peppercorns, cognac and cream is sublime, but the fish, fresh from the market, is to die for. Shame about the lack of atmosphere, but the service is friendly and the food so good you won't even notice you're the only people in.

Mangerie

164 Church Road, Hove

☎ 01273 327329

One of Hove's best kept secrets, the Mangerie eating experience is always a joy. The walls are adorned with paintings by local artists which adds to its cosy but aesthetic interiors. A starter of delicious whitebait with garlic mayonnaise, followed by lemon sole meuniere, or beef fillet with pepper sauce, served with scrumptious potato dauphinoise and a large plate of steamed vegetables, will cost you a mere £13.75 if you bring your own wine. The portions are generous and the puddings yummy. Choose from banoffee pie, tarte tatin and creme brulee. Booking is essential as the space is small but intimate. Mangerie is BYO and credit cards are not accepted.

La Marinade

77 St George's Road, Kemp Town

☎ 01273 600992

Extraordinarily good French cuisine tucked away in the residential end of Kemp Town. More like a front room than a restaurant, the three tables on ground level give the impression that you've been invited to some posh dinner party which the hosts have left you to enjoy by yourselves, while the maitre'd/chef silently oversees your night's feasting. Three sumptuous courses (£20.50) might include poached sea bass with a lemon and saffron butter sauce and tarte tatin flamed with Calvados.

La Petite Fourchette

East Street, The Lanes

☎ *01273 711001*

North African posh nosh and blackboard fish from Pascal at the Big Fork down the road. More of a patisserie when we popped in than anything Pascal told us it would be, but the paint was still wet at the time...

One Paston Place

1 Paston Place,

Kemp Town

☎ *01273 606933*

Formerly Langans when Michael Caine owned the keys, the owners now pride themselves on buying the best ingredients money can buy. The food is fabulous: light langoustine soup with sorrell and caviar (£9.50), Dover sole with baby squid, mussels, jus mariniere, potatoes with spring onion and olive oil (£21). The wines match to perfection, but the atmosphere is stifling, the music and ambience dull, the waiters can't answer the simplest of questions, and questioning the bill had us banned. Make sure you know your poulet de Bresse from your Hoads Farm.

Victors

11 Little East Street, The Lanes

☎ *01273 774545*

Proper posh French with hours between courses and the kind of food which can only come from the love of a good chef. Victor is Mr Hugo rather than the chef, Rosario, whose food and personality people cross oceans for. Ask him to plan your three courses and wine to match and you're in for a treat, as well as his (divided) attention throughout the evening. The scallops in saffron jus, medley of sea bass, monkfish and salmon with dauphinoise potatoes followed by tarte tatin had us drooling like babies. Two course meals are £19.95 and three courses are £21, but give Rosario your budget and he'll prepare an appropriate feast. He's open for lunch, but only if you book first.

indian

Ashoka

95-97 Church Road, Hove

☎ *01273 734193/202112*

Takeaway or eat in at the Daily Mirror's Indian restaurant of the year. OK, so that was in 1995, but in Brighton and Hove it still deserves its title. The proper job flock wallpaper and piles of beautifully presented, gleaming balti dishes filled with exactly what you'd expect from an Indian restaurant, make it fantastically popular even in midweek midwinter. Prices are also what you might expect (Tandoori chicken masala £7.45), there's also a large vegetarian menu and the food matches its reputation. Listen, if it's good enough for Cliff Richard, whose pictures shaking hands with the ecstatic manager adorn the walls, it's good enough for us.

Chilka House

69 St James Street,

Kemp Town

☎ *01273 677085*

Few Kemp Town folk make it past the takeaway counter to the tiny, but cosy and friendly restaurant area. The food is more varied than most Indians, with Goan dishes a speciality. A bite to eat rather than a big night out.

Goa

4-5 Richmond Parade

☎ *01273 818149*

There's plenty of xacuti and peri peri at this Goan restaurant hidden around the back of the Pressure Point off the Old Steine, but the Bangladeshi waiters reckon that it all tastes Indian to them. Apparently the nearest they get to Goa is the fact that the (Bangladeshi) chef was trained by a bloke from Candolim. Still, it's worth a visit if only for the fantastic animated waterfall painting, the likes of which are rarely seen outside New

Delhi. It's BYO, but you can get your booze from the Pressure Point. Students can eat as much as they like for £6.50 every Tuesday between 6pm and 11pm as long as they bringID.

Bayleaf

104 Western Road, Hove

☎ *01273 722280*

Indian restaurant serving traditional and modern British Indian food without the flock wallpaper and sitar muzak. Bayleaf serves locals an offbeat menu in purple shirts and matching paintwork. No one's going to persuade us that cheddar and mozzarella can be used in Indian cuisine, but their more traditional food is better, and the Habitat crockery shows that at least they're trying to pitch a groovier crowd. Try the takeaway too; if everyone else is too busy, chances are that your korma will be delivered by the boss in his Mercedes and Indian livery. Averages £15-£18 per head.

Indiana Tandoori

4 Church Road, Hove

☎ *01273 731354*

Smart blue interiors and halogen lights give Indiana a sophisticated feel. This is a quality Indian and the tandoori dishes, barbequed in a clay oven and marinated with mustard oil and yoghurt are superb. Try the tandoori shaslik, grilled with onion, tomato & pepper (£6.95), or the succulent king prawn kashmir (£7.25).

Kemp Spices

51 St George's Road, Kemp Town

☎ 01273 623331

An unusually modern local Indian with brasserie-style cane furniture, starched uniformed and courteous service and tablecloths which set it apart from the local takeaway. The menu is what you'd expect, but the spices are well marinated and the meat and fish is freshly cooked. A rich red carpet and dark blue ceiling creates a soothing atmosphere. Kingfisher lager is on tap and takeaway is available. Averages £10 per head.

Zamdani

216 Church Rd, Hove

☎ 01273 722216

There are very few notable Indian restaurants in Brighton and Hove but Zamdani is almost worth crossing town for. The interiors attempt plush class, and the waiters are typically polite, but the menu rises above the crowd with dishes you probably won't see anywhere else in town. Chicken is not just Korma'd or Tandooried, Dupiaza'd or Madrased; this is where it gets the Hydrabadi, Nawabi or Methi Kalia treatment. You'll almost certainly never see the like anywhere on the Sub Continent, but who needs India when you've got Hove?

italian

Al Duomo

7 Pavilion Buildings, Brighton

☎ 01273 326741

Italian favourite among families with young kids, and a perfect lunch break after a visit to the Pavilion. The pizzas are delicious and big enough for two, and the choices of pasta, carne and pesce are good enough to come back for more. The service is friendly, the welcome generous, and the atmosphere cosy. Set menus for lunch and dinner are around £10, including a glass of wine which makes it one of the best value Italians in town.

Ask

58 Ship Street, Brighton

☎ 01273 710030

Tasty if unadventurous Italian food served in modish blue and white surroundings. Popular with business folk and ladies who lunch. A convivial atmosphere and excellent service adds to its charm. The thin crust pizzas compare nicely to Pizza Express, but don't expect anything outstanding. Try their Di capra (£6.95) or the penne con pomodoro secchi - sundried tomatoes, artichokes with green chillies and a light tomato sauce (£5.90). Other merits include garden and separate non-smoking room.

restaurants indian • italian

Bella Napoli

2-4 Village Square, The Marina

📞 *01273 818577*

Packed with Italian families at the weekend, this Neapolitan family run business will twirl its pizzas, kiss your babies and entertain your little ones all day while you quaff your way through their wine list. Excellent (and genuine) Italian ice-cream - and the coffee is straight out of Naples.

The Brasserie

15d The Village Square,

The Marina

📞 *01273 818026*

So huge are the portions that you could almost forgive them for charging so much for your dinner. If anyone is ever that hungry, it could be a good deal, but as the only posh Italian in the Marina (the only posh anything in the Marina - apart from the yachts) it does a roaring trade. On a beautiful day, the tables are shuffled out onto the waterfront and if you half close your eyes, you could almost imagine that you were in the Bay of Sorrento. £25 per head for 3 courses.

Donatello

1-3 Brighton Place, Brighton

📞 *01273 775477*

Bright and breezy family of Pizzerias with Italian largesse and small bills. The food and the waiters are unreconstructed Italian, so the service is friendly, children are welcome, and the pizzas are damn fine. The biggest of the brothers commands an impressive presence in the heart of the Lanes, with nooks, crannies, conservatories, lounge bars and enough space to seat a Sicilian extended family. Pinocchio's, its theatreland sibling, is across the way in New Road and boasts one of the best loos in town. Their special menu is £7.90 for three courses without wine with a la carte options.

Latin In The Lane

10 Kings Road, The Lanes

📞 *01273 328672*

Brighton's favourite restaurant with a price range to suit every pocket, and service to please everyone from babies to grannies. Two floors of goodies offer the kind of Italian food you could take an Italian to, with a counter of the freshest oysters and fish greeting you at the door. The menu is enormous: carpaccio of swordfish (£6.95); spaghetti vongole (£8.95); baked sea bream cooked in sea salt (£10.95); scallops with parmesan and white wine sauce on saffron rice (£15)... It goes on. One for food fans.

Leonardo

55 Church Road, Hove

📞 *01273 328888*

Voted the best restaurant in Brunswick and Hove a couple of years ago, this is a firm favourite among Friday-nighters and Sunday-lunchers, despite the slow service. The food is good when it finally arrives - the sardines are fresh and grilled to perfection, the pizzas are thin and crispy, the choice of pasta is boggling - but the service lets it down. We had to ask twice for our drinks, twice for our rocket salad and beg for some garlic bread to munch on while we waited the 50 minutes for our main courses (£10-£15 per head).

Mamma Mia

68-71 Preston Street,

Brighton

📞 *01273 326823*

One of the best Italians in town but, like its ex-partner, Alfresco, it falls down on the service; we were turned away from an empty restaurant at 6pm on a Saturday night because we hadn't booked. But once we promised to be out by 7pm (of course we'd be out within the hour; what do they expect from kids of four and one?), the food was gorgeous. The risotto Italia (£5.95) was rich with parmesan and sweet with red pepper and sun-dried tomato, the mussels were New Zealand (although not green-lipped) and the prawns (also £5.95) paddled delicately in their garlic butter.

Piccolos

56 Ship Street, The Lanes

📞 *01273 203701*

Extremely popular Italian for a Pizza restaurant which doesn't boast an Italian family ownership. Particularly child friendly with two floors for them to run around in. The pizzas are good too and they do take away.

Pieros

30 Spring Street, Montpelier

📞 *01273 329426*

Just off the Western Road, this authentic family run Italian has been serving up its traditonal take on what Brits want from their pasta for 15 years or more. Lots of insalata tricolore, chianti and good old fashioned Italian fussing.

Pinocchio's

22 New Road, Brighton

📞 *01273 677676*

Part of the Donnatello chain (see above), Pinocchio's specialises in classic Italian fare. The atmosphere is both lively and welcoming, and appeals to a good cross section. Pinocchio's excels at making children feel extra special; go for a birthday treat and you'll receive the standard Pinocchio treatment of a cake lit with a sparkler and a silver plate dropped on the floor in an ear-shattering clatter! Try their pescatora, tomato, mussels, peppers, tuna and garlic pizza (£5.10), or All' arrabiatta fusilli, with tomato, chilli, garlic and herbs (£4.95). Get in there quickly before The Treatment Rooms turns it into a temple of hedonism.

Pizza Express

22 Price Albert Street, North Laine

☎ *01273 323205*

Part of the national chain, Pizza Express offers the best pizzas in town at an average of £5 a go. The staff are endlessly patient with children; in fact it's the place to take young kids if you know they're going to throw their food at the wall. If you don't want to be surrounded by young families, don't go on a Saturday or Sunday lunchtime. By night, the lights dim, and the atmosphere is more chilled. Also at 107 Church Road, Hove (01273 770093) where the jazz is live from 7.30pm every Tuesday.

Sole Mio

64 Western Road, Hove

☎ *01273 729898*

Italian posh nosh set in the airy surroundings of the lovely old Nat West bank opposite the floral clock. The Italian chef has a bit of a penchant for all things Spanish, hence the patatas bravas (£2.95) and paella (£9.95) standing proudly next to the anti-pasti and pizzas on the menu.

The food is excellent and the service is what you'd expect from a more expensive restaurant. The Argus reckons it's got the best garlic bread in town (although we prefer Pizza Express's) and the squid is sumptuous. Instead of the House Red, pay an extra pound and try the Chianti Frescobaldi (£10.95).

Terracotta

28 Church Road, Hove

☎ *01273 328837*

Friendly little Italian serving extremely good value lunches (country sausages with mashed sweet potato at £4.50) and not such a bad value dinner (fillet steak with thyme and oregano butter; grilled tiger prawns with lime and chilli sauce, both £8.50). The service is genuinely Italian and, stuck in the middle of Hove's tiny eating quarter, it's one of the best.

japanese

Moshi Moshi

Bartholomews, The Lanes

☎ *01273 719195*

Conveyor belt sushi blazing a trail of Asian food from London Town. Sister to the Liverpool Street and Canary Wharf restaurants, Moshi has stamped its chopsticks in the heart of Brighton, rebuilding its original shell into the glowing lanternesque

Octagon in Bartholomews. Cool (sake cocktails?) stylish and the best fast (and healthy) food in town with sushi from £1.20 - £2.90 from the conveyor belt and hot dishes from the menu.

Oki Nami

208 Church Road, Hove

☎ *01273 773777*

Stylish little Japanese which sits quietly at the Hove end of Western Road, doing very nicely thank you for the best part of six years. Rather too stark for a two-hour evening, with absolutely nothing to look at other than your food, your partner and the straight lines of the benches and tables, it could do with the fascinating focus of the sushi bar generally found in such places. They even provide a little origami to help pass the hours, but the food is fab: try the Tsunami set meal (£21.95 per head) to have your tongue tickled as the five courses of sushi and teriyaki build like the tidal wave it's named after.

Sapporo

38-40 Preston Street, Brighton

☎ *01273 777880*

Not so long ago, this was a tame Japanese with so-so food in the street of so-so food, and apart from the extraordinarily over-the-top central sushi bar where you'll be entertained by the juggling of pepper pots and

tossing of prawns, it still is. Taking tips from The Mongolian Brasserie and chefs from The 'let-me-entertain-you' Philippines, the owners have made sure that chicken teriyaki will never seem the same again. As the flames shoot and the crowd whoops, the diners in the cheap seats vow to book the hot spot next time or go to Oki Nami for the real thing. Averages £15-£20 per head.

lebanese

The Fountain House

60 Queens Road, Brighton

☎ *01273 888860*

A Lebanese run by Iranians? Listen, we tried to review it because it was so highly recommended from so many of you, but as it was closed for refurbishment, we can't comment. Apparently they do the shiha thing and you should avoid the kibbeh.

Kambi's

107 Western Road, Montpelier

☎ *01273 327934*

Authentic Lebanese in the heart of Western Road which, to a less discerning eye, looks like the kind of kebab takeaway which might serve an inebriated clubbing crowd. Peek inside to find a genuinely Middle Eastern atmosphere with gentle and unassuming service and vegetarian and meat mezzes to make your mouth water. The fare is what you'd expect in towns where there's more of an Arabic connection than Brighton; even the signs on the loos are in Arabic. After dinner, ask to partake of the shiha, a kind of elegant version of a bong, and you're in for a truly Alice in Wonderland experience. Averages £15 per head.

mexican

Los Amigos

60 Church Road, Hove

☎ *01273 778777*

Excellent Mexican and Italian food cooked by a French chef and inspired by the Iranian owner. The chimichangas, enchiladas and tijuanas sit happily next to the spaghetti marinara, the atmosphere is informal but classy, and Gloria Estefan provides the only touch of South America in Hove. Now that Boris has gone to his more spiritual home at C Restaurant, the service is not quite so entertaining. Averages £15-£20 per head.

Blind Lemon Alley

41 Middle Street, The Lanes

☎ *01273 205151*

Boasting a funky location tucked away at the end of an alley in The Lanes and an upstairs room with lounging facilities perfect for birthday celebrations, this is a hit with students. The vibe is cool, with Phil Mills, the celebrated slide guitarist, playing every Sunday night, but the Cajun/Southern influenced food is not cheap and isn't as tasty as the menu promises. A beefburger with fries is £6.95, and tortilla served with salad, sour cream and guacamole is £7.95. The charming staff and warm ambience makes up for the food's shortcomings however. Booking is essential.

The Cactus Canteen

5-20 Brighton Square, The Lanes

☎ *01273 725700*

Big servings and kicking music have the weekend crowd thronging their way into these Tex Mex banquettes in the heart of the Lanes. 12oz steaks go for around £13.95 and there are plenty of veggie fajitas (£10.95) and enchiladas (£9.95) to make the Brighton crowd happy. It's also a top choice for a kiddy friendly lunch.

The Grapevine

29-30 North Road, North Laine

☎ *01273 703985*

There's an impressive range of traditional Mexican fare on offer at this cool cafe/bistro as well as inspired daily specials, which invite your tastebuds to a party quite unlike any other. The honey-maple roasted parsnip, butternut squash and goats cheese chimichangas with black bean hummus and tortilla chips are a bargain (£8.95). The Grapevine is not licensed, but you can bring your favourite tipple for £1 per bottle. A tasty meal in equally tasteful surroundings (no dancing chillies wearing sombreros in sight) without the ceremony of most restaurants.

El Mexicano

7 New Road, Brighton

📞 *01273 727766*

One of the handful of genuine Mexican restaurants in the UK, El Mexicano doesn't do the Tex Mex thing with its chimichangas. In fact it doesn't even do chimichangas. Instead, you'll get a bitter green tomato salsa which we think is delicious but which is probably an acquired taste, and a hot chilli salsa to spice up your own enchiladas (£7.95). Some of the dishes you may never have come across before: Mole (£9.95) is a chicken bathed in over 100 ingredients, including chillies, nuts and chocolate, but the Margaritas and the Sols, the big party bookings and the Latino music are more of what you might expect. Top service makes the night a friendly one.

modern british

Arundel Restaurant

The Metropole Hotel, Brighton

📞 *01273 775432*

Posh nosh in faded grandeur, but probably only for those with dowager aunts willing to foot the bill. The food is excellent (artichoke hearts with mushrooms and truffle essence (£6), corn-fed chicken stuffed with mozzarella (£16), pan-fried sea-bass with fennel and shallots (£17), lemon and passion-fruit torte with raspberry coulis (£4.90), all served old-style on silver platters with complementary sorbets between courses. Yet despite the magnificence of the high-ceilinged Georgian banqueting hall, the atmosphere is dismal: piped muzak, 'Wines of the World' posters and the unpleasant salmon-pink decor all detract from what could be a grand eating experience.

Barry's At The Tureen

31 Upper North Street,

Montpelier

📞 *01273 328939*

Barry Would has been entertaining a loyal clientele in this intimate little restaurant for the past 15 years, serving calves liver and gossip on the same plate. Chef, maitre d' and wine waiter, Barry is Queen of The Tureen; invite him to join you on quieter nights and you're in for a treat. The caramelised red onion and sundried tomato tart ("I copied it exactly from a recipe in *The Evening Standard* and now it's my best seller," says Barry) is a dream, and the blackberry liqueur souffle with summer fruit terrine is why he's able to make a profit in this unlikely little set-up. Book to make sure he hasn't gone home. Averages £25-£30 per head.

C Restaurant

Blanch House, 17 Atlingworth Street, Kemp Town

☎ *01273 645755*

Glamorous, stylish and hidden away in the brand new hotel of hedonism, Blanch House, C Restaurant is what happens when the guys behind Grouchos, Pharmacy and Great Eastern Hotel get bored with London and come to live in Brighton. White leather benches spread across the length of a Heavenly white retro basement designed by Amanda Blanch and run by Cass Titcham and Anthea McNeil while Boris, fresh from Los Amigos, swells with pride in his new role as Maitre'd. The menu changes every day so you're unlikely to enjoy our crab, leek and parmesan tartlette with watercress, seared scallops with coconut and coriander chutney and caramelised banana and almond pudding with vanilla ice cream (the colour of a vanilla pod). It might cost the earth, but save up – it's worth it. Dinner is £29.50 for three courses or £24.50 for two courses. Brunch £10 per head.

English's

29/30/31 East Street, The Lanes

☎ *01273 327980*

Brighton's oldest fish restaurant celebrates its antiquity with the walls of its Red Room almost whispering stories from the Edwardian gay days. A favourite with Charlie Chaplin and Lawrence Olivier, it is housed in three fishermen's cottages dating back 400 years on the edge of the Lanes, and creaks with authenticity. Inside for a posh dinner, it delivers, but don't try the cheaper weekend lunch menu if you want to sit outside and watch the jazz band in the square. It's consistently poor and lets the whole place down badly.

Fruit De Mer

42 Waterloo Street, Hove

☎ *01273 733733*

Small fresh fish restaurant styled in soft creams and lit by fairy lights. There are only half a dozen or so wrought iron tables, which makes eating at Fruit De Mer an intimate dining experience. The food is Modern British with a twist of the Far East and they serve meat and vegetarian dishes as well as fish. The dishes are exquisitely presented with complimentary crudites and glass of kir while you browse through the menu. There are two two-course menus to choose from; try the Thai fish kebabs grilled on lemon grass sticks with cucumber and chilli dipping sauce followed by coconut chicken with basil and coriander with jasmine rice for £18.50, or the sweet potato and coriander soup with cumin followed by smoked haddock on a bed of wilted spinach with chive and butter sauce for £11. The £11 menu is not available on Saturday nights.

Gingerman

21a Norfolk Square, Hove

☎ *01273 326688*

Tucked away between Western Road and the sea is the Gingerman, one of Brighton's gourmet treats - particularly for meat fans. A simple yet elegant decor creates an atmosphere of calm, enhanced by efficient and helpful waitresses with nice little extras like the delicious olive oil and home baked bread and post dinner homemade chocolates. The menu includes seared peppered salmon with herb creme fraiche, feuillete of snails and chorizo with grilled baby peppers for starters. A main course might include fricassee of artichokes with air-dried ham and roasted foie gras, corn-fed chicken breasts with roasted garlic mash, garlic and thyme sauce. You should book well in advance and expect to pay around £30 per head for a three-course meal with wine.

Quentin's

42 Western Road, Hove

☎ *01273 822734*

One of the least pretentious of Brighton's fine eateries, the atmosphere is understated but convivial with large untableclothed wooden tables and smiley waitresses. At £19 for three courses or £17 for two, the choice of dishes looks good, but beware the hidden costs. The house champagne is £55, and a bottle of West Chiltington's finest impersonation is £49. Our roast seabass was undercooked while the breast of duck was done to more than its turn, and we were seriously put off when we realised that the appetisers we'd been tucking into turned out to be skewers of kangaroo. You can book the downstairs room for parties.

Terre A Terre

71 East Street, The Lanes

☎ *01273 729051*

A local favourite even among meat eaters, Terre a Terre is one of the best vegetarian restaurants in the country. The decor is funky, the vibe original and the waiters set a standard with their wit, charm and food and wine know-how, rarely seen this side of Melbourne and Sydney. Last year's Juicy Restaurant of the Year, the menu is global, eclectic and designed to keep the staff amused (saltimbocca funghi -

wild mushroom confit wrapped in creamed polenta, cased in sunblushed tomatoes and seared, served with truffle potatoes and garlic puree, toasted pearl barlen, braised cazolo and fino jus @ £11.35) Even the wine and kids food is organic (and there's a toy box to keep them entertained). Booking essential.

Whytes

33 Western Street,

Brighton

01273 776618

Revamped last year by its ebullient host, John Anthony, Whytes is a cosy (if sometimes cramped and often precious) fine dining experience. The perfect presentation of the breast of duck, roasted pink with glazed peaches and a cinnamon sauce set against the starched white of the linen tablecloths and the quiet muttering of the satisfied clientele as they tuck into their grilled calf's liver with shallots are why it's booked solid when the Tories come to town. Starters are all £4.95, main courses £12.50 and deserts £3.95.

moroccan

Coriander

5 Hove Manor,

Hove Street, Hove

01273 730850

It's probably too early to pass judgement on this new restaurant in Hove. They've taken some care with the décor and done it up in a classic, minimalist style and earthy colours reflecting the region, but we presume they're still unpacking the boxes and haven't got round to replacing the 1970's carpet. The Bed and Breakfast style crockery and tablecloths could set a standard in post modern Hove chic. The staff are friendly and sweet though and committed to using the best (and if possible, organic) produce in their Moroccan influenced dishes. On a cold rainy Sunday lunchtime, the tagines looked tempting, but the organic Sunday roast (£10) was deliciously home-spun and the fresh fruit skewers with honey and rosewater syrup and homemade ice-cream (£4) hit the spot.

spanish

Casa Don Carlos

5 Union Street, The Lanes

01273 327177

Every day is a holiday at Carlos's house with Carlos and Ramon taking turns to provide the unrelentingly authentic Spanish service to a backbeat of Ricky Martin and (natch) the Gypsy Kings. The food is fab and inexpensive - marinated anchovies and prawns with garlic mayonnaise (both £3.95), patatas bravas (£2.95), calamares (£4.25) - which means the place is always packed. Book if only to check that there's no Sangria-swigging birthday party in that night.

El Porron

14 Ship Street, The Lanes

☎ *01273 737322*

New tapas bar next to the Sussex Arts Club which promises much and because of the hideous acoustics and lack of ambience, delivers little. The food's fine; the gambitas a la sarten (£4.50) are suitably garlicky and lemony, but with Casa Don Carlos down the road packed to the gills with folk who come for its Ricky Martin vibe, such a cool competitor might find it has a short run.

thai

Aumthong Thai

60 Western Road, Hove

☎ *01273 773922*

Always packed and one of the most popular Thai restaurants in town, but the staff exude a Zen-like tranquillity even when faced by large numbers in the party mood. Expect authentic Thai food served with great style. The staff dress in beautiful traditional outfits and the cutlery is gorgeous. Memorable dishes include spicy prawn cakes served with sweet & sour sauce (£4.50), crispy fish served with dry curry sauce (£6.95), duck marinated in special Thai sauce (£6.50).

Muang Thai

77 St James' Street, Kemp Town

☎ *01273 605223*

Takeaway or sit down in the heart of Kemp Town. All the favourites are here from green and red curries to Phad Thai and Tom Yum, and the service is typically humble, courteous and attentive. The average price for a main course is £4, but the (huge) set menus are between £28 and £33 for two with the vegetarian version at £25. More of a last minute idea than a birthday treats for no reason other than its position in the heart of a quiet residential area.

Shada Thai

4 Lewes Road, Brighton

☎ *01273 677608*

Unassuming little Thai on the outskirts of Hanover where the soups are hot and the prices are good. Its location means that it feeds a local or passing crowd and tends not to buzz with the birthday parties you'll find at Aumthong Thai (see below). But the food is consistently fine, the service is what we've come to expect from the gentle Thais and that's more than you'd get at most restaurants in any town. Averages £10 per head.

Thai At The Pond

49 Gloucester Road, North Laine

☎ *01273 621400*

Good Thai food in a little room over the Pond Pub just off the Queens Rd. It's what we've come to expect from Thai menus: red and green curries, sweet chilli sauces, noodles - all with good vegetarian options, and The Pond does it as well as anyone. But unless there's a birthday party in, forget the idea of any ambience. On a rainy night out of season, the thump of the music (Kylie from the pub downstairs) can be the only soundtrack to your evening's feasting. Under a £10 per head.

world

Black Chapati

12 Circus Parade, Preston Circus

📞 *01273 699011*

Oh how we'd love to love this place. The food is fabulous, the chef is said to be the "father of fusion" - in this country at least - but despite it all, eating at the Chapati is a sour experience. The waitresses seem terrified of chef Steve Funnell which means that any questions about the food or wine has them quaking at the prospect of asking him on your behalf. Service can take an age, and the spraying of Mr Muscle on the next table is as off-putting as the shouting from the kitchen. Unless you just have to taste the genuinely exquisite food, save your money; there are so many nicer places in town.

Havana

32 Duke Street, The Lanes

📞 *01273 773388*

World menu (roast pumpkin pie, peppered curd and pear and fennel jam at £5.50, sweet chilli salmon, yam sauté and yellow curry soup and spring onion noodles at £12.95), Havana is Brighton posh with a decor hinting at memories of colonial Cuba. One of the few expensive restaurants in Brighton where you don't have to dress up and where the space and new cocktail bar gives it a much more informal, younger vibe. For an endless stream of first dates, birthday and anniversaries, it does a bustling trade.

snacks, take aways

Like pubs, everyone's got their favourite takeaway. So what that it's usually only in your heart because it's round the corner or on the way home from the pub? It's yours and that's all that counts. Here are a few of ours.

Agra Tandoori

263 Ditchling Road, Fiveways

📞 *01273 503676*

Recommended by Rosario from Victor's restaurant, so it must be good.

The Cheeky Chip

Eastern Road, Kemp Town

Pukka pies (including chicken balti curry pies), great chips with extra friendly service and about the only deep fried Mars bars outside Glasgow.

Delhi Darbar

40 St George's Road,

Kemp Town

📞 *01273 606677*

William G is the only proper job Indian chef in the whole of Sussex and is keen to let everyone know that, although he was the architect of the now famous Nishat, he's since left to set up his own empire in Kemp Town. Nishat still his uses his menu, but not his culinary prowess and the best of Goa is now in Kemp Town.

The Market Diner

19-21 Circus Street,

Carlton Hill

📞 *01273 608273*

All nighter for those tipping out of the Ocean Rooms

Jethros Organic Chicken

Queens Road,

Brighton

📞 *01273 325888*

Surprisingly successful for such an ambitious project with its promise of home delivery (within reason) of freshly cooked organic chicken in any style from Thai to French with delicious roast potatoes. Book early if you do want the delivery, or pop in and watch to see just how fresh it is.

Nishat Tandoori

58 Preston Street, Brighton

📞 *01273 321701*

Since Julie Burchill mentioned in The Guardian that Nishat is the Goa of the South East, the queues stretch both ways down the seafront and back to Preston Park - which galls its ex chef, William G who has since set up at the Delhi Darbar in Kemp Town. The menu's the same, so it's worth ringing a couple of hours ahead to make sure that you get your curries before midnight.

Sea Breeze

Southover Street, Hanover

No phone number that we can find, but it's worth taking a trip to Hassan and Melika's on the right as you go down Southover Street for the best fish and chips this side of town. They also do North African take away, although you might have to twist their arm a little to do you a special.

Spice Nutriment

66 Queens Rd, Brighton

📞 *01273 777746*

Midfield General's favourite Indian if that colours your judgement.

Woodingdean Fish Bar

6 Warren Way, Woodingdean

📞 *01273 303061*

The sign outside proclaims it 'The

best fish and chip shop in town". Is there another chippie in Wooding-dean? Whatever, the fish is fried in fresh oil and the chips are excellent. Mr Papadopoulos will also fry the fish of your choice while you wait. There is a selection of pasties, spare ribs, homemade American chicken, battered sausages, fish cakes, onion rings, pickled onions and soft drinks. Large Cod & chips, (£3.60) Fish cakes & chips (£1.19).

cafés

On a sunny day when the tables are on the street, Brighton looks like it hasn't got anything better to do than sit around watching the world go by. Brighton - unlike Hove - is a café society, and has a feeling of the Continent that somehow other towns can't quite muster. And it's no new thing. Ask anyone who was here in the Fifties when coffee first arrived from Italy. These days, the coffee bars have a turned into cafes, and the coffee has turned into mochachino, but the song remains the same. The cafes themselves range from the post modern to the greasy spoon, the food from the vegan to the full American plateful, but the feel is always Brighton.

cafés introduction

Alice's

113 St George's Road, Brighton

☎ *01273 691790*

Homely, very clean, friendly cafe, serving a good range of lunch time grub in a non-smoking environment. Roast chicken and mayonnaise baguette (£2.65), jacket potatoes with cheese and onion (£2.95). The American breakfast is particularly scrummy: two grilled bacon, two hash browns, griddled egg, toast, tea or coffee (£3.95).

The Bagelman

Bond Street, North Laine

☎ *01273 704407*

Julian Egelman is the Bagelman and

has brought the best bagels and friendly and informed service to Brighton. Also at Sussex University, The Bagelman does exactly what you want to your bagels with the freshest ingredients, and doesn't charge a fortune. No need to stray from smoked salmon with dill, lemon and pepper on a poppy seed bagel, but if you must, the prawns are a delight too.

Becky's Cafe

Elm Grove, Brighton

☎ *01273 628184*

You can't miss Becky's London Underground sign and splendid racing mural right opposite the race course. The place to go for quality fry-ups. If you want to pig out try their Gut Buster: two eggs, two rashers, two sausages, bubble and squeak, black pudding, mushrooms, chips, beans, tomatoes, toast, and tea for £4.50.

Billies

34 Hampton Place, Montpelier

📞 *01273 774386*

🎵 *runner-up, best café,*

latest juicy awards 2000

The place for all day breakfast in Montpelier. There's no chance that a normal person will ever finish one of the enormous hashes which come in a staggering variety from farmhouse (eggs, bacon - the works on top of a hash) to Ranchero (salsa, guacamole and sour cream on top of your hash) and all for a mere £4.90, but the effort is worth it. At the weekend, you'll be lucky to get in, and if you've got a buggy or a wheelchair, forget it. But a little tip: pop into The Hampton's pub next door (the back room has a small garden and is kiddy friendly), and Billies will bring your food over.

Concept

53 Coleridge Street, Hove

📞 *01273 719513*

🖥 *internet access*

Internet access, software and hardware suppliers, repair and network systems, and if you're wondering what they're

doing in a section like this, they do coffee too. A loungey kind of place to email your mates while pondering on the colour of your next computer.

Costa Café

42 Market Street, Brighton

📞 *01273 329575*

Couple of spacious cafes offering a blinding array of coffees to an increasingly bean-and-steam-literate clientele. As the sun moves round, so the mood changes as bustling workers grab their take aways, lazy shoppers watch the world go by, before a buzzy afterwork crowd cranks up the energy. Too much of a chain to be truly cool in Brighton, but more coffee in town can be no bad thing. Also at *2 Dyke Road, 01273 725124* and *32 Bond Street, 01273 772024*.

The Curve

Gardner Street, North Laine

📞 *01273 603041*

Another café in the heart of the North Laine. Big and cavernous, handy but maybe not the place for that cosy chat. For a food review, see the Food section.

The Dorset

28 North Road (corner of Gardner Street), North Laine

📞 *01273 605423*

A bustling Brighton institution which

chucks its tables out on the street the minute the sun shines, joining the mix of chic and scruffy cafes which mark Gardner Street as the heart of the North Laine. On Sundays it's packed with families who come for a post Kids@Komedia lunch because they do good food for kids and throw the crayons in for free. By night the vibe is more Red Snapper than Little Mermaid, and the food's getting better all the time.

Feedwells

325 Kingsway, Hove

📞 *01273 417705*

Basic, cheap but ever so tasty, fry ups, roast dinners and steam puddings. gammon steak, egg, chips, and toms (£3.90), scampi and chips (£3.50), steamed toffee pudding (80p).

Good Bean Coffee

39-40 Bond Street, North Laine

📞 *01273 723912*

Light, airy café chain, with a seductively pervading aroma of coffee. The list of different types of coffees is endless, if slightly ridiculous, but try the hazlenut latte (£1.75 - £2.30 depending on size), a sublime mix of hazlenut syrup, espresso and steaming milk. The vivid Rothkos, cool clean interiors at Bond Street look a little like a Habitat showroom, but the papers are free, you can take the kids

and you know you'll get a good cup of coffee. Also at *16 Prince Albert Street, 01273 727726* and *41 Trafalgar Street, 01273 674608*.

Grinders

10 Kensington Gardens, North Laine

📞 *01273 684426*

You won't come to Grinders for the food which is very average and deeply unimaginative (baked potatoes, and pasta) considering the enviable position it commands in the heart of the North Laine's busiest Saturday street. Instead, you'll come to sit on its balcony high above the teeming mass of market traders and weekend shoppers, and dream of a cool smoothie or freshly squeezed orange juice. Grinders sits idly by, forgetting to clear its tables, oblivious to the seriously good deal it could offer its begging clientele.

Hove Tea Bar

Station Approach, Hove Station

You can always tell a good café by the taxi cabs outside, and the Hove Tea Bar is a real taxi drivers café. It serves the best hot, chunky, sarnies and rolls in town. The fried egg and sausage rolls, (£1.30) served on thick white bread are unbeatable. On a cold day, sit outside, sip a steaming cappuccino, and savour the succulent flavours of fried egg, sausage and soft bread.

Hove Tea Rooms

Hove Museum and Art Gallery

19 New Church Road, Hove

☎ *01273 290200*

A sweet tea and cake place in the museum where parents, kids and little old ladies are particularly welcome.

Infinity Café

50 Gardner Street, North Laine

☎ *01273 670743*

Workers co-op offering a sit down and take away service for fans of its exceptional organic foodstore around the corner in North Road. All the food is organic, the salads crunchy and deeply wholesome, and on a sunny day, the tables tip onto the pavement to join the buzz of the North Laine. In the bleak midwinter, the smell of goulash and freshly made soup lures shoppers and locals into its small but cosy café where the coffee is not only delicious, but fair trade and organic. An average lunch is just over £4 (take away is much cheaper) and the cakes can be sugar free and vegan. Try the mezze plate and a smoothy on a hot summer day.

The Juice Bar

2 Brighton Square,

Brighton

☎ *01273 734810*

▤ *www.liquid-lounge.co.uk*

Brighton's very own Australian juice bar. Sit on one of J Spot's ultra modern stools and choose from a invigorating selection of juices, smoothies and home-made vegetarian soups. The Juices have three prices: small (£1.25), medium (£1.50) or large (£1.75). Try the water melon and strawberry, or the celery, apple, beetroot and parsley. The smoothies are either yoghurt or sorbet. Small (£1.50) med (£2.00) large (£2.50).

Kensington's Café

1 Kensington Gardens, North Laine

☎ *01273 570963*

Open Mon-Sun 9.30am-5.30pm

Lunar Bar and Café

5a Castle Square, The Lanes

☎ *01273 220014*

Open 11am-11pm

Formerly Disco Biscuit, Zel have scooped up the bits and transformed it into an alien theme bar. Stranger things have happened in Brighton.

Mac's Cafe.

30 Arundel Road,

Kemp Town

☎ *01273 692621*

Mac's is that rarity - a proper institution. The best fry-up breakfast shop in town, it opens at some ungodly hour and is always but always busy. Cabbies and drivers, people who know about these things, they're here.

The Meeting Place

Hove Sea Wall, Kingsway, Hove

(opposite Brunswick Square)

☎ *01273 738391*

It's a top place to meet friends - hence that clever name - and you can't miss the bright yellow wind barriers on the seafront. Open all year, this is the hardiest of the seafront cafes and deserves its loyal clientele, There's an outside heater lamp and great toasted sandwiches, so blow those cobwebs.

The Mock Turtle

4 Pool Valley, Brighton

☎ *01273 327380*

Tea, egg and cress sandwiches and the best cakes in Brighton. Very traditional with table cloths and the works, but the cakes are fabby. Take away if you haven't got time to watch the world go by.

Nia Café

87/88 Trafalgar Street, North Laine

☎ *01273 671371*

A touch of culinary class in Trafalgar Street's caféville. Big wooden tables, great coffee and wadges of ciabatta with big food too such as the Chicken with Red Pesto sauce, Roast Parnips and Mange Tout (£6.70). The specials tend to be more vegetarian but Sausage and Mash is always on at £6.50. No alcohol, but they're applying for a licence.

Philippe De France

69 East Street,

Brighton

☎ *01273 220691*

The decor is minimal, the ambience is urban and the menu is mouth watering. Philippe De France offers a huge range of tantalising French delicacies, including patisseries, coffees, home-made chocolates, ice-cream and savoury snacks. Try the croute Provencal, French bread, tomatoes, garlic, olive oil, black olive tapenade, anchovies and melted goat's cheese (£5.95) or the Charlotte aux fruits frais, vanilla mousse on a sponge cake, soaked in vanilla punch and topped with fresh fruits (£2.25).

Puccinos

1 Bartholomews,

Brighton

☎ *01273 204656*

Comfortable, friendly café in the Lanes which teems with breast feeding mothers and young children in the Lizard Lounge upstairs by day, and chills into a feet up, sofa seated bar by night. The windows disappear as long as the rain stays away, lending a laid back, watch-the-world kind of feel as you scoff their very fine cakes. There's also a branch at the train station, and now on the Victoria trains themselves. So that'll give you something to do while you wait.

cafés

Redroaster

1d St James Street, Kemp Town

☎ *01273 686668*

European style, spacious cafe decorated in muted yellows and greens along with leather sofas for lounging. Tasty choice of coffee, croissants and a delicious selection of baguettes: try the Pear, Pecorino and Watercress on walnut bread (£2.20) a yummy fruit smoothie for (£1.20). Only complaint is the service which is appallingly slow considering they do not serve hot food.

The Rock Street Café

7 Rock Street, Kemp Town

☎ *01273 697054*

Known more affectionately as Sally's, The Rock Street Café is a haven of tranquillity at the quieter end of Kemp Town. Sally's cakes and comfy sofa offer refuge to the area's writers and actors who idle away an afternoon, playing Solitaire or Back-gammon. Mediterranean Sardines and creamy cheese toast are the best in town. Sherry takes over the reins on friday evenings and changes the menu, in a very Kemptown style job share.

The Sanctuary Café

51 Brunswick Street East, Brighton

☎ *01273 770002*

🚹 **best café, latest juicy awards 2000**

Funky but friendly Vegetarian café where Brighton meets Hove. Late night coffee and cake on the ground and upper floors with poetry readings, in the Beatnik basement, and sunny lunches out of windowless windows. The look is sculpted Boho, the vibe predominantly gay. Best café at last year's Latest Juicy Awards.

Scene 22

129 St James's Street, Kemp Town

☎ *01273 626682*

Just off the Old Steine, Scene 22 is Brighton's only gay shop and coffee bar. It's fully stocked with club wear, safe sex aids and toys for both men and women. Those looking for accommodation in gay friendly households should make Freddie's noticeboard first port of call.

Starbuck

210 Western Road (next to M&S), Brighton

☎ *01273 324097* and

18/19 Market Street, The Lanes

☎ *01273 328157*

America's latest export, promising to make coffee the new tea, has hit town, serving up its dizzying array of the stuff in The Lanes and just off Churchill Square. The sofas upstairs in both make you stay for another coffee and offer a nice alternative venue for business meetings.

The Usual Cafe

115 Dyke Road, Seven Dials

📞 *01273 328858*

Groovy looking café in the heart of Seven Dials.

Waikika Moo Kau

11a Kensington Gardens, North Laine

📞 *01273 671117*

Open Tues-Sun 10am-6pm

Average per head : £5

A Juicy favourite in the North Laine with a welcome to complement the size of the meals. Order a mezze for the entire family and you'll be pushing it to finish the plate. Despite its popularity, the laid back staff don't try to move you on once you've finished your coffee, and the smiles are genuine. Could be the influence of all those buddhas and gods on the walls.

Zerbs

2 Gardner Street, North Laine

📞 *01273 685248*

Keep the corporate coffee giants with their long skinny lattes at bay and try this friendly little café in the heart of the North Laine which stoically sits it out as the Coffee Big Boys recognise the growing café culture in Brighton and nudge their chrome tables ever closer to its loyal clientele.

cafés

pubs

Pubs and bars, bars and pubs; the city is heaving with both. And in Brighton, at least, there's enough of a crossover to send a small minority screaming about the sanctity of the Great British Tradition. In particular, Zel and C-side, who have recently been bought out, have been the architects of a new genre of pub-bar offer a welcome blend of the best of bar and pub culture, making Brighton and Hove the distinctive place it is. If it's pub walks you're after, that lunchtime meal thing, check out the Days Out and Pub Walks chapter.

The Basketmakers

12 Gloucester Road, North Laine

📞 *01273 689006*

Not a virgin wall in sight. Cigarette cases, Victorian toffee boxes, photographs and old posters compete for space in one of Brighton's best loved pubs. Popular with art students, lecturers and the sort of clientele who appreciate its intimate atmosphere and cask-conditioned ales.

The Bath Arms

4-5 Meeting House Lane, The Lanes

📞 *01273 329437*

Saturated with old Brighton memorabilia, The Bath Arms offers plenty of space to stretch your legs after a shopping trip around The

Lanes. Attracts a young crowd who somehow manage to chat above the deafening background music.

The Battle of Trafalgar

34 Guildford Street, Kemp Town

📞 *01273 327997*

Tucked away down a cobbled alley, this is a proper, old-fashioned victuallers. It's worth a visit just to see the cast of oddball punters who frequent the place and if you like bar billiards and the unexpected, then this is the pub for you.

The Blue Parrot

New Road, Brighton

📞 *01273 889675*

More a cocktail bar than pub, this is

where you'll want to sip your Long Island Tea and gaze at the gorgeous Pavilion by night. Right next door to the Theatre Royal, it's a late night option to The Colonnade Bar after sitting through the evening performance.

The Bristol Bar

Paston Place, Kemp Town

📞 *01273 605687*

The Bristol's punters range from the cool and collected, to Kemp Town dignitaries and singleton women. Set just across the road from the sea, The Bristol has wonderful views and they serve proper coffee all day long, so why doesn't the landlord turn the largely unused car park into a garden?

The Charles Napier

57 Southover Street, Brighton

📞 *01273 601413*

Longstanding local community pub with great beer that makes it very popular with the forty-something social worker and teacher crowd.

Chequers Inn

45 Preston Street,

Brighton

📞 *01273 329922*

A hard-bitten pub worth a visit on a Sunday night just to see the oldest DJ in town in action. Rocking Bill has been spinning his discs for more than

30 years and it's said that the Fatboy learnt everything he knows from this man.

The Colonnade

10 New Road, Brighton

📞 *01273 328728*

Gloriously luvvie and packed to the gills with actors in residence at the Theatre Royal next door. Expect to see famous faces and wannabes alike merging with the many portraits adorning the walls.

The Constant Service

96 Islingword Road, Hanover

📞 *01273 607058*

A favourite among Brightonians, The Constant Service is more of an evening experience than a daytime haunt. The warm, welcoming atmosphere attracts a mixed crowd and the ultra-efficient, but courteous staff will put you at your ease, whoever you may be.

Coopers Cask

3 Farm Road, Hove

📞 *01273 737026/736945*

For the personal touch you cannot beat the Coopers Cask. One of the most unusual pubs in Brighton, drinks are brought to you at the table and they come round regularly to check if you need a refill. Exotic, but cheap menu is real value for money.

pubs

The Cricketers

15 Black Lion Street, The Lanes

☎ 01273 329472

Graham Greene's favourite haunt, the Cricketers is the oldest pub in Brighton and the Victorian interiors are gorgeous. Popular with tourists and office parties, but cooler Brightonians tend to avoid it.

The Dragon

58 St Georges Road, Kemp Town

☎ 01273 690144

Bordering on the Gothic, expect a mixed-age grungy crowd, tables lit by dripping candles, a weekly backgammon competition and live music. They also do a great vegetarian Sunday lunch

Dr Brighton's

16 Kings Road, Brighton

☎ 01273 328765

It looks like a run-of-the-mill, traditional seaside pub, but it's quickly obvious that looks can be deceiving. Dr Brighton's is a legendary welcoming local without the cliqueyness of other gay pubs. Official host of the pre-Wild Fruit shenanigans, there's no room for mundane traditions here. Regular drink promos and the temptations of 12 different flavoured Schnapps on offer, Dr Brighton knows how to warm up the revellers and get the party jumping.

The Druid's Head

9 Brighton Place, Brighton

☎ 01273 205065

Close to the Open Market, The Druid's Head used to cater solely for market workers but that's all changed now. Music mags are scattered over the tables and it likes to play its music, loud, loud, loud. Popular with students, the staff will not only wait on your table, but also give you a free lolly-pop when you leave!

The Evening Star

55-56 Surrey Street, Seven Dials

☎ 01273 328931

For sublime real ale, you can't beat The Evening Star. The landlord changes the barrels every two days. A must for those who crave the real beer-drinkers experience.

The Fiddlers Elbow

11 Boyces Street, Brighton

☎ 01273 325850

Authentically Irish as opposed to some of those themed pubs, The Fiddler's Elbow is more chilled than its hectic neighbour The Full Moon, but it's still decidedly happening. Punters are a mix of students, trendies and lovers of all things Irish. It also has live Gaelic music.

The Fortunes Of War

157 Kings Road Arches, Brighton

📞 *01273 205065*

Maybe it's because this pub is so reliant on passing tourist trade that it lacks atmosphere, but seafront places often do. Never mind, you can't have everything. The Fortunes is always popular as a meeting place in the summer to sit outside and bask in the Brighton seaside atmosphere.

The Full Moon

8 Boyces Street, Brighton

📞 *01273 328797*

A Brighton institution, the Full Moon is the hangout for Brighton's young and beautiful who go for its relaxed vibe and gorgeous organic Sunday roasts. The bar is mostly a chemical-free zone with organic beer, wine and cider on offer.

The Great Eastern

103 Trafalgar Street, North Laine

📞 *01273 685681*

The Great Eastern is high on the list of the most popular pubs in Brighton. Professionally run, its quiet and relaxed ambience make it a firm favourite with the young and stylish, but is equally welcoming to the less sartorially inclined.

The Grey's

105 Southover Street, Hanover

📞 *01273 680734*

✉ *mike@greyspub.com for the live music newsletter*

🖥 *www.greyspub.com*

Once renowned for its Belgian chef, the food is no longer the reason to hide away in The Greys. Sad but true, even if the new chef, 'Spats' Picken, is enough of a character to get away with it. But the legend of live music lives on, and Mike Lance still books the bands more out of a love for greatness than a dollar sign in his eyes. The Belgian beer menu is comprehensive enough to confound the CAMRA crowd, and with the kind of bar staff who know about music and an old-fashioned welcome, it's no wonder that this dark little hostelry in the heart of Hanover is still one of the best pubs in town. All shows are 9pm, except 8.30pm Sundays.

The Hanbury Arms

83 St Georges Street, Kemp Town

📞 *01273 605789*

A cracking new comedy night has rejuvenated the Hanbury Arms. Shaped like an Indian temple, the drinking space is minimal but does great party nights, including the infamous Margies Party night.

The Hand In Hand

33 Upper St James Street, Kemp Town

📞 *01273 602521*

pubs

The weeniest, teeniest pub in Brighton. Oozing with character, the Victorian ceilings are splendid, as is its incredible collection of ties hanging from every available space. Popular with ageing Thespians and sea captains, it is worth a visit if you can find a place to squeeze in at the bar. Live music and comedy too.

The Heart In Hand

North Street, North Laine

☎ *01273 624799*

A stone's throw from all the action in the busy North Laine this is a quiet pub to hide away from the crowds. It's popular with the market-traders of Upper Gardener Street so there's always the chance of securing a bargain over a pint. The H in H is a small but comfortable pub with a superior selection of beers and nibbles and a jukebox stacked with classics from Marvin Gaye to Tim Buckley.

Hectors House

51-52 Grand Parade, Brighton

☎ *01273 688869*

Lively starting point for a night at the Ocean Rooms and jumping with students and late teens most nights of the week.

The George

Trafalgar Street, North Laine

☎ *01273 681055*

Word has it that The George serves the most expensive beer in Trafalgar Street, but as it's always packed, nobody seems to mind. The food is fab -much of it vegetarian and organic - and the roaring fires make it the cosiest pub in the North Laine. Though frequented by a cool crowd, the no smoking policy until 8.30pm every night means that kids are welcomed so it is a must on the family pub list.

The Lion And Lobster

24 Sillwood Street, Montpelier

☎ *01273 776961*

Cosy, traditional pub extremely popular with a thirty-something crowd, so get there early if you want a seat. The lager is organic (Bittburger and Warsteiner), and the live Irish music on Sundays helps the two-course roast lunch (£5.50) go down a treat.

The London Unity

Islingword Road, Hanover

Part of the Hanover pub Mafia, the Unity is beloved by locals who come for the warm atmosphere, roaring fire, original stripped floors and the sounds of hippy hits from times gone by.

The Marlborough

4 Princes Street, Kemp Town

☎ *01273 570028*

pubs

Tucked away behind the bustle of Pavilion Parade, The Marlborough is a friendly local for Brighton's lesbians. Split between two bars it's a good place to pick up info on gay goings-on in town. During the week the Marlborough's mellow air makes it a popular spot for a quiet chat over a few pints, while on Friday and Saturday nights DJ's provide the musical entertainment. There's also a theatre above the pub available for hire to budding Thespians.

Mash Tun

1 Church Street, Brighton

01273 684951

Funky pub with two floors depending on your mood: slouching sofas upstairs and more prim pew-like chairs below. Deliberately employing the best-looking bar staff helps to give the place a bit of a buzz. 'Friendly food, tasty staff' boasts the blurb outside, pretty much summing it up really. During the day there are newspapers on tap and coffee served. Just the way it should be.

Mrs Fitzherbert's

25 New Road, Brighton

01273 682401

A cosy and intimate atmosphere, you can eat tapas, canoodle in the cubby holes, or just enjoy drinking in central Brighton.

Nan Tuck's Tavern

63 Western Road, Hove

01273 736436

Rather kitsch and Gothic theme pub perfect for drama queens. Attracts a mixed crowd of students and business people who come to let their hair down after work.

The Nelson

36 Trafalgar Street, North Laine

01273 695872

A proper, old-fashioned local. The beer is excellent and the staff well trained.

No Man Is An Island

106 Lewes Road, Brighton

01273 622310

DJs include Ninja Tune's Bonobo on Thursdays and DJ Ziggy on Fridays. Slapbang in the centre of the Lewes Road junction, the place is loud and proud with pre-clubbers and party-lovers. Student food and large screen videos pack them in on a cold winter's night.

The Office

8 Sydney Street, North Laine

01273 609134

A young person's pub in the heart of North Laine complete with feet-tapping dance music that's never intrusive. Noted for its spirits, which include cachaca, a Brazilian sugar

pubs

cane-based drink, as well as a fine selection of different tequilas and all the proper vodkas. The food is getting a bit of a fine reputation here too. The chef from Wok Wok has recently joined the kitchen.

The Open House

146 Springfield Road, Brighton

☏ *01273 880102*

The latest of the Zel regeneration where the distinction between pub and bar merges in that peculiarly Brighton way. The mosaics, paintings and sculptures and the area's famous Open House weekends during the Brighton Festival reflect the clientele's penchant for all things arty. The decked garden is splendid for a spot of lunch in the summer (plate of humus, olives and ciabatta for around a fiver) and the lounge bar is cosy and child-friendly in the coldest days of midwinter with its Chesterfields and low-slung tables. The promise of large-screen videos will bring the cosy Fiveways community even closer together. The kitchen is open late and Sunday's DJ (Chuck Maverick) is particularly cooking.

Park Crescent Pub

39 Park Crescent Terrace, Elm Grove

☏ *01273 604993*

High on our great pub list, the Park Crescent sits in an exquisite location in the middle of a Regency estate. It has a lively, friendly atmosphere and boasts a wonderful garden.

Pressure Point

33 Richmond Place, North Laine

☏ *01273 235082*

To friendly, clubby Brighton bods the Pressure Point is a relaxed place to have a few beers and a chat. Regular drink promos and decent pub grub mean that it's also a popular alternative to the nearby Student Union. The main bar is the scene of much merriment when the hum of daytime drinkers turns into the buzz of a wild night fuelled by an inspired cocktails menu. After 11pm, the club and live music venue upstairs is a tempting option for the hedonists already in the house.

The Prince Albert

48 Trafalgar Street, North Laine

☏ *01273 730499*

Unassuming little pub just down the road from the station, it's also the preferred watering-hole of Brighton's clubbing giants. The Prince Albert shares its owner with the exceptionally hip Concorde 2, so anyone wanting tickets for whatever the Next Big Thing is can ask for Chris.

Prince Regent

29 Regency Square, Brighton

☎ *01273 329962*

Step through the door and enter a time warp. It is as though this pub has been frozen in the era of Prince Regent - you can even imagine the man himself downing a few beers at the bar. Probably then, as now, this is a relaxed haunt for a mix of gay and straight drinkers. The no-frill's style of most of Brighton's pubs hasn't touched The Regent, where recreating the grandeur of a royal hangout is more the theme. Ornate brassware and cheeky cherubs adorn the walls and there are no DJs in sight.

The Prodigal

80 East Street, Brighton

☎ *01273 748103*

Long, extra-friendly grey bar situated right on the seafront. Popular with students in the week, but on Friday and Saturday nights the place is jammed-packed with all and sundry.

The Pub With No Name

58 Southover Street, Hanover

☎ *01273 601419*

Juicy Award winning pub in the heart of Hanover. There's no sign outside but you'll know it when you find it. The wooden tables, guest DJs and cool ambience attract the young and hip crowd, as well as large sections of the Hanover community. You'll find a seat mid-week, but at the weekend the place heaves with pre-clubbers. At the weekends families move in, attracted by the covered deck for kids at the back.

Queen's Head

10 Steine Street, Brighton

☎ *01273 602939*

If the Freddie Mercury picture hanging outside isn't enough to tempt you inside this gay local then the home-cooked food will. The Sunday roasts are one of the best hangover cures in the book! At all other times the Queen's Head is a quiet spot to hide from the Kemp Town shoppers on one side and the seaside day-trippers on the other. At the weekends it's a lively place to drink before cruising round the corner to Zanzibar or Revenge.

The Regency Tavern

32 Russell Square,
Brighton

☎ *01273 325652*

Wonderfully camp pub tucked behind Regency Square where landlord Chris Ryan is more Bet Lynch than Alex Gilroy and serves his pints under the watchful eye of a bunch of gold cherubs. At last orders, a glitterball replaces the standard lighting as the PA croons a midnight tune to its largely gay clientele. Sunday lunch is exquisite (two courses for £6.95),

pubs

although Chris compares it to the first day at the Harrods sale. No booking so get there early! The vegetarian menu is a big pull and the loos are possibly Brighton's most glamorous.

Royal Pavilion Tavern

7-8 Castle Square,

Brighton

☎ *01273 827641*

A Regular Joe kind of pub which harbours a well kept secret upstairs in the form of the Tavern club. Once the bar shuts it's time to shimmy up the stairs for a Sixties showdown on Saturday nights, or a no-nonsense stomp with Gogglez on Wednesdays. Fresh on Friday caters for a mixed gay and TV crowd, while MFI (Mad For It) celebrates everything Mancunian mid-week.

The Rock

Rock Street, Kemp Town

Rather quaint pub in a quiet street with a small, heated patio. Even though the floors are fashionably bare it exudes an old-fashioned atmosphere and boasts two roaring fires, one of which is in the rather gentrified lounge bar. Perfect if you want a quiet drink and a chat.

The Shakespeare's Head

1 Chatham Place, Seven Dials

☎ *01273 329444*

Only in Brighton would you find a pub with a tiled bar, giant Elizabethan-clad dummies, purple walls and backgammon tables lit by night-lights in glass jars. The perfect place to hang out with friends, while instrumental jazz plays in the background.

The Sidewinder

65 Upper St James Street Mews,

Kemp Town

☎ *01273 679927*

Hip yet unpretentious, The Sidewinder is popular with students, media types and all those who crave an urban atmosphere. The fabulous large garden is perfect to spend hot summer evenings in or afternoons with the family. Refectory tables and comfy sofas that meet most needs, it also supplies a large range of mags and newspapers. One of the best places for a quiet lunch in Kemp Town, the mezze of olives, roasted peppers and humus goes down particularly well.

St James

16 Madeira Place,

Kemp Town

☎ *01273 626696*

Huge choice of spirits including rare stuff not found elsewhere in Brighton. The newly designed menu is to be organic by with a wide range of veggie options. DJs play seven nights a week for a mixed bag of drinkers.

The Station

Goldstone Villas, Hove

📞 *01273 733660*

Cool drinking den next to Hove Station for youngsters who don't care about the chilly atmosphere.

The Star Of Brunswick

32 Brunswick Street

West, Hove

📞 *01273 771355*

The Star of Brunswick is something of a Brighton-drinker's institution. For those who want a late night, there's the option to pay £2 and you can booze till 1am.

The Sussex Cricketers

Eaton Rd, Hove

01273 734541

Previously a down-to-earth local pub with a focus on sports events and a pleasant lunch-time garden, Graham Greene's old favourite has now been transformed into a rather predictable, chain-run bore. In trying to be all things to all people, the end result tries way too hard. Imagine stark Swedish interiors meets trad pub décor (especially the carpets), with a handful of open fires, a stack of chopped logs and display units full of irrelevant artefacts and you've got the picture.

The Sutherland Arms

Sutherland Road, Queens Park

📞 *01273 603059*

Popular with sexy rock chicks in their forties, ageing musicians and members of The Levellers.

The Wagon and Horses

10 Church Road, Brighton

📞 *01273 602752*

Similar feel to The Mash Tun but not so self-consciously trendy. It is small, lively and the perfect place to meet up before a night on the town.

Walmer Castle

95 Queen's Park Road, Queens Park

📞 *01273 682466*

The Walmer Castle is an increasingly groovy environment to drink in with the young and the gorgeous. Expect it to be lively whatever night you go.

The Western Front

11 Cranbourne Street, Brighton

📞 *01273 725656*

It's impossible to miss this canary-yellow pub right next door to Churchill Square shopping centre. One of the best of the Zel pubs, it's conveniently located for chic shoppers in need of liquid refreshment or a light snack. The perfect spot to mull over a potential purchase, it's also a lively place to kick-start a night out.

pubs

bars

In Brighton, where so many clubs fill to capacity even before midnight at the weekend, bars are a popular alternative for a night out, particularly as many have a license until 2am. The majority are not attached to a chain so there is more scope for impressive and original style and design to dazzle you while you sip. Don't be surprised to find a queue outside the more central bars, and arrive early if seats are a priority.

Alfresco

The Milkmaid Pavilion

Kings Road Arches, Brighton

📞 *01273 206523*

More restaurant than bar, although because of the attitude of the management, we recommend skipping the pizzas and having a drink on the terrace over some rather unexciting olives with feta, enjoying the sunset and moving on. As such, it is Brighton's best sunset viewpoint, with its circular glass domed restaurant and terrace overlooking the West Pier.

Ali Cats

80 East Street, The Lanes (behind The Prodigal pub)

📞 *01273 220902*

Go down the stairs and into a dark den. Where are the windows? There are no windows. Where's the air? No air. Ali Cats is, in every senses, an underground dive. But if louche lounging is what's in your heart, this is the place for you. There's regular DJ spots, cult movies every night and reasonably priced booze. Get there early enough to grab a sofa.

Amsterdam

11/12 Marine Parade, Kemp Town

📞 *01273 688825*

Based on the tried-and-tested bar and sauna formula, the Amsterdam has managed to create a relaxed atmosphere for its mixed gay locals. With a predominantly wooden décor, this bar has an uncluttered vibe while still feeling fairly intimate. The seafront location makes the Amsterdam a convenient pre-club detour as well as a real suntrap, ideal for those summer drinking sessions.

Bababalabar

7 Albion Street, Brighton

📞 *01273 699840*

Behind the Pressure Point sits the Honey Club's own pre club bar, providing cheap drinks, love spuds (with salsa and soured cream) and fizzy vibe before a free mini bus transports the revellers down to the seafront club for the night, every night. Anyone can turn up (the bus leaves between 10.30 and 11.30pm) but regulars will get VIP invites. Stamped hands at Bababalabar allow for queue jumping for anyone who prefers their own form of transport.

Bamboo Bar

10 Kensington Gardens,

North Laine

📞 *01273 684426*

Much needed revamp of the shabby Grinders cafe which perched arrogantly above Kensington Garden's bustling market refusing to clean its tables and serving horrible food. This, the younger and hipper sister of the louche Fringe Bar downstairs, is as welcome to the Gardens as a waggy tailed puppy at a kids' party.

Candy Bar

St James' Street, Kemp Town

📞 *01273 622424*

Sister of the legendary lesbian Londoner, The Candy Bar is what Kemp Town kittens have been waiting for. Blokes are allowed in as long as they're a guest of a suitably oriented female.

Casa

155 North Street, Brighton

📞 *01273 738763*

Strange mix of style and girls out on the town (at the weekend at any rate). Tends to attract the central town post work crowd more than most, and heats up to a pre-clubber as the night goes on. It spreads across two floors with a swanky mezzanine for diners who can order their food over the Net before they arrive.

Charles Street

8-9 Marine Parade,

Kemp Town

📞 *01273 624091*

A slice of metro-chic reaches Brighton's pub-based gay scene at last with this new two-level bar (Charles Street) and club (Pool) on the seafront. The downstairs bar is where most of the money has been spent, and here you'll find tables, sofas, strategically lit standing room (you'll see) and a glam walkway for that all-important entrance. Teeming at the weekend with the pre-Revenge crowd, this bar has dragged Brighton's scene into the 21st century. A down-to-earth and reasonably priced food menu, served to your table by cute bar staff, an oh-so-cool unisex bathroom, beautiful people and prime location (there's a terrace for the summer too) look set to keep the place packed. The upstairs club, Pool, although clearly the poorer sibling, still exudes bags of style. So it's a shame that it will be offering 'cabaret' (ie drag) most nights of the week - when this is already well catered for elsewhere in Brighton's traditional boozers. The television screens advertising drink promos were a little off-putting and brought a slight whiff of tackiness to an otherwise stylish ensemble.

Circus Circus

2 Preston Road,

Preston Circus

📞 *01273 620026*

Standing loud and proud on the Preston Circus junction, this is the closest thing to a style bar in the area. All the key ingredients are there: large spacious bar, brash and bold walls and the odd settee. The location dictates that this will probably remain a nice place for a few pints before nipping over the road to the Duke Of York's cinema.

Easy

9 Cranbourne Street, Brighton

📞 *01273 710928*

Slap-bang in the centre of town next to Churchill Square, this is a straight forward, no nonsense pop-in-for-a-pint sort of place, somewhere to avoid the crowds during a busy weekend shopping spree and enjoy an unhurried beer. The sofas and gimmicks of other style bars have been shelved in favour of a simple more neutral look.

Fishbowl

74 East Street, The Lanes

📞 *01273 777505*

Another of The Honey Club's official pre club bars, with privileged queue jumping for those who hop to the sounds of the regular DJs before making it across the road. (See also Restaurant section).

The Fringe Bar

10 Kensington Gardens,

North Laine

📞 *01273 623683*

Exotic and sumptuously designed new restaurant-bar in the main artery of the North Laine. The leopard skin chaises and elegant low level tables where the beautiful people sip their champagne cocktails served by waitresses with flowers in their hair, are owned by the rather more

bars

studenty Bamboo Bar cafe upstairs, presumably designed for the folks they believe their punters will grow into. The Thai spiced crab and prawn cakes with chilli soy dressing (£4.75) were disappointingly gluey and the roasted tomato, basil and mozzarella tartlet with Mediterranean chutney (£4.25) was stunningly dull, but beauty doesn,t always have to be more than skin deep.

Gemini Beach Bar

127 Kings Road Arches, Brighton

📞 *01273 327888*

The largest and liveliest of the bars on the seaside strip, Gemini's epitomises summer in Brighton. Chrome seats spill out onto the promenade where carefree drinkers get an unrivalled view of the sea. Impromptu skate boarding stunts and live jazz bands help give the continental atmosphere a Brighton twist. By dusk the party's moved inside the cosy bar where securing a seat is as important as being noticed. The small capacity makes Gemini's fairly exclusive at weekends when the rich and famous come to mingle in the mellow ambience.

Greens

62 West Street,

Brighton

📞 *01273 778579*

A cocktail bar type of affair with wannabe chic that looks very smart. Maybe too smart. Still, it's dead central and, as they say in the old country, you can never have too many bars.

Guarana Bar

36 Sydney Street,

North Laine

📞 *01273 621406*

Not so much as café as an all purpose guarana shop, but while you're there stocking up on your energy bars and natural stimulants you might as well have a coffee or (maybe better) a 'guarana tea'.

Lanes End

54-55 Meeting House Lane,

The Lanes

📞 *01273 729729*

Only open at weekends, this is a stylish and approachable bar to while away an afternoon or kick-start a night out. Decorated in a cool, calm and collected shade of blue with subtle lighting, the open plan design gives Lanes End the feel of a hip loft conversion. The regulars are a mixed bag of drinkers ranging from sophisticated socialites to slouching students. There's no particular music policy at this bar, so don't expect to be treated to pre-club DJs, instead go for a serious drink and save the dancing 'till later.

bars

Legends

31 Marine Parade, Kemp Town

☎ *01273 624462*

Actually the bar for the seafront New Europe Hotel, but don't let that put you off. Its vibrant, funky design complete with sumptuous marble tables makes it well worth visiting. Bright and airy, it's particularly popular with gay men but all are welcome. In the evening there's cabaret acts (although the bar staff are known to break into song at all other times) and on Wednesdays it's a full house for the bingo night. Legends is the official warm-up bar for Revenge and there's usually some free tickets up for grabs if you ask behind the bar.

The Polar Bar

114 Western Road, Montpelier

☎ *01273 733245* and

St George's Road, Kemp Town

☎ *01273 683334*

Shows how fast things move in this town that The Polar Bar should have become an institution after being open only two years. A relaxed place to hang out during the afternoon or a steaming place by night, it's the business with its friendly service, architectural flower arrangements and cool Chesterfields. The newer Kemp Town version is more laid back, less the weekend madhouse, and a cool choice for a midweek drink.

Riki-Tik

18a Bond Street,

Brighton

☎ *01273 683844*

▤ *internet access*

Playstation junkies, Internetters and dressed up clubbers adorn this stylish drinking den. Primarily a pre-club bar where glamour and lager are dished out in equal measure, Riki-Tik is a lively spot to start the night. A host of DJs from Brighton's clubland get the young and hip clientele going around six nights a week. On Fridays fight through the crowded ground floor and relax with a cocktail in the more salubrious upstairs lounge bar. Those who find it all too much can ask at the bar for a Playstation and pretend that they are actually alone in their front room.

Shark Bar

57 West Street,

Brighton

☎ *01273 822555*

Inside, the purple exterior, it's minimal chic, and is a swanky space to stand and sip in style rather than lounge unnoticed in the corner, though the tiny shoe shop style stools make slouching a physical impossibility. Club class DJs man the decks seven nights a week and reaffirm the Shark's reputation as a full-on warm up to all the big nights.

Skid Row

20 Preston Street, Brighton

📞 *01273 326408*

Frequently receiving the accolade of 'Best Bar' by The Latest magazine, Skid Row successfully combines the creature comforts of a local with the full-on music policy of a banging pre-club bar. It's easy to see why this is a Brighton favourite. Renowned for its quality resident DJs' who serve up top tunes six nights a week, this is a friendly wooden-walled bar which is refreshingly unpretentious enough to welcome both party animals and home birds. And we haven't even mentioned their sponge cakes.

Squid

78 Middle Street, Brighton

📞 *01273 727114*

Squid is a stylishly designed spot to charge-up before a night out. Vibrant orange walls help soften the metal bar complete with Mexican style mosaic on top. Popular with a funky, laid back crowd who happily hang around while enjoying bargain priced shooters and chilled tunes on the stereo, its central location makes it a natural choice for clubbers heading to the Zap or the Honey. There's also a large bay window ideal for checking out the crowds already heading to the seafront while you soak up the pre-club atmosphere at its warmest.

St Peter's Bar

York Place,

Brighton

(opposite St Peter's Church)

Originally this was just as much a celebration of all things Russian as a bar named after the huge church opposite, but the new owners have updated and gone for a younger crowd, swapping blinis for breakbeat. Despite its proximity to the University, this laid back pre-club bar attracts a cooler breed of student eager to sample the cutting edge tunes while sipping cheap drinks. A good place to pick up flyers for house and hip-hop nights as well as info on Brighton's more alternative clubs.

Sumo

9-12 Middle Street,

Brighton

📞 *01273 823344*

On a mission to be first in the style bar stakes, Sumo's doing rather well. Spread over two floors there's space to dance to the DJs downstairs, although gentle toe tapping on your classy yet uncomfortable stool is more Sumo etiquette. This is where the fashion conscious converge, kick back and generally look cool. Sumo also benefits from having an extended licence, leaving plenty of time for another G&T, darling.

bars

Sussex Arts Club

7 Ship Street, The Lanes

📞 *01273 727371*

Brighton's members-only media hang out is no Groucho's, although the Chesterfields and all day licence do give its members a very relaxed venue for meetings. Membership has just gone up to £80 per year, but to their credit, they have introduced a worker's lunchtime membership of £10 a year which offers a fine place to have meetings between 12pm and 4pm. But £80? To have somewhere nice where you can do your after hours drinking, it's worth its weight. There's a ballroom in the back which seems to exist in its own time zone, and the often bizarre events from poetry readings to salsa nights to proper white weddings keep the place just the hip side of naff.

Tiger Bar

98 Trafalgar Street, North Laine

📞 *01273693377*

Tiger is a more restrained warm-up for the clubber who wants to start the evening in a laid back style and one of the few bars to visit if you fancy a few quiet beers. Listen, you can always meet here and go on to somewhere wilder if you want. (see restaurants)

The Tin Drum

95-97 Dyke Road, Seven Dials

📞 *01273 777575*

and

43 St James Street, Kemp Town

📞 *01273 624777*

The Tin Drum is more than a bar/restaurant. Spacious and chilled during the day, parents flock in with their toddlers after it opens its doors at midday and workers pop in for a veggie goulash or wild mushroom risotto (both £5.95). By night, it's a hopping venue where Seven Dialers and Kemp Towners end their day with poetry readings, live DJs and a good dinner.

late night drinking

It is the curse of the occasionally sociable. Getting a drink after hours is still, for some strange reason, a test of ingenuity in this country. If you're not a member and you're not in with the crowd, it sometimes seems absurdly difficult. However… apart from the clubs, hotels and restaurants, there are a few places where you can get a drink after hours. The legal ones are listed here and, OK, so you'll need membership for some of them. So test that ingenuity.

Charles Street and Pools

8-9 Marine Parade,

Kemp Town

📞 *01273 624091*

See main Bars section.

Brighton Marina Yacht Club

The Marina

☎ *01273 818711*

Greenhouse Effect

63 Church Road, Hove

☎ *01273 204783*

Grosvenor Casino

88-92 Queens Road, Brighton

☎ *01273 326514*

and

28 Fourth Avenue, Hove

☎ *01273 720261*

Membership is free if you give them 24 hours notice and take in your driving licence or passport. Or phone 08080 212121 and they'll send a form.

Hanrahans

Village Square, The Marina

☎ *01273 819800*

Hectors House

51/52 Grand Parade, Brighton

☎ *01273 682422*

The pub better known for being below the Pressure Point.

Hove Lagoon Watersports Centre

Hove Lagoon,

Western Esplanade, Hove

☎ *01273 424842*

International Casino Club

6,7,8 Preston Street,

Brighton

☎ *01273 725101*

King Alfred Suite

King Alfred Sports Centre,

Kinsgway, Hove

☎ *01273 738112*

Komedia (basement)

44-47 Gardner Street,

North Laine

☎ *01273 647100*

Kruze

5-7 Marine Parade,

Kemp Town

☎ *01273 608133*

Plaza

44-45 Kings Road, Brighton

☎ *01273 325229*

Pussycat

176 Church Road,

Hove

☎ *01273 735574*

🖳 *www.pussycatclub.co.uk*

Rendez vous casino

The Marina

As we write the builders are bulding. Maybe by the time you're reading this the roulette wheels will be spinning. Maybe.

bars

Star of Brunswick/ Vats Bar

32 Brunswick Street West, Hove

📞 *01273 771355*

Lurking beneath the unsuspecting Star Of Brunswick club there's the Vats Bar, dark and small and all things that an after hours bar should be. You can get food past midnight and sometimes there are DJs and entertainment.

Sumo Bar and Lounge

9-12 Middle Street, The Lanes

📞 *01273 823344*

See main Bars section.

Sussex Arts Club

7 Ship Street, The Lanes

📞 *01273 727371*

See main Bars section.

The Smugglers

10 Ship Street, The Lanes

📞 *01273 328439*

Tiger Bar

98 Trafalgar Street, North Laine

📞 *01273 693377*

See main Bars section.

clubs

clubbing in Brighton & Hove
by Lady Laverne *(the whore on the door at The Honey Club)*

Dear Clubbers,

If you're looking for a night of debauchery on the club scene, I'm just the girl to help you paint this town red.

First stop as you come down Grand Parade is the Ocean Rooms, oddly situated next to the fruit and veg market. Nights here are aimed at the slightly older, groovier clubber - well, 23 plus. Thursday is school disco night with Tanya Love and Sister G playing everything from Chas'n'Dave to the Birdy Song. Friday is always sold out due to Grand Central and Off Centre's residency with their breakbeat and hip-hop sounds. Saturdays is Boy, Girl, for boys to meet girls and vice versa while DJ Jacques Le Cont plays funky House music in the white room. The club also has a luxurious red room which serves as a VIP room/Cabaret/pre-club room from 6pm. Blag your way in via Miss Kimberley or The Perv.

Next stop is Zanzibar off The Old Steine for a mixed gay/student crowd who'll crush you against the bar on a Thursday for the two for one policy (that's drinks, darling) and regular pop icon. The weekends are hosted by the lovely Julie and Emma - yes, real women with their own in-house DJ spinning chart topping dance tracks.

Move down into Marine Parade for the

Escape where its new promoter Dan Boorman has opened a new chapter. Red Light Rush is still three on a Wednesday, another two for one deal, but only when the red light flashes. The menu for entertaining the attendant glitterati will focus on past winning formulae with a new and exciting, deep and dirty underground vibe on a Saturday. It's said to be a very sophisticated night out.

Come further with me to Madeira Drive below the Victorian Lift and we're at the Concorde II where a funky street wise crowd in acres of denim with low slung crutches dance the night away in a purple haze. The biggest night is Phonic Hoop (also at Enigma on Saturdays) where Mr Scruff plays a wicked six hour set on the first Friday of every month. A close second is the fortnightly Big Beat Boutique where Fatboy Slim occasionally plays. Other regular nights to watch for include Positive Sounds, Funkt, Experiments, Legends of the Dark Black and Knowledge of Self.

Let's go back along the seafront past Brighton Pier to the Honey Club, my spiritual home on a Saturday night, for Seven Sins, the best night around with Tall Paul, Daniele Davolli and top name DJs whipping the crowd into a frenzy. An extremely gay friendly venue and host to Kinky Booty on Fridays hosted by Stephanie Starlet with up for it punters getting down to the best house tunes. If Indie is your kink, Pop Starz on the first Wednesday of every month is not to be missed. And it boasts the poshest toilets this side of the Thames. It's open seven nights a week with Sundazed ending the weekend with a bang.

Going away from the sea front back up to town is The Gloucester, with its new lick of Jade Dulux not detracting from its Seventies underlit dance floor. Frequented by a mostly indie student type with a glam rock and heavy metal clientele (from the old Hungry Years), Lust for Life on a Friday is a joy. On Tuesdays, it's Sindrome with cheap drinks for weird and wonderful clubbers in leather mini-skirts and negligees. And that's just the men!

I'm off home now to get my beauty sleep. See you on the scene.

Lady Laverne

Bar Centro

3 Ship Street, The Lanes

☎ *01273 206508*

Home to Salsoteca dance school during the week, this is more a pre-club bar than a full-on club, but don't be fooled into thinking this is a quiet way to wind down the weekend, the vibe here is as crazy as in any club. But there are plenty of drinks offers to keep the momentum going.

Barracuda

139 King's Road Arches, Brighton

An occasional club with an 'unlicensed' status, the Barracuda switches between gay nights, alternative dance and some of the best trance and techno in town.

The Beach

Kings Road Arches,
Brighton

📞 *01273 722272*

Open door beach bar/cafe by day, closed throbbing heart of the seafront by night, everyone goes to The Beach at least once. Partly due to its name but mostly due to its location, The Beach is a favourite haunt of weekend trippers and anyone looking for that authentic Brighton clubbing experience. To locals, it's more the baby brother of the legendary Concorde Club, it was the temporary home of Friday night favourite Big Beat Boutique until it was claimed back. Still, it's always a good night out - just be prepared to queue.

Blue

100 Kings Road Arches, Brighton

📞 *01273 770505*

Relaunched as Blue, Cuba was always 'that other club on the seafront', but that's in the past. Blue - another split level club - has developed into a hot, jumping scene of its own. Young, sprightly and not so pretentious.

BN1

Preston Street, Brighton

📞 *01273 323161*

If you're into drum'n'bass and you want a nice small club to dance and chill and hang loose, this is the place for you. The decor could do with chilling a bit too - all that stark white paint and black lighting, it's hard on the eyes - but it's got a loyal following so obviously they don't mind.

Casablanca

Middle Street, Brighton

📞 *01273 321817*

The place for jazz and funk lovers. A biggish place spread over two floors, Casablanca gets the nod over most other places because the music isn't just a bloke with his record collection - it's sometimes actual people with actual records. Yeah, I know it's an odd idea. It'll probably never catch on.

Catfish

19-23 Marine Parade,
Kemp Town

📞 *01273 698331*

A club that's a bit on its own in Brighton town. Run by DJ Carl

'Rumble Chillin' Moses (a proper job character), the music veers towards R'n'B, Seventies blues and things that are played with proper instruments and sound real - Curtis Mayfield and James Brown and that kind of thing - and there's no age grief. People of all ages turn up and feel none the worse for it.

Concorde 2

Madeira Drive,

Kemp Town

☎ *01273 606460*

Brighton's legendary Concorde club re-opened January 2000, and not before time. Harry Hill, Eddie Izzard and Phill Jupitus all stood up in the Concorde's pre-fab comedy scout hut by the Pier, and Skunk Anansie played to a rapturous audience for a mere £30 in another time. Primal Scream practically lived there. Now down at the Black Rock end of the beach in a building which was originally a bus shelter, then a Victorian reading room and latterly a bikers cafe, and has a Victorian lift which is the oldest in the country linking the lower Madeira Drive to the road above. But does it work? Home to the fabled Big Beat Boutique night on Fridays. For tickets, ring or pop in to The Prince Albert in Trafalgar Street (01273 730499) to find out who's selling them this week.

Core Club

12 Kings Road,

Brighton

☎ *01273 326848*

Deep electronica in a small basement next to Dr Brighton's pub.

Cream

Aquarium Terraces,

Madeira Drive,

Brighton

It's a measure of Brighton's status in Clubland that when Liverpool superclub Cream decided to set up in another town, they chose Brighton. Last year we wrote this: "At the time of writing it's not open yet (it was due to open April 2000) but we know what to expect from these superclubs by now. Should be a treat." It's still not open. What can you say?

Enigma

10 Ship Street,

Brighton

☎ *01273 328439*

OK, so I'm biased, but Phonic Hoop might well be the best night in town right now. Home to the Ninja Tune beats, Phonic (Saturday nights) is all jazzy breaks, hip hop beats & all those other things that make us feel warm.

Escape

Marine Parade, Kemp Town

☎ *01273 606906*

Away from the seafront, The Escape is probably Brighton's most successful club. Set in a perfect Art Deco building just the Kemp town side of the Brighton Pier, it is young but not too young, hip but not too hip and dangerous but not too dangerous. Deep funk rules the roost but the most fun to be had is on Saturday night when the all-female DJ crew Dolly Mixers theme up the joint and get going. Maybe the place if you're 18 and looking for somewhere in between the big Paradox type places and the hipper seafront clubs. But beware, there's always a queue.

The Event 2

West Street, Brighton

📞 *01273 732627*

There's two ways of looking at this: we could say it's honest and unpretentious or we could say it's a bit of a meat-market. Either way, you know what we mean. Huge and cavernous and full of Seventies disco schtick like brown carpets and disco balls. You've got the idea by now, haven't you?

Funky Buddha Lounge

169 Kings Road Arches, Brighton

📞 *01273 725541*

ℹ *best club, latest juicy awards 2000*

The winner of last year's Juicy Award, the Funky Buddha is small but

perfectly formed. From the funky dance floor to the chilled out lounge, it's just there and feels just right and though a relative newcomer, it's already a favourite. Created with an eye on design - it's one of the few clubs to take it's shape into consideration - it boasts state of the art light and sound equipment but doesn't let any of that clubland hipper than thou preciousness get in the way of a good night out.

The Gloucester

Gloucester Place, North Laine

📞 *01273 688011*

The Gloucester's been going since before the game began and so deserves its place in history. If it's an unpretentious good night out you're after rather than a seat on the cutting edge, this could be for you.

Honey Club

214 King's Road Arches

📞 *07000 446939*

Remade and remodelled, the Honey Club is a sophisticated and stylish haven for dance types, and until Cream opens (whenever, if ever...) this is the closest in Brighton to a 'super club' with three gleaming bars, tardis-like toilets and a spacious chill out room in the back arch. There's a new balcony bar to watch the revellers while for the more adventurous there's enough podium space for those eager to strut their funky stuff.

The Jazz Rooms

10 Ship Street, The Lanes

☎ *01273 321692*

If modern jazz is your thang - jazz funk, Afro-jazz, Latin jazz, whatever - this will be your Nirvana. Down in this small, dark basement DJ Russ Dewbury - the man behind the Brighton Festival Jazz Bop - spins a sweat-soaked array of discs that, thanks to a conversation-killing sound system, sound fab. It's the sort of place where people go to dance and be friendly, not show off and be seen. Tuesday is dub reggae night. Surf Fm on a Sunday night is where you can hear Russ' music if you can't take the heat.

The Joint

West Street, Brighton

☎ *01273 321692*

Smoky basement club with kitsch, cosy seating and an intimate feel (it's that red lighting that does it) that aims to emulate that boho beatnik vibe. If you're into lounge and all that easy listening thang, then this is the place for you.

The Ocean Rooms

Morley Street, Kemp Town

☎ *01273 699069*

Said to have the best sound system in town, this is a three tiered night out with enough massive red sofas and velvet walls to reinvent Lounge Music. There's a cushioned-walled restaurant on the middle floor and a basement bar spruced up by glowing UV tabletops where a newly seduced clientele of art students idle during the week before the cocktail quaffers join them at weekends. As well as some of the best salsa lessons in town, Everyday People (featuring the very cool Ashley Slater) spin the discs once a month.

The Paradox

West Street,

Brighton

☎ *01273 321628*

Big and bold and brassy, The Paradox is the high end of the High Street nightclub. Chart, disco and Hi-Nrg share the space with the smart but casuals who are out for a good night. Next door is Club Barcelona, the same sort of thing but pitched a little older. I guess the idea is that when you hit 25, you can just move over.

Pool

8-9 Marine Parade, Kemp Town

☎ *01273 624091*

Charles St Bar's upstairs club, Pool, is clearly the poorer sibling, but still exudes bags of style. So it's a shame that it will be offering 'cabaret' (ie drag) most nights of the week - when this is already well catered for elsewhere in Brighton's traditional boozers. The television screens advertising drink promos were a little off-putting and brought a slight whiff of tackiness to an otherwise stylish ensemble.

The Pussycat (at the Zap)

Kings Road Arches, Brighton

☎ *01273 202407*

Five years and going strong, this is a one-nighter that's been going so long it's an institution. The Pussycat operates every Friday night at the Zap and kicks out a disco friendly mix of hard house and kicking glam.

Revenge

32, Old Steine, Brighton

☎ *01273 606064*

The largest gay club in the south of England, Revenge has a faithful following of gay men and women and their straight guests. It also has a reputation for consistently wild soirees (and considering it's open 6 nights a week that's some feat!). There are two floors to check out with two different styles depending on your taste. Friday's Lollipop is a party extravaganza and always pulls the crowd. The atmosphere is happy and hedonistic - the ideal start to the

weekend. Less room to move on Saturdays when it's hands in the air dance anthems 'til 2am. If all that's not enough, the second floor has panoramic views out to sea and over the floodlit pier.

The Shrine

11 Dyke Road, Seven Dials

☎ *01273 208678*

Gothy kind of place for those who think that life begins and ends with a kohl pencil. Fine by us.

The Tavern Club

Castle Square

☎ *01273 827641*

The place where the indie kids get their kicks because Thursday night is Indie Night at The Tavern. Friendly and open and unpretentious in that way that indie clubs are.

Underground

West Street, Brighton

Like The Shrine, Underground is a touch Gothicy round the edges, though maybe a bit more Velvet Underground than Sisters Of Mercy. Dark and a little bit pokey - just as these things are supposed to be.

Vats

32 Brunswick Street West, Hove

☎ *01273 771 355*

A late night drinking haunt where you

can get down and shake your booty should you feel so compelled. But really, it's more a bar than a club, so if it's that Wild Fruit you're after... look again.

Volks Tavern

Madeira Drive, Kemp Town

☎ *01273 682828*

Volks always was the perfect antidote to both the big, showy nightclubs and the hip beachfront places. It was the place you would go if you wanted a good night free of poseurs and tourists. Happily, it still is. Despite opening the basement and expanding, it's still groovy and slightly down-at-heel. Bargain beer prices and cheap entry have long attracted a loyal following of friendly up-for-it clubbers. Music wise, every night's a winner but highlights include Lunarcy's melting pot of techno, trance, jungle, D'n'B and general madness every Friday

Wild Fruit (at the Paradox)

West Street, Brighton

☎ *01273 321628*

On the first Monday of every month, something strange happens to the monolithic Paradox. Out go the lager-fuelled 18-year-olds and in comes Wild Fruit, a wild, glamourpuss of a night that was originally set up as a gay thang, but has become so popular that it's crossed over. It's still predominantly hi-energy gay and very camp.

Zanzibar

129 St James Street, Kemp Town

☎ *01273 622100*

This bar-cum-club a stone's throw from the Old Steine celebrates every camp cliché known to man. A bad thing? Not necessarily, no. Regular drinks promotions (check out Thursday's 'Crush Bar'), and the promise of cabaret acts strutting their stuff, mean that you'll pop in for one and end up staying all night.

Zap

Kings Road Arches, Brighton

☎ *01273 202407*

🛈 best club, latest juicy awards 2000

The oldest and maybe the best. With two main rooms and a maze of arch shaped corridors to explore, the Zap is the juicy award-winning original raver's playground. A true favourite among party people there's a variety of full-on nights to cater for every taste, and from the student friendly Eighties midweekers to the heaving Ibiza babefests at weekends it's obvious why the Zap has stayed such a popular club.

club listings

by John Chittenden at *surf 107.2*

monday

Club Tropicana
@ The Zap

Now where else, other than Brighton, can you get away with going to a club and dancing your pants off to Bros, Tiffany, Chesney Hawkes and Five Star? Well, maybe Leeds, but still. This is the ultimate 80's pop classics night, so if you're worried about your image, best go in heavy disguise. Presented by Filton, who bears an uncanny resemblance to Gianni from EastEnders. *Admission:* Free before 11:30 with a flyer, £3 after and £2 with concessions.

tuesday

The Funk Club
@ Casablanca

DJ Laughing Boy (ask him to tell you the one about the two nuns and the broom stick) plays a night of classic funk flavours (note I didn't say "flavas", cos how sad is that). Another top night and it's FREE!! At the weekends, the club features some really cool live music, plus some of the best-looking blokes in the city and they all go like trains... so I've heard. *Admission:* Free.

wednesday

Red Light Rush
@ The Escape

Two floors for the price of one, so no wonder it's popular with the students. Means they can spend more money on beer. Upstairs, Richie D and Dolcie Danger play club classics, while downstairs Dave Godding and Neil Silk Roden (he's just so smooth) spin the latest in up-front house. The tiled floor downstairs has come right off the set of the El Dorado. Nice. *Admission:* Free before 11:30, £2 after and £1 with concessions

thursday

Dynamite Boogaloo
@ The Joint

Hosted by Dynamite Sal, Boogaloo Stu and DJ W****r (and we all know what he's good at), the night promises the best in pop, indie, trash and disco. I've been there when they've played the themes to Wonder Woman and Cagney and Lacey and the dancefloor has gone mad. If you take your clubbing seriously, you'll want to commit suicide by the end of the night, but if you want a laugh, you'll get your money's worth - times ten.

Don't go before you catch the cabaret with Dolly Rocket, who is so overly-endowed, it's actually ridiculous. The fire brigade are often called to rescue men who are trapped deep in her cleavage. *Admission:* £4 or £3 with concessions

friday

Pussycat Club
@ The Zap

Now careful not to get confused here, cos there's a club in Hove with a similar name. At that club, things are a bit more fishy - if you get my drift. This one though is hosted by Sadegh and Jan, Brighton's answer to Richard and Judy. The club is what Brighton's all about. An up-for-it, no attitude, mixed crowd. The best house music. Guest DJ's have included Boy George, Judge Jules, Sonique and thankfully not a whiff of Peter Powell. *Admission:* £8.50 or £8 with concessions.

saturday

Phonic Hoop
@ The Enigma

Here you'll find one of the friendliest crowds on a Saturday night. Resident Rob Luis (who is just the nicest guy) has a bit of a thing with Mr Scruff (but not in that way), cos he's often guest DJing at the night and that's well worth checking out. Expect breaks, jazz, hip and drum'n'bass -

basically everything except Westlife. In the back room, you can play original versions of Atari and Pac-man. I can't wait for the day when they get that old Binatone game, where you can play tennis with yourself. *Admission:* £6 or £5 with concessions.

sunday

Sundazed
@ The Honey Club

This is definitely for the hardcore clubber. When most of us are at home watching Heartbeat and Ballykissangel (OK, so that's just me then), there are some animals who can keep it up all night (now that does sound more like me). DJ Jose, Little Jon (he's tiny), John Weatherley and Krunchie spin a popular night of techno and hard house. It makes me sound like my dad, but whenever I've gone, all I think is, God, these people have to get up for work tomorrow! *Admission:* Voluntary £2 contribution to cover costs.

John Chittenden is the co-host of *surf 107.2*'s daily breakfast show

teenage

13+

Brighton & Hove is a truly great place for teenagers, providing a wide range of entertainment and activities. So whatever you are in to you will always find a place to hang out. The selection of places to eat and drink is huge, whether it be a light snack or a heavy meal you're sure to find it.

by Beatrice Warren, aged 16

Busy Bee

Market Street, Montpelier

☎ 01273 205979

Small, cosy inside seating area plus tables and chairs outside where live bands are often playing. Reasonable prices and friendly people.

Mac's Cafe

30 Arundel Road, Kemp Town

☎ 01273 692621

If you are into a real cooked breakfast then this is for you. Cheap and cheerful with generous helpings.

Esprit

41 Market Street,
Montpelier

☎ 01273 748801

Popular, modern cafe, expensive but delicious. Often queues but large indoor and outdoor seating area.

Yum Yums Noodle Bar

22-23 Sydney Street, North Laine

☎ 01273 683323

Upstairs from the Chinese restaurant mini market. Good prices, a nice range, great tasting food and friendly people.

Waikikamoocau

11a Kensington Gardens,
North Laine

☎ 01273 671117

Vegetarian cafe. Cosy and colourful. Nice food but not cheap. Sofas and relaxed seating. Very friendly people.

Riki-Tik

18a Bond Street, North Laine

☎ 01273 683844

Lively modern internet cafe. Great place to sit down, surf the net and have a coffee.

Kensington's

1a Kensington Gardens, North Laine

☎ *01273 570963*

Friendly and affordable vast range of simple delicious foods. Many seats also balcony seating. Live music.

other activities

• If you are up for going out dancing then Brighton's club scene is absolutely brilliant. But don't despair if you are under 18 because the clubs Paradox (☎ *01273 321628*) and Event 2 (☎ *01273 732627*) offer a great night for young clubbers.

• If you are into Skateboarding, Blading, or BMX biking, then you will find ramps and grids at the Level, Brighton's small skate park. There is also a small ramp at Woodingdean, just outside Brighton. Serious BMX riders should check out Sheepcote Valley on the seafront where they often hold BMX championships.

• Brighton's seafront provides a volley ball court in the summer and a basket ball court all year round. Summertime, and most teens hit the beach generally near groynes to jump off. Watch out for Blading and skating competitions on Hove Lawns usually held at weekends. For windsurfing or sailing go to the Hove Lagoon clubhouse.

other useful organisations

Brighton Youth Theatre

☎ *01273 673211*

Brighton Youth Orchestra

☎ *01273 6433450*

• Winter indoor activities include: Ten Pin Bowling and Bowlplex at Brighton Marina, Virgin Cinema complex and the Odeon cinema's. Also, don't forget the fabulous Palace Pier and its many rides.

• If you want to buy some 'extreme sports' clothes or products, the best places to go are:

Fat Mamas

15 Sydney Street,
Brighton

☎ *01273 685110*

Independent skate shop, that sells all and everything to do with skateboards: stock includes, Flip, Birdhouse, Unabomber, Vans, Innes and Death and Clown.

Mambo

West Street

☎ *01273 323505*

Route One

Bond Street

☎ *01273 323633*

teenage

Bone Idol

125 Kings Road Arches

☎ *01273 770666*

Legends

Western Road

☎ *01273 204872*

Re-al

Dukes Lane,

☎ *01273 325658*

tweenage

My six fave places in Brighton

by Hayley Sensicle, aged 9

1. Churchill Square

Superdrug is the BEST, because of the hair and make-up stuff.

2. Brighton Pier

I love the doughnuts, the rides, but most of all the sweets.

3. The Boardwalk

on the seafront near Brighton Pier

It has great food and I love the milkshakes.

4. Browns

Duke Street

The best [and I mean the best] restaurant in Brighton. Great food and cool service.

5. Pine Secrets

East Street

This is a great shop selling gorgeous Bagpusses and loads of cuddly beanies, this shop also sells Pokémon and Digimon accessories.

6. Last, but not least, **the Seafront**, I like the beach because it's a place where you can hang out and chill.

teenage & tweenage

neighbours & neighbourhoods

Life in an estate agent's office has changed since The Juicy Guide became the relocator's bible. "*These days out-of-towners know more about the neighbourhoods in Brighton and Hove,*" says Paul Bonett, a local agent who deals more than most with prospective London buyers. "*That means they're more focussed on specific areas and it makes life a lot easier for everyone.*"

For others, the story remains the same as it did BJ (Before Juicy). "People spend more time choosing a video recorder than they do a house," Peter Gladwell of Halifax Property Services told us. "On day one, my clients tell me that they want a period character house with garden, garage and seaview. Very often, by the third day of looking, their specification will have changed completely; they realise that a period house near the seafront in Brighton will get them a patio garden and nowhere to park their car so they start thinking about the bigger, newer properties towards the north side of Hove. They think Brighton and end up in Hove. They think seafront and they end up near a park. They think Victorian and end up Thirties. But many haven't got a clue about what a town's really like to live in."

Which is why we trawled through Brighton and Hove's properties, parks, schools and playgrounds. We've reviewed the restaurants, bars and cafes like all good guidebooks, but we've also talked to the locals about what it's like to live here. House prices are obviously only a guide and have gone up since our first edition came out in May 2000. Prices were checked as we went to press at the end of March 2001, but Brighton and Hove is a city moving up in the world, and as more people decide to chill-out by the seaside, the prices will rise again. Until fairly recently, estate agents would tell sellers that a Londoner would pay anything you ask. No longer; while it's true that the proceeds from a small flat in Central London would buy a mansion in Brunswick Town, there's still a lot of sharp intakes of breath.

The different areas will probably maintain their identity despite the influx of out-of-towners. Social workers and teachers head for the pubs and community feel of Hanover. Expensive cars and big wallets go for the swimming pools of Withdean and Hove Park. And the gay crowd feast on the bars and clubs of central Brighton and Hove. We've stereotyped our friends and neighbours shamelessly, but what you've got here is from the horses' mouths.

So how do you find your tribe? House prices alone won't tell you; you won't find many pop stars in the million pound mansions of Tongdean, or many lawyers in the Millionaire's Row where Norman Cook and Zoë Ball, The Jamiesons and Nick Berry rub shoulders. The Greek statues on the front lawns of Withdean's castles might let on that there's money in them there hills, but if you're looking for the local pub or a late-night grocer, this is not your patch. Kemp Town with its bohemian reputation won't seduce many born and bred families with its patio gardens and three-storey houses, but its increasingly Boho feel and Council-funded facades has tempted the likes of Noel Gallagher and ex-Spice Girls' manager, Simon Fuller, in the past year. Even Posh and Becks have managed to save up for a little pad in one of those gorgeous crescents.

If it's Londoners you want to live with, chances are you'll buy in London-by-the-Sea, the seafront and streets stretching back to Davigdor, Seven Dials and some roads in Hanover. If it's Sussex and Home Counties you feel comfortable with, go for Hove Park, Tongdean and Withdean. If your people are the Brighton and Hove families who've lived here forever, you'll find them in Hanover, Queen's Park, outer Hove, Hangleton, Westdene, Moulsecoomb, Hollingdean, Bevendean, Woodingdean and Patcham. Listen, we told you at the beginning of this chapter about the stereotyping.

But first things first: are you a Brightonian or a Hoveite? If you think that Hove is for the elderly or the very rich, Brighton for the gay community, students and London refugees, think again. Once upon a time, Hove was famous for its zimmer frames and blue rinses, but as Brighton's star shone brighter attracting more folk to come and join the party, Hove with its gardens, bigger houses and quieter feel was able to soak up those who wanted to play in Brighton and get a good night's sleep in Hove. But don't be fooled; behind those muslin curtains, there's stuff going on that you don't want to know about. Well, Julie Burchill lives there so what do you expect?

If the main point of buying in Brighton and Hove is to make money on the deal, or to buy yourself the kind of space you could only dream of in your past life, think bedsitland. A fair few enormous houses split into bedsits or flats are still available and could be transformed into the mansion of your dreams - if you have the cash. The Council has a policy of maintaining the multiple occupancy dwellings, the sort of places those with a get-rich-quick mentality might kill for. The bottom line is that if it can house eight families, why allow a family of four to knock down the walls to make space for a bigger dinner party? The loophole is to be found in the old buildings that would cost the Council too much to maintain to meet fire regulations.

The Council also runs a scheme for those who want to make a bit of cash by buying a second property here. There are still lots of flats going for around the £80,000 mark which could easily be rented out to pay the mortgage. For those who want to stay true to their liberal politics, the Council will guarantee the rent if you agree to house an otherwise homeless family. In a City, which has the biggest homeless problem in the South East outside London, it's one solution which still safeguards your pension.

If you're driven by the need to have a garden, get yourself an ordnance survey map to see exactly where the gardens are. The roads north of New Church Road in Hove are where most gardens are to be found, as well as Arundel Road in Kemp Town, both with easy access to the sea and City centre. Once in the centre, you'll get little more than a yard or, if you're lucky (and loaded), a roof terrace. But before you dismiss the idea of a backyard, visit the gardens shown off as part of the Open Houses scheme in May's Brighton Festival (see The Season for details). The creativity is inspiring. There are also plenty of allotments available, so ring the Council for details.

A word about parking. Once upon a time, parking in Brighton and Hove was easy. Now it's about as easy as finding a space in central London. Traffic is increasing and the wardens are smartening up their act, and worse (or better - you decide) the residential streets in Kemp Town, Queen's Park, Hanover and Hove have recently, or are about to be, allotted residents' parking bays, although non-residents can park here for up to four hours at a time. The standard tariff is £80 a year to park your car.

Estate agent Paul Bonett points out that there are still areas in Brighton and Hove where houses with gardens are affordable - even on a limited budget. "To the east is Whitehawk, close to East Brighton Golf Course, the Racecourse and The Downs, while north of Queen's Park is the Queen's Park Estate. Beyond Elm Grove are Bevendean, Moulsecomb and Coldean Estates, handy for the universities, with Hollingdean Estate beyond Hollingbury and near the golf course. Over into Hove,

sponsored by **University of Brighton**

city art

Brighton and Hove is a city characterised by its art, with an infrastructure that respects and - sometimes - supports it. From the Open Houses, the informal exhibitions in artists' own homes which has been part of the Brighton Festival for the past 15 years, to the University of Brighton which produces a stream of new talent and South East Arts, the Arts Council body which awards the funding, the message is that art is a vital part of the spirit of Brighton and Hove.

City Art is our own exhibition space that shows off some of the great talent living here. All the paintings are for sale - or at least they were when we launched in May. Contact us via the website: www.juicyguides.co.uk if you would like to put your offer in and we'll put you in touch with the artist. If you're too late, you'll also notice that we've got a gallery on the website, and we'll be updating it regularly to show off the wealth of great work that's coming out of this city.

For dimensions and sales information on the art shown on these pages, visit **www.juicyguides.co.uk**.

SARA HILL GALLERY

1st floor, Risby Butler, 'The Designers'
42, Church Road, Hove 01273 749933

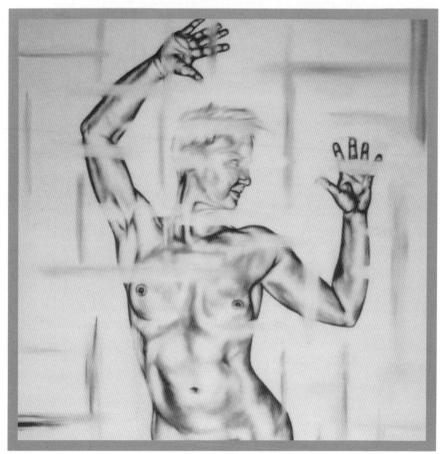

tuesday-saturday 10-6
original oil paintings • exhibits change regularly
www.risbybutler.com • www.artisticlicense.co.uk (artist register)

Sara Hill Over 30 regularly changing works are on display from this internationally selling artist at The Sara Hill Gallery including colourful, energetic figures and mesmerising abstracts in oil. Prices range from £100 to £1000.

Sponsored by **Rigby Butler and Avard Estate Agents (01273) 696000**

Ann Gardner trained at the Slade at both undergraduate and postgraduate level. In 1993 she won the Windsor and Newton Young Artist of the Year Award and for two consecutive years she was a National Portrait Awards finalist. More recently she received a David Bailey scholarship to study painting in South West France. Ann's work is held in public and private collections.

Ann Gardner trained at the Slade at both undergraduate and postgraduate level. In 1993 she won the Windsor and Newton Young Artist of the Year Award and for two consecutive years she was a National Portrait Awards finalist. More recently she received a David Bailey scholarship to study painting in South West France. Ann's work is held in public and private collections.

Ann Gardner

Natalia Lara Stevenson-Oake trained at Brighton University. Natalia is an award winning artist specialising in printmaking. Her work featured here is from a series of monoprints called "Distortions" inspired by dance and movement. Each work is on sale for £500.

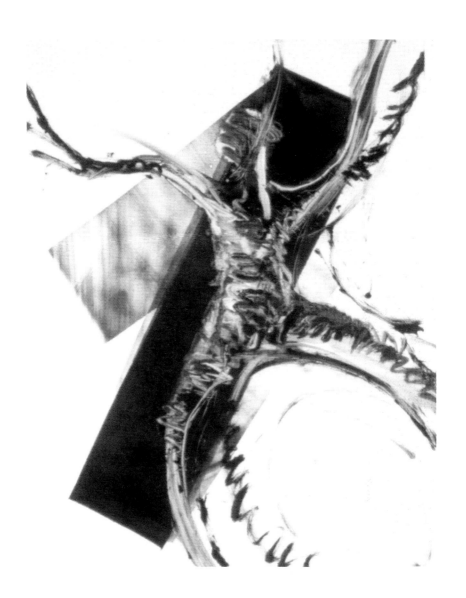

Natalia Lara Stevenson-Oake

area map of the city of
brighton & hove

SARA HILL GALLERY

1st floor, Risby Butler, 'The Designers'
42, Church Road, Hove 01273 749933

tuesday-saturday 10-6
original oil paintings • exhibits change regularly
www.risbybutler.com • www.artisticlicense.co.uk (artist register)

Sara Hill Over 30 regularly changing works are on display from this internationally selling artist at The Sara Hill Gallery including colourful, energetic figures and mesmerising abstracts in oil. Prices range from £100 to £1000.

Sponsored by **Rigby Butler and Avard Estate Agents (01273) 696000**

Artist in residence at Gallery 73, **Katje Lelic** specialises in quirky handpainted relief woodcarving. The gallery also shows an eclectic mix of jewellery, ceramics, sculpture and greeting cards.

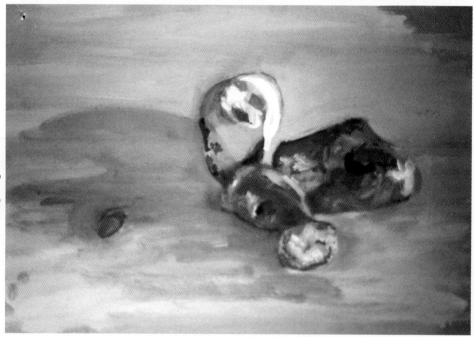

Lucy Timmer is an interior design student, exhibiting watercolour and oil paintings. She is interested in commissions for architectural drawings.

University of Brighton

Anthony McIntosh is a mature fine art student with a background in psychiatric and general nursing. His work is concerned with the creation, storage and retrieval of human memory.

University of Brighton

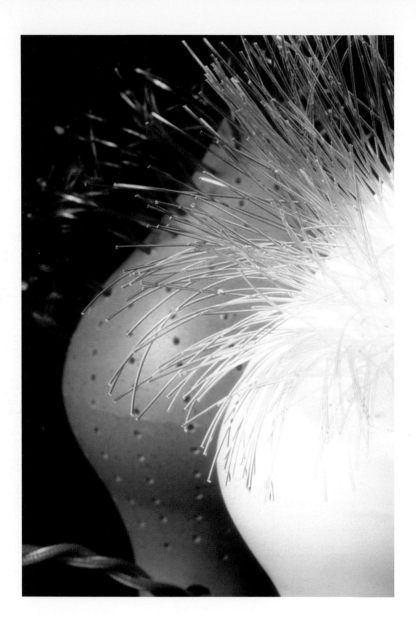

Frances Doherty's work, *Dandelion Light and Porcelain and Monofilament*, is an example of the exceptional designs which come out of the University's 3D department.

University of Brighton

Moira McNair is a mature fine art student who came from a primary school teaching background. Her oils and watercolours are inspired by the process of decay and regeneration.

University of Brighton

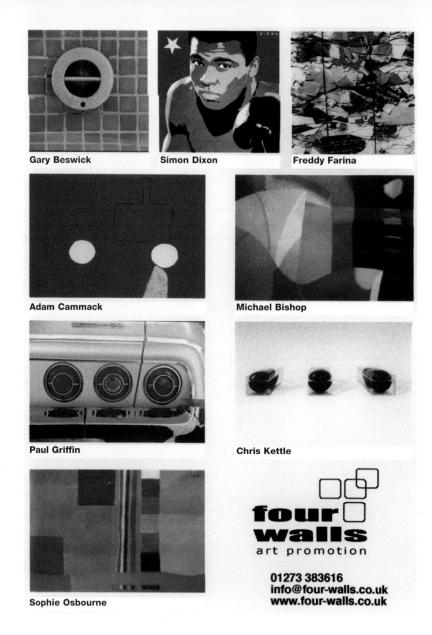

Gary Beswick

Simon Dixon

Freddy Farina

Adam Cammack

Michael Bishop

Paul Griffin

Chris Kettle

Sophie Osbourne

Lara @ Four Walls is a mover and shaker in the local art world, exhibiting her artists in some of the best bars in town. She was responsible for making sure that Simon Dixon's work was prominently displayed in the Tin Drum at Kemptown when Eastenders was shooting there earlier this year.

there are estates in Hangleton close to the Downs leading towards Devil's Dyke and the countryside."

Paul suggests families look at Patcham and Westdene, both of which have strong communities linked to the primary and junior schools. "I sold a gorgeous 18th century cottage in Patcham Old Town and a lovely flint-fronted wing of a 17th century mansion house. The family who bought it had moved from Queen's Park to get more of a garden. And they've got access to the best baker in town, Patcham Bakery, which sells the best doughnuts and curry pasties you've ever tasted!" Portslade is also a good place to look for cheaper properties. "A new three-bed semi with a garage and garden will cost you £150,000. And it's two minutes away from the A27 and about 15 minutes into the centre of Brighton."

Saltdean, a three-mile hike from Brighton and Hove is becoming increasingly popular, particularly with the Hanover types who want to buy a bigger house, but find themselves trapped in the property boom. As a result, a community of young families seems to be taking over, with the local toddler groups and primary schools the epicentre of social life. Rentals are hard to come by, but a three-bed house with garden is around £900 a month. To buy, three-bedroomed houses - most of them detached bungalows with loft extensions, front and back gardens and plentiful parking, on or off road - begin at £125,000.

An ambulance siren can only mean one thing in Saltdean: another property on the Market (it's no coincidence the estate agent is next door to the funeral parlour). As oldies move out feet first, young families, wanting more garden and parking spaces for their money, move out of Brighton and into Saltdean. Gay couples have also discovered it, bringing a cosmopolitan vibe to what was once a sleepy retirement resort. It's still a resort (evident by every shop selling ice-cream), but with a strong community spirit. A dedicated group known locally as the Saltdean mothers run the pre-schools, toddler and baby sessions and support the excellent primary school. Their latest project involves transforming the oval park, the green heart of Saltdean, planting trees, replacing the slide and building a tea hut to sell even more ice creams.

MARINA BAKER, *author of* Spells for Teenage Witches, *lives and works in a 1930s mansion in Saltdean*

Take some time out to sit in the cafes, pubs and parks to ponder where to buy in Brighton and Hove. More than anywhere, parks are where you will find your particular tribe. Eavesdrop or join in at St Ann's Well or Queen's Park, cheer the football teams at East Brighton and Preston Parks and reminisce about the old days with Hove's born and bred at Hove Park café. People-watching is never more fun than when kids are involved, and the parenting skills of St Ann's Wells media dads is the stuff of sitcoms. It may seem as if all the best properties are being snapped up, but relax and enjoy the varying vibes of Brighton and Hove before you ring an estate agent.

montpelier

Aesthetically, Montpelier is one of Brighton's most appealing areas, and in a city with so much stunning architecture, that's saying something. Large white houses lurk in streets of pastel hues lending an atmosphere of style rather than wealth, a feel of Mykonos rather than Belgravia. Montpelier is about as close to central Brighton and Hove as you

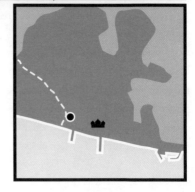

can get. The luvvy of Brighton neighbourhoods, it buzzes all year round, leaving little peace for its chic, funky residents. But that's why they choose to live here: this is where the action is, and most have the money to pay for it.

Montpelier is small enough to negotiate and close enough to everything for access. If you live here, you walk. What's the point of the car anyway? Residents pay £80 a year for a parking permit, there are precious few garages or off-road parking, and by the time you get in to your car, drive, find somewhere to park, you could be where you want to be. Montpelier people walk to the shops and the sea. They walk to the schools, to see friends or St Ann's Well Gardens. Soho apart, it's rare to find a community feel in the centre of a city, but Montpelier pulls it off.

Montpelier Villas is one of Brighton's most gorgeous streets with its Mediterranean-style houses and spiky yuccas leading the eye down to the sea. Montpelier Terrace and Montpelier Place leading to Upper North Street has a typically Brighton mix of small, but beautifully decorated houses and large villas. In the Clifton Conservation area, a large four-bedroom house will cost around

Typical Day of a writer and performer living in the Montpeliers... Get up at the crack of midday and walk along Clifton Terrace past St Nicks church where my mother is church warden. I push my way through hundreds of McGann brothers (in leisure slacks), and the cast of Eastenders as I make my way to the Brighton Natural Health Centre in Regent Street. Once there before I settle down to writing I submit to a torture session of gyrotonics with my 'trainer' Laurie Booth (famous dancer and capoeira expert). Emerge cursing but about 4 foot taller and say to the people lining up to do yoga or 5 rhythms or bellydancing, "Just popping to Infinity." Which is an hilarious joke in anybody's language. Infinity and Neals Yard just opposite are where I spend my happiest hours buying healthy snacks and remedies. Neals Yard is brilliant because you can moan on about your symptoms for centuries and they are still nice. On Fridays I do love to go to the Regency Fish bar on the seafront. Sometimes Red Ken goes as well and we chat about old times when he and I ran London. (Well, we both wrote for the Evening Standard. And I admire his safari jackets..er... and ultimate power over people).

LOUISE RENNISON, *writer and performer*

£475,000, a medium-sized, three-bedroom house will go for between £250,000 and £325,000 and a two-bedroom one will cost between £170,000 and £215,000. Powis Square, with its elegantly distressed balustrades and peeling white paint, still exudes a Georgian grandeur and attracts a hip but wealthy resident. Set in the heart of the Montpelier/Clifton area, the five-storey houses (some with 30-foot gardens) are worth between £350,000 and £650,000, despite the neglected state of the central communal garden which is a much-loved play area for the local kids. Flats and converted maisonettes are a better buy (and tend to be in better condition), and go for around £145,000.

seven dials

Seven Dials is a self-contained pocket of sophistication, which revels in its autonomous culture. It has become a prime location for commuters being only minutes away from Brighton station, while Hove Station is only a short bus ride away. Estate agents are keen to stress to prospective buyers that you can buy anything you want here. On Dyke Road you'll find a couple of excellent

Confessions of a London refugee

There are at least 20 yoga classes taking place at any given time of the day in this city; I can bend my body into contortions for less than a fiver, in a Buddhist Centre, an African artefacts warehouse, a church hall, a healing centre, a front room. At any time of day, I can go out for a loaf of bread and be gone for hours, simply because Giovanni, the Italian greengrocer in Seven Dials has decided to sing the five verses and four choruses of Santa Lucia whilst serving me with olives. And I can walk back from the beach ,with my towel under my arm on a late summer's evening, smugly content in the knowledge that all those "trippers" are stuck in a traffic jam in Croydon on their way back to the metropolis.

JOANNE GOOD, *breakfast presenter, BBC Southern Counties*

delicatessens, a late-night chemist (Ashtons), a designer florist and an organic greengrocers. The Tin Drum, the coolest bar/restaurant in the neighbourhood, puts its tables on

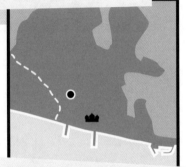

We love living in Brighton because it's full of people who think they are living in Spain! There's nowhere else in England where you would nip to the shops for a pint of milk and end up on the beach (having just signed up for guitar/yoga/Spanish lessons), a cocktail in one hand with three new friends and a fabulous new outfit! It's the first place ever where we've actually hung out with our neighbours, been on first name terms with our newsagent, deli-man, postwoman, greengrocer etc (we even know the name of the local traffic warden, but you couldn't print it!) Fabulously funky little hotels so we can still have our 'dirty weekends' here. Well, where else is there? You could eat in a different place and drink in a different bar every day of the year - and believe me we've tried!!! And we couldn't live without Pussy, our favourite shop, and love being verbally abused by Gwen. The calm of the sea, the drama of the Downs, the weird, wonderful, colourful, glitteringly wild population (and that's just our neighbourhood). Only the truly boring could ever be bored by Brighton!

JULIE GRAHAM, *actress*

the street pavement when the sun shines, attracting a visible coffee-drinking, paper-reading weekend crowd and enough of an evening buzz to pull the locals in for a Sea Breeze.

Almost all the Regency and Victorian houses have been divided into flats. This year, the wannabe roads are still Vernon Terrace where you'll find a two-bedroom flat for £125,000 and the busy Denmark Terrace where some of the high ceilings and large rooms are magnificent. Beware the shamelessly chopped-up Eighties developments, though. A one-bed in the ever-popular Chatham Place will cost around £70,000. If you want real Regency style with balustrades and balconies, you might just pick up a maisonette in Compton Avenue for around £175,000. Nosey neighbour and creative director of Latest Homes Andrew Kay reckons that Dyke Road is the area to watch. "There's a fabulous 5 bed Tudorbethan house just off Dyke Road with sauna and jacuzzi, outside pool, garden and double garage going for £285,000".

Well I was born on one side of Hove Park and now I live on the other, so how handy was that to move? I am one of few Brighton folk to be born here and having lived in Ireland, Scotland and the USA, the lure of mussel and the odd cockle was just too much. Favourite pub (this week anyway) has to be The Colonnade, right next door to the Theatre Royal. It was probably quite fashionable about 50 years ago, but it's still fascinating looking at the faded signed photos of various E-list celebs who've been on stage at the Theatre (check out the sexy picture of Playaway's Brian Cant). It's the best place to chill out after a long day's work (but keep that to yourself). Once we've got the engines burning, a trip to The Honey Club is in order. I don't know about you, but there's nothing more off-putting than going to a club where everyone's a complete minger. Well not at The Honey Club. It may have been in the ladies toilet, but I've met male models and the like in there. Gorgeous. Saturday nights are the best because they'll bring the best-looking people to the front of the queue. Hence I normally get in the club about 3:30am.

JOHN CHITTENDEN works at Surf 107.2, as the producer of the Breakfast Show and editor of the website. He lives just off Dyke Road.

As much as the sea and the piers, The North Laine makes Brighton what it is with a plethora of simply fabulous and quite extraordinary shops where you can buy anything that your heart desires - as long as it's funky. From hippy, dippy, grunge gear, to post-modern garden equipment, you can get it here, and if you want it in pink Day-Glo fake fur, all the better. If

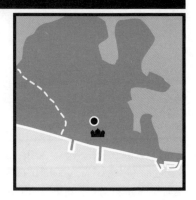

you love kitsch, you'll be in Heaven. Sit in any one of the chic cafes or bars and watch the world go by: it's better than anything you'll see on the telly.

Living here is a buzz - certainly at the weekend and in the summer when the party barely stops. In some of the quieter roads such as Titchbourne Street and Queens Gardens, the residents find their tranqulitiy in their tardis like homes - a top buy if the Jubilee development gets the go ahead. The grand plan is to open up the back of the Komedia Theatre to extend their cabaret space and rehearsal rooms, and create a glass fronted box office on Regent Street. If they get permission, Botanica, the garden shop next door, will join The Komedia's extension, creating a winter garden conservatory out the back overlooking the new Jubilee Centre with the children's library attached to the Prince Regent swimming pool.

Plans for the Centre itself include an alfresco cafe-fest, 15 "niche" retailers and an organic supermarket in keeping with the of spirit of The North Laine. A brand new twitten will be created to link Regent and Jubilee Streets with workshops, a doctor's surgery and pharmacy keeping the community feel. Loft-style apartments will be built on top of them to house the cafe society that is the North Laine, and a four star hotel is planned for the southern end of the new Square for anyone who just can't bear to leave.

You may not find a garden, but you are right in the centre of town where a small terraced house might cost anything from £140,000 to £350,000. A family house in Pelham Square will cost around £285,000 plus. Despite the changes, the active North Laine Community Association prides itself on retaining its roots. Local historian Jeff Mead describes North Laine as 'Islington on Sea', but stresses that though it has become gentrified, it upholds the tradition of embracing the diverse and unusual. Similarly, the cost of property for retailers is much lower than

Why do I live in Kemp Town? From the train I can ring Paul at Brampton's the butchers and order a leg of lamb before he closes. He'll take it to Protos, the fruit and veg shop opposite, who'll pay for it for me until I pay them back. Then I go for a drink in the Polar Bar, which rescued the old Burlington from sub-Victoriana chintz and cheese by creating a modern pub where you can have a pint without getting stuck to the carpet. Then I can wander back home along the front past one of the great Regency seafronts in the world. Part village, part city grandeur where the sea and the buildings square up to each other, creating a frontier of unending ambition on which to live. So why would I ever move? Kemp Town. The World.

SIMON FANSHAWE, *writer and broadcaster*

in central Brighton, and the North Laine Traders ensure that rents are kept low. In a truly Brightonian move, the Association advises potential shopkeepers on leases that will benefit them as well as the landlord.

kemp town

Inevitably called Camptown, this village of students, gay folk and London media refugees stretches east from the Brighton Pier to the Marina. It has some of the most beautiful Georgian architecture in Brighton including Sussex Square, Marine Square, Chichester Terrace, Lewes Crescent and the gorgeous Royal Crescent, an exquisite half-

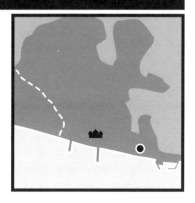

circle of black and white Regency buildings dating back to 1807. Nestling behind these extraordinary squares is the shopping area, a multi-cultural feast of Chinese medicine, transvestites' naughty nightwear, Dolly Parton-wannabe frocks and the most entertaining Safeways in the country where Kemp Town's magical mix buys its cornflakes.

In April 1999, the Kemp Town Business Association raised more than £250,000 to build a symbolic "village square" called Fish Market Square. To celebrate Brighton's diverse cultural life it was decided to bury symbols from different religions: a Jewish scull cap, a Hindu prayer book, a palm cross, a wooden cross, a silver earth goddess, a crystal from Glastonbury, Japanese wishes of good luck, pebbles and toys put in by children and lastly Tibetan prayer papers. All these were placed under the design of a mosaic fish that was designed by a local artist. The Kemp Town business community has also pledged its support for caring for the vulnerable, and many shopkeepers work with the police and careworkers to provide support for the mentally ill.

The Council has poured money into a regeneration project that has attracted new business, restaurants and bars to the area. New bars like the Tin Drum and The Candy Bar haven't so much changed the character of the place, but they have succeeded in luring more Kemp Towners out at night which makes after dark in St James' Street a very different experience.

Home to Scene 22 café, Brighton's gay information centre, St James Street turns the corner into St Georges Road, as camp takes second place to more ordinary village delights. Here the Aladdin's Cave of Brighton Fleamarket sits next to The Kemp Town Deli, The Fish At The Square, Protos, the greengrocer, and Brampton's, the oldest - and some say the best - butcher in Brighton. And, of course, Kemp Town Bookshop, one of the last bastions of independent bookselling.

Sussex Square, part of the Kemp Town conservation area, vies with Clifton Terrace as the best address in Brighton. In the main, the houses have been divided

New York was out of the question, so in September '99, I moved to Brighton, spurred on by London property prices and a disinclination to live in a flat the size of a bus shelter. I had a "woman-by-the-sea observing dramatic sunsets, hair billowing in the breeze" kind of vision of myself, but sadly this came with deeply neurotic undertones; what if I make no friends, never go out, become sad and lonely and start harassing naked men on the beach? I shouldn't have worried. My house is a seven minute walk to the beach - on a good day, i.e. not a day following a night of several vodka and Redbulls too many, nor a day that started with a champagne brunch. This louche existence means that I've haven't seen much of the sea or the Downs, but that I have met some absolutely gorgeous people. Brighton's size allows for the sort of spontaneity Londoners can only dream of. It's just not the sort of place where you have to synchronise diaries at 20 paces. Three months in and not only do I feel totally at home, I'm having a complete ball. And I've even started baking.

ANNA ARTHUR, *42, has a PR company (Anna Arthur PR) in London and lives in Kemp Town*

into flats and the rooms vary enormously in size. What makes Sussex Square unique is not only its beautiful exterior and sublime seaviews, but also its incredible five-acre communal gardens split in two by Eastern Road. The lower lawns hide a secret rose garden and has its own tunnel leading to the beach, the spot which, according to local legend, inspired one-time resident, Lewis Carroll, to write Alice Through The Looking Glass. Residents in Sussex Square, Lewes Crescent, Arundel Terrace and Chichester Terrace are automatically given a key. Prices have risen dramatically in recent months, so expect to pay up to £140,000 for a ground-floor, one-bedroom flat, and watch out for maintenance payments on these Grade One-listed buildings. You can add zeros as you add bedrooms, the same as in the Brunswick area.

One thing to remember about Lewes Crescent and Sussex Square is that Thomas Kemp, the architect of Kemp Town, only built the facades of the sweeping white Georgian buildings which give the neighbourhood its distinctive character. He sold the plots themselves to a number of different property developers which means that there's an enormous difference in style from one house to another, with some accommodating swimming pools in their sub basements while others remain extremely humble flats.

Down the seafront on Marine Parade, the architecture is positively palatial and the flats boast awesome seaviews. If you're seduced by Kemp Town's proximity to the sea and its village atmosphere, beware: prices are going through the Grade Two-listed Georgian roof - something which won't be helped by The Independent listing it as one the most desirable places to live in England. A five-storey Regency house will set you back anything from £350,000 to £1 million. And there's always that rumour about Posh and Becks.

The Kemp Town Carnival, a fund raising day: bed races through the streets, Morris Men, funky floats and live music, has become a yearly 'must do' for the locals.

queen's park

Queen's Park has been called the heart of Brighton - and you can see why. It is a family place; couples move here who have grown out of their flats and want more space for the kids with easy access to both Kemp Town and the centre of town. Queen's Park itself - maybe the most beautiful park in Brighton - was designed and built as an ornamental garden in 1824, and is flanked at each end by two formal arches and built in a deep hollow giving the park dramatic views sweeping down to the sea. It is beautifully laid out, with a wild garden, landscaped stream, tennis courts and bowling green, and facilities for the elderly and the disabled. There's also a well-equipped children's playground that heaves in the summer with queues for the swing and the café. The park remains one of the most relaxed meeting places in town and while you don't have to have kids, it helps.

Queen's Park is a strange cross between Kemp Town and Hanover. Some of the biggest gardens and most expensive properties are here, but you can get a three- or four-bed property with seaviews for anything from £180,000 to £300,000, depending on how grand you want to be. Purpose-built flats such as Carn Court go for £60,000 to £100,000 and are unusually spacious. And with views from the top of the hill over the English Channel, you might want to think again about that dive in Montpelier.

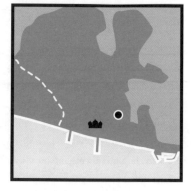

East Drive and West Drive, which curve around the park, are the area's best addresses with their large, semi-detached Victorian houses and some of the biggest gardens in Brighton. Expect to pay in the region of up to £500,000. Freshfield Road runs from Eastern Road and up past the Racecourse towards the Downs. The towering Victorian houses make great family homes and go for around £285,000, although the three-bedroom terraces further up towards the race course go for around £180,000 to £200,000. Even the more recently built Thirties houses have increased in value as this area becomes ever more popular. You might be lucky and get a four-bedroom house for under £200,000. Canning Street falls in the middle of Queen's Park and Kemp Town area. Canning Street residents love their plants and virtually every exterior cascades with greenery. Popular with families, the Victorian three-bed houses range from £155,000 to £185,000.

hanover

Hanover is a dense spread of Victorian houses that wiggles down from Queen's Park Road to The Level. Originally built to accommodate the train and carriage labourers working at Brighton station, the small terraced houses have historically fostered an intense community spirit. The houses are generally too small to convert into flats - apart from Ewart Street, with its 'older style, purpose-built' flats, some with small gardens. This has built a strong owner/occupier community that still exists, and today Hanover has its own website complete with area pub guide and

Why do I live in Brighton? Where else could I encounter giant jelly fish gliding on the low tide on an otherwise uneventful Sunday morning, accompanied by a string quartet, and presided over by our own resident mermaid? Where else could I take the children on the beach every day in the summer until the sun sets, and watch the herons and dolphins, or feel the thrill of the race course on race days in my lunchtime. Here I can sip my tea in the Meeting Place Cafe, and wonder if those four elderly ladies sitting opposite you in identical twinsets, pearls, ill fitting wigs, and large snap shut handbags are really bank managers from Surbiton.

JULIE JENNINGS, *39, single parent and ceramicist, lives in Elm Grove*

even its own guidebook.

Hanover Lofts, the beautifully designed flats sculpted from the Old Finsbury School by former It Girl Tara Bernard, and her new hubby, Manhattan Loft magnate John Hitchcock, cleverly tap into what Hanover may well become.

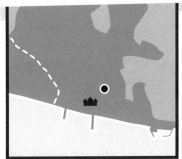

Hitchcock is said to be the man who spots how we want to live before we know ourselves, and if that's the future for Hanover, get saving. They're all sold, of course: £150,000 for a one-bed flat up to £400,000 for a two-bed flat spread over 2100 square feet. But keep an ear out for the patter of tiny feet that will send all those sexy Hanover Loft couples off to Queen's Park in search of a garden and open the communal door to a stream of New Hanoverians.

Hanover is well placed for schools, with access to Queen's Park, Elm Grove, Fairlight and St Lukes which keeps the kids in the community. Life revolves around the great pubs - Hanover's pubs are legendary - and the Hanover Community Centre in Southover Street (01273 694873) where an eclectic range of events are held from the Hanover Beer Festival (held annually on October 23), to yoga, toddler groups and live music. In the middle of August, Hanover celebrates as the streets are closed to cars and a good, old-fashioned street party takes place. For the rest of the year, the party never stops in Southover Street, which boasts an unnatural amount of good pubs. Walking down the steep hill, the first pub you come across is the Pub With No Name where the beers are said to be unsurpassable by those in the know. Stumble past The Napier to The Goose That Flew Over The Water, with its candlelit garden, and on to the eatery and music venue, The Greys. There's a cute story that The Geese Have Gone Over The Water used to be called The Geese but the signwriter commissioned to paint the sign couldn't paint a goose and rather inventively painted a stretch of water instead. Could be true.

Hanoverians - characteristically social workers, teachers and first-time Brighton buyers - used to say that you live here until the kids force you to move to Fiveways or Queen's Park. That's changing now as Brighton and Hove become too expensive and locals are beginning to complain about being trapped by the property boom. Not so long ago, Hanover was a haven for first-time buyers, but the prices are moving swiftly upwards and a two-bedroom in Stanley Street will cost upward of £120,000. Hanover Crescent, which is part of the Valley Conservation area, is the smartest road in Hanover with its 24 listed buildings, but it is rare to find a flat or house for sale these days especially with its proximity to the station. Estate agents value flats there from £90,000 depending on room size, and the houses start at around £300,000 - one sold in 2000 for £700k!

Dee and I moved from London more or less on a whim in 1975... hard to believe, but there's so much to do in this city, if you have enthusiasm and energy, and suddenly its 25 years on! Looking out the kitchen window on a clear day and seeing the sea in the distance - it's brilliant. One day we'll move and get a full-on sea view...that would be nice. We're at last getting spoilt for choice for restaurants, although years ago it wasn't like that... and of course, just crossing the road for a bottle of wine from The Butlers Wine Cellar - too handy! The worst thing about living here is the number of interesting things you never get to see, because of the other interesting things you do get to see... can't be bad. And what about the mix of people... the world in microcosm; and, I promise, Brightonians are getting more tolerant. Our now grown-up children could hardly think of a better place to be - that says a lot about this unique place. The only other choice for me would be deep in the country - I don't think we're ready for that!

PAUL BONETT, *estate agent*

elm grove

As Hanover's property market reaches saturation point, first-time buyers are looking at Elm Grove, the area on the other side of the hill behind Brighton's racecourse. From Elm Grove's lofty peaks you can clamber up on to the South Downs and look out to sea, or take a surprisingly beautiful walk through to one of the cemeteries off Bear

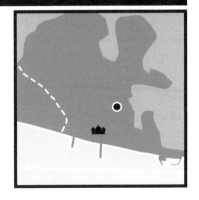

Road. Although Elm Grove doesn't zing with community spirit, it's a deceptive area, and within its boundaries lie some lovely streets. In De Montfort Road the larger houses are fabulous with substantial gardens. A house here will set you back upwards of £150,000. In Hartington Road you can still find gardens, but they tend to be behind the Victorian houses which cost around £160,000 and some for £215,000. The tree-lined Brading and Bernard Roads are also popular, and a house here will cost around £150,000. Elm Grovers agree that although The Grove has no centre and little ambience of its own, it is close enough take advantage of its more vibey neighbour, Hanover, and that the houses with gardens are substantially bigger here.

Traditionally, landlords have bought along the Lewes Road and let their properties out to students; the Universities of Brighton and Sussex are both based around here. These are still extremely good buys for anyone interested in a spot of DIY before landlords cash in on the boom. A one-bedroom flat in Whippingham Road will currently sell for £65,000, while a two-bedroom maisonette in Milner Road, off near the Lewes Road, will cost around £75,000.

The Patch - officially The William Clark Park - is one of Elm Grove's best-kept secrets. Directly behind Bonchurch Road and Elm Grove School, it provides Elm Grovers with their own park and children's play area. If you live in Bonchurch Road you can walk straight out of your back garden into the park.

preston park

The well-heeled of Brighton and Hove who care not a jot for a seaview will make their way to the Victoriana of Preston Park. The park itself is a large green space with a clock tower, a scented garden for the blind, two cafés, a playground, a cycle track where kids can learn to throw away the stabilisers and enough squirrels to keep the dogs happy. The two cafes are the Floriana Rotunda with manicured lawns and perfect flowerbeds, serves roasts and proper teas from 9am to 6pm from March until the nights draw in, and the Chalet where you'll get a cuppa even on a wintry afternoon. The tennis courts, running and cycle track and

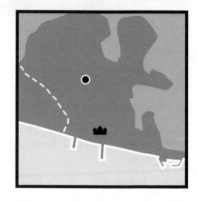

bowling green are well attended and well maintained, and on a warm summer's evening, the sight of all that activity off the London Road is a tonic to those who've left the rest of the world behind on the M23.

The area tends to attract professional couples and parents-to-be moving down from London. For most buyers here, the huge pull, apart from the larger Victorian houses and its smart profile, is the local schools. Despite the no-catchment policy, Balfour infants and junior schools and Dorothy Stringer secondary school are said to be the best (academically) in Brighton and they can - and do - pull the net tightly around the local area. See the Schools chapter for what local parents think of them.

The triangle from Preston Park to Preston Drove and Stanford Avenue are where the biggest houses with gardens are to be found. A two-storey, two-bed house with 25-50 foot garden will go for around £150,000, while a house with loft conversion in Cleveland Road overlooking Blakers Park, might go for about £275,000. But there are some exceptional bargains in the area; some of the smaller-looking properties in the triangle can be deceptive. "They're like the Tardis," a resident of Edburton Avenue who grew up there, told us.

Neighbouring Florence, Rugby and Surrenden Roads with houses ranging from £200,000 to £375,000 or even more, depending on size and garden, can accommodate the bigger families. The prices come down again for the slightly smaller Victorian terraced houses (£140,000 - £175,000) in the Preston Drove area, and the people tend to be a little less precious. Estate agents will tell you that the Preston Drove divide will cost you £30,000, with the neat rows of well-maintained homes on the Blaker's Park side lending a more genteel air. There really is very little difference to the houses themselves, so if you've got a child who might excel in the academic halls of Balfour, do yourself a favour and go for the north side of Preston

Drove which will almost certainly fall inside the ever tightening net. But before you buy one of the tiny two-bed terraced homes with postage stamp gardens which are flooding the market, remember that many of them have been rented out to students with little maintenance over many years, and will need a whack of cash spent on them. Around the Lowther and Hythe Roads, estate agents are also scooping up the few tiny houses here where elderly Preston Parkers spent their last days. With their Sixties gas fires and miniature gardens, the average price of £145,000 means that they are not the best bargains in town despite their access to Balfour.

preston village

This is not what we expect from a village these days with no shops, village square or real sense of community. In fact, it is no more than six roads off the London Road, stretching from South, Middle and North Roads with their older Victorian cottages and gardens worth between £150,000 and £190,000, to Clermont Road and Terrace at the

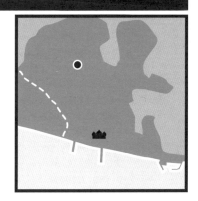

back of Preston Park station, where substantial houses can set you back anything from £200,000 to as much as £400,000. A hop and a skip from a commuter station, it's beginning to attract more London buyers.

Beyond Clermont Road are the later Victorian, three-storey houses, some terraced, but most have been converted into flats. The houses are currently worth around £200,000 to £350,00 and the flats £60,000 to £200,000. From there, Withdean's Thirties, Forties and Fifties housing, mansions and architectural experiments lead out to Westdene with its Fifties and Sixties estates, bungalows and upside down houses with sitting rooms leading from basements on to sloping gardens. If you're mad enough to commute by car, the main routes out, the A23 and A27, are close by. It's also the way to Devil's Dyke with its panoramic views of the South Downs and English Channel.

fiveways

Stretching from one end of Ditchling Road to the other, Fiveways refers to the junction of Stanford Ave, Preston Drove and Hollingbury Road, and is, according

My first taste of Brighton came as I walked out of the train station. It was a beautiful sunny day, and catching sight of the blue sea at the end of the road, I was taken. When I had the choice between moving back to London or moving to Brighton - well, no contest. My first home was a fantastic garden flat in Tisbury Road just up from Hove Town Hall. Owned by two women artists, it had a gallery bed which could only be reached by a ladder. With huge rooms, high ceilings, wooden floors and large oil paintings everywhere - it fulfilled my expectations of Brighton as a crazy, creative place. I used to get up for an early swim at the King Alfred Centre, take a brisk windswept walk along Hove promenade followed by breakfast outside my back door, if it was sunny. Since then I have always lived in Hove. With its wider streets and less frenetic atmosphere, it's the perfect place to live in this city. Taunts that it is populated only by OAPs are patently untrue - nowadays Hove is increasingly trendy, there are great places to eat (including Oki Nami and La Piazza), and great places to shop. Unattached? Check out Waitrose. Cullens is for celeb spotting, and since the pedestrianisation of George Street, an influx of trendy bars and coffee shops means it's no longer just charity shop city. Forget the tourist ridden streets of the town centre, Hove is on the up, although with that parking has become a nightmare!

NIGEL BERMAN, *editor, The Insight*

to local mythology, where the Guardian readers of Kemp Town and Hanover move to when they have more kids. In the past few years, as the reputations of Downs and Balfour school, Dorothy Stringer and Varndean have grown, the Guardian

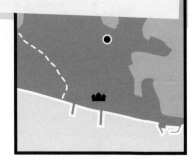

readers have skipped the Kemp Town bit completely and headed straight for the large semis, terraced Victorians and windy roads heading across to Hollingbury to avoid the dearth of secondary schools nearer the sea.

Preston Park and Blaker's Park are within walking distance if you can manage the hills, and Hollingbury Park and golf course stretches out towards the South Downs for the serious walkers. Brighton is one of the few places where the golf courses are public and open to dog walkers. Keep to the edge and watch out for flying golf balls and you'll find some of the most beautiful walks in town.

Ditchling Road, a long straight thoroughfare out to Hollingbury's bungalows and older community and on to the A27, hosts a motley collection of houses. The few detached houses with enormous gardens hover on the edge of the Friar and Surrenden areas, secluded off-the- main-drag communities with a 4WDs parked on most of the driveways. The terraced Victorian homes perched on the wide pavements stretching down towards the Fiveways junction are home to middle-class, middle-income, thirtysomethings who spend their spare time doing up their houses and hanging out with parents of their children's friends.

The community is children-oriented with a distinct lack of focal points from shops or pubs, largely because both parents tend to work, do the shopping in their lunchtimes near the office and come straight home to play with the kids before bedtime. Someone could (and will) make a fortune by opening a deli/café at Fiveways to scoop up the new parents and Saturday crowd who would otherwise get the bus to the North Laine or hang out at Seven Dials. Zel have already spotted the gap and filled It with The Open House, a lounge lizard of a pub with mosaic patio for Sunday barbecue lunches nestling in the residential streets around Downs Infants and Junior schools.

hove

Brighton's quieter, more refined sister is only a stone's throw from the main action, but by the time you've marvelled at the Peace Statue and the manicured lawns which mark the boundary, an air of tranquillity really does seem to descend. The breathtaking architecture of Brunswick and Palmeira Squares leaves the showy, gaudy anomalies of

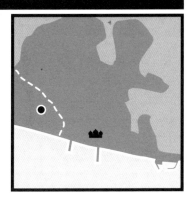

Brighton's seafront such as the Brighton Centre and the tacky eateries paling into insignificance. It all looks impossibly grand and graciously residential.

Hove prefers to do its shopping, eating and clubbing in Brighton, if only to keep hoi polloi off its doorstep. Its long stretch of high street is Church Road with its floral clock and pretty trees silhouetted against the horizon, but don't expect to find anything much more interesting than a few nice clothes shops and a few reasonable restaurants until you get to George Street, the pedestrianised epicentre of Hove.

Many of the enormous houses you'll find here have been converted into flats, and occasional ones will boast roof gardens with the best views in town. The original Hove was known as Brunswick Town, and these days Brunswick Square and Brunswick Terrace is still known to many as the centre of the universe. Since the 1850s and the development of Albany, Medina, Osborne and Ventnor villas next to Adelaide Crescent, Hove moved west as the Stanford family built its estate. Compared to Brighton, Hove is a baby, with few buildings dating back before 1825, meaning properties here can have the garages and gardens which Brighton's Regency town houses lack. Hangleton, Portslade, Aldrington and West Blatchington were former villages and even if they have been absorbed by the blanket of Hove, they still retain their respective identities.

brunswick

If you're young(ish), free and single with a bit of disposable cash, you're likely to go for the area north and south of Western Road around the Brighton/Hove boundary at York Road. The prices might have risen since Nigel Richardson immortalised the area in his book Breakfast In Brighton, but it's still well worth a look. Most properties are converted flats - some with fantastic little patio gardens.

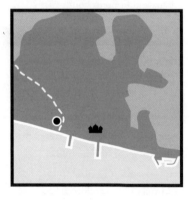

In the last five years, most of the people who have moved to this part of town are likely to have sold their one-bed flat in London, made £50,000 on the deal and ploughed it into their £85,000 one-bed or £125,000 to £145,000 two-bed flat. They buy their interiors from the shoppers' heaven that is the North Laine and build an architectural garden out of nothing more than a slab of east-facing concrete and some serious creativity. But fear not: they may have moved from the designer-fest of Islington, but keeping up with the Joneses hasn't been encouraged in Brighton and Hove since the days when the Prince Regent first stamped his own individuality on the town. Finding your own style, making it rather than buying into it, being your own person is what life is about down here.

On the seafront itself, the Regency two-bed flats in Brunswick or Palmeira Squares, push the property prices into the £250,000 bracket. A four-bed without a garden will easily go for £275,000. But the bargains are still there: a first floor flat with a balcony might cost £160,000, while a roof conversion in the same building will go for £120,000, and both will look out over the Channel. Seafront Hove is a different planet from Hillside Hove. Its streets are avenues - Grand, First, Second and Third, and The Drive and Upper Drive which are still the best addresses this side of the statue. Up the hill, the houses are slightly smaller, but the average price is in the £300,000 to £400,000 mark, with walled gardens and the kind of signals to the world that those who live here have arrived. (See Tongdean and Withdean.)

new church road

A seaside address is still a seaside address and even if it is not in the shade of cool Brunswick, it is still a seaside address. The streets south of New Church Road which stretch down to the sea and look over the Western Lawns are where you'll find large houses with gardens for about £300,000, with those north of New Church Road going for £190,00

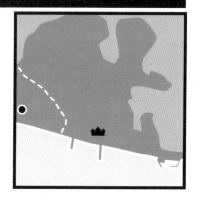

upwards. It may seem a bit suburban, but the difference between buying in Hove and buying into Terry and June suburbia is that you can walk along the seafront to some of the best clubs in the country. Teenage kids can get a cheapish cab home, parents can walk their younger kids to school, and you can save a fortune on petrol because Brighton and Hove thinks it's a good deal bigger than it is. You can even park your car on the street for free or in its own garage. A Kent developer is marketing two very stylish converted flats here for around a quarter of a million. Is Hove starting to emulate Kemp Town?

In Hove, most residents prefer to promenade along the seafront, and parks are few and far between. Davis Park is no more than a rose garden and a set of tennis courts belonging to Dragons Gym. Aldrington Rec is little more than a collection of rugby posts and a small children's playground. Wish Park between New Church Road and the seafront is a big enough space to kick a ball around, and towards Portslade, Vale Park is also a nice place to take the kids. But it's only when you get up to Hove Park and across to Preston Park and Queen's Park that you'll find the buzz, the trees, the bigger playgrounds and the cafes which a good park should be about. But Hove is a small town, and nowhere is too far from the glorious St Ann's Well Gardens with its café, tennis courts, winding paths beneath ancient elms, the enormous children's playground and heavenly scented garden

st ann's well gardens

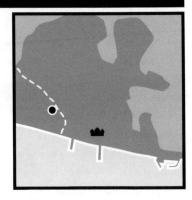

This is the area of leafy and not so leafy streets that border Montpelier, Seven Dials and central Hove. It is one of the genuine communities in Brighton and Hove, largely because at around 8.45am and 3pm, the streets are awash with parents and kids trekking to and from Davigdor, Somerhill, Brighton and Hove High School for Girls, Cottesmore, Cardinal Newman, Blatchington Mill and Hove Park. The area is dense with schools and people rather than the shops, pubs and clubs which characterise the rest

After the removals van goes, we peer out of the front window of our new house near St Ann's Well Gardens. At a quarter past three the schools chuck out and the pavements are filled with children. This is good: like so many others we have moved here because, with two small kids, London becomes less and less like the place we feel like calling home. And then, the grown-ups: one skids down the pavement on a skateboard. Another has vivid, pink-dyed hair. We have fallen into a neighbourhood of cool-looking couples. People we want to know. Brighton has become a geography of choice. We like-minded people flock to this wild colourful city because we are the kind of grown-ups who like to still play at being 18, and this is the perfect place to do that. Looking through where our curtains will one day hang, we are suddenly a little scared. We move here because we believed it was a smaller version of London. But in London you inevitably rub up against strangers from all corners, from any class. This is going to be an altogether different adventure. The people in our neighbourhood look oddly like us.

WILLIAM SHAW

of Brighton and Hove, and its heart is in St Ann's Well Gardens where the community comes to play.

Houses here vary from late Edwardian semis to large, detached Thirties buildings. One of the best selling points of the area, apart from the school and the park, is the size of some of the gardens that average between 50 to 100 feet in Somerhill and Nizell Avenues. But it does mean that they're not cheap, ranging from £290,000 to £450-500k. Around Highdown and Lyndhurst and a number of roads off there are the less expensive Edwardian four-bedroom houses with 20 foot square gardens which are currently on the market for between £190,000 and £295,000. The County Cricket Ground is a walk away at top of Salisbury Road, as is Hove station.

hove park

Above Withdean Stadium where Brighton and Hove brought back The Albion, the prices and the houses leave the real world behind. Hove Park, according to some estate agents and the people who live there, is the best place to live in Brighton and Hove. Safe, expensive, middle class, and not made up of the London types who are a feature of

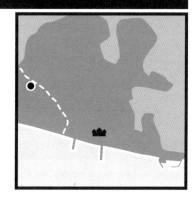

Preston Park railway station at 8am. "There's a lot of Brighton and Hove people who inherited properties in the Eighties, sold them and moved up here," Peter Gladwell of the Halifax told us. "It's a real community of butchers, bakers, candlestick-makers made good." Eighty per cent of the houses bought here are by local folk, according to Peter. "London people want London-by-the-sea. The people here are dentists, lawyers, people who've made a lot of money one way or the other. Airline pilots move here when they are based at Gatwick. That's the kind of person you'll find around here."

The park itself is a large, rolling, well-kept expanse of space hedged by the Old Shoreham Road. It is designed to please with a café, kiddies' playground split in two for the large and small, bowling green and recently revamped tennis courts. The miniature railway is run by volunteers and is open in the summer, and the cycle track makes it a perfect stroll for those with buggies and wheelchairs.

tongdean & withdean

Tongdean Avenue has been described as the Beverley Hills of Hove. Houses here will go for an average of £600,000 to £750,000 with the odd beauty selling for more than £1million. According to Nigel Richardson in the Saturday Telegraph, their status is measured by the "inches of their Doric columns" although his snobby estate agent

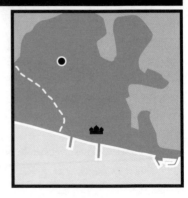

source added that he found this area "insufferably vulgar". The other most sought-after addresses are Tongdean Road, Dyke Road Avenue and Barrowfield Drive. The local choice of school here is not so likely to be Blatchington Mill or Hove Park, but the private Mowden School for boys, Hurstpierpoint College or Roedean. Surrenden Field, originally 5.65-acres of open space belonging to Home Farm (and once upon a time, Brighton and Hove Rangers, the forerunners to B&H Albion FC) runs across the bottom of Surrenden Crescent, neatly tying up the area with the boundary of Preston Park.

poets corner

The Bohemian area of Hove which leads from the station to Clarendon Villas, as far west as Alpine Road and down to Portland Road, may be slightly dilapidated, but could be one of the areas which will double in price in the next 10 years. In the meantime, this is where the young marrieds or happy singles buy their two- to three-bed Victorian middle

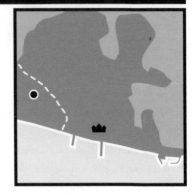

terrace houses or flats for between £125,000 and £175,000. East of Sackville are some two and three-storey Victorian houses which are going for about £165,000. Poet's Corner is near the station, too far from the sea and just more than a short walk to the nearest park. But it's a foothold on the property market, and the starting point for many families who might move to New Church Road when the kids get too big to share a room. Pedestrianised George Street is the centre of the community, the Dieppe Market with its French goodies visits twice a year, once more than its festival trip to Bartholomews in Brighton, confirming the local interest in delis and all things cosmopolitan.

renting

costs

- Average agency fee: £100 for referencing, inventory, check in/out and finding fee (some are cheaper).
- Average one-bed: £120; top end is £900 for one bed.
  Two-bed: £140pw -170pw.
  Studios: £80 - £100pw.
- At the moment, rental prices in B&H are high. Try and share a bigger property with more people. Three to four bed share is hard to find though.
- Demand is still outstripping supply and turnover of properties is high. Keep in touch with agents rather than waiting for them to call.
- Money Down - You'll need to put one calendar month (4.3 weeks) down. That's £560 on £130pw, plus five weeks deposit (£650), plus £30 "Finding fee' and £68 "Referencing". That's a grand total of £1,308.

tips

- Ask about hidden fees in administration charges. For example: extended tenancy agreements, checking out, further referencing.
- Get parents as guarantor if first property (parents have to live in England or Wales to comply with law).
- Learn how to look after a house - it'll save you a fortune if you know, for instance, how to turn off the stopcock...
- Check inventory. If it's written down - it's better in the event of a court case.
- Check it and return within five days. Make comments, for example, what is fair wear and tear?

expectations

- Plain décor, fitted carpets, cooker, fridge
- Agents advise landlords to provide unfurnished

neighbours & neighbourhoods renting

- The biggest problem is getting landlords to return money. ARLA (01494 431680) and NAEA (01926 496800) are self-regulatory bodies which agents subscribe to. Neither can get your money back if agent runs off with deposit, but they can fine their members and discipline them, but won't give that money to the tenant. You have to go to Small Claims Court.

- If agents are prepared to go through the rigmaroles of becoming members of ARLA or NAEA (accounts audited etc, fees paid), they are more likely to be sound, but don't be put off if an agent isn't a member - there are ways of dealing with problems which are more local and more likely to reap rewards.

- Council's Duty Housing Advisors (01273 293157) deal with legal rights of private tenants (and landlords), rent increases, validity of agreement, harassment etc. Will liaise with solicitors on tenant's behalf on caseworker approach, writing letters on tenant's behalf and visiting solicitors with tenant etc. Free.

- Brighton and Hove Housing Trust (01273 234737) covers Shoreham to Patcham to Peacehaven. FREE drop-in sessions on all housing issues but prioritises homelessness cases. If you can afford your own solicitor, you won't get help here.

PARSONS SON & BASLEY

32 Queen's Road, Brighton BN1 3YE
Tel: 01273 326171 Fax: 01273 821224

• *Chartered surveyors since 1825*

• *Surveys and homebuyers reports*

the surveyor

Nigel Bamford
St. Johns Building, 76 Hollingdean Terrace,
Brighton. BN1 7HA
Mobile 07956 247392
Fax/Messages 01273 298344

Loft Conversion Specialists

Complete service including Preparation of plans
for building control and planning permission.

the builder

MILES BRÖE ARCHITECTS

Coronation Studios, 104 North Street,
Brighton, E Sussex BN1 1YE
tel 01273 625911 fax 01273 625411
email bbc@topcentre.co.uk

PRIVATE RESIDENTIAL & OFFICES •
SOCIAL HOUSING • RESTAURANTS & BARS •
INDUSTRIAL • RETAIL • COMMUNITY

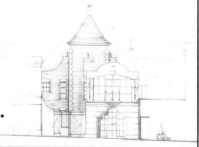

the architect

BRIGHTON HOUSE DOCTORS
Realise the potential of your house

*For professional advice on how to style
and present your home for selling.*
Contact Roland or Jonathan
on 01273 241538

the designers

WILLIAM GREEN

*landscape and garden
designer*

tel 01273 493076

2, Lime Kiln Cottages, Woodmancote, Nr Henfield, W Sussex

the garden designers

the business

introduction by Simon Fanshawe, head honcho in the successful city bid campaign

December 18th 2000. Announcement from the Queen via Tony Blair. Brighton & Hove, you are a city. December 19th wake up wondering if it feels any different. Was it all a horrible mistake?

And no, it wasn't. It's just, like the campaign, it's a process and not an event. In the short term it does confirm that Brighton and Hove is the capital of the South East, a world destination for tourists and conferences, and where most people in the surrounds come to work. Formally becoming a city gives us the kind of prominence we deserve in Europe, which is good for business and thus jobs. But the real benefits will arrive bit by bit.

Most people down here really wanted to win. And we did. And that does make us proud about where we live and if we love where we live, we'll work together to improve it. Grand, groovy and great though it is, we have problems. We've never ducked that. Keith Waterhouse once described it as "a town that looked as if it was helping the police with their enquiries". Brighton & Hove might be the place to be, but like your younger brother's bedroom, it needs a right good tidy up. What city status has done is to give us confidence to start sorting those things out. It raises the city's eyes above the horizon and opens our minds to our aspirations.

Winning city status gives us the chance to create a new and different kind of European city for a new century. Unusually in Britain, our prosperity in Brighton & Hove is inspired by our quality of life. That's why we love living here and it's what attracts companies, artists and creative business people to the city to stimulate jobs and work. Being a city will inspire us to take that even further, to make great buildings in the city, to build a heritage of the future, to regenerate the areas that have fallen behind and sustain an environment for everyone which is healthy, beautiful and clean.

City status is a milestone in Brighton and Hove's climb onwards and upwards towards being one of Europe's great urban areas. We have the fun (some of the country's best clubs, the beach and the shopping), the food (finally some top restaurants), the sea (new improved and without tampons), the jewel in the rococo crown of camp (the Pavilion..... or the gay scene... take your pick).... It's a catalogue of delights. And being a city can only inspire us to greater achievements.

Working in Brighton and Hove - particularly if you're setting up your own business - is easier than you might think. Making money can be a bit more difficult; Brighton and Hove may be a City, but if you're looking for investment, you'll probably find yourself heading London-bound - for a while at least. But it's compact enough to network easily and devoid of the kind of pressure which makes you want to tell small untruths about yourself. And there's enough of a support structure to make you think that you really can make a million in this town.

Much of this feeling of confidence is generated by The Sussex Innovation Centre (SINC), set up in May 1996 as a response to the enormous potential for wealth creation in the area. With the universities of Sussex and Brighton among the leading institutions producing around 40,000 students in further and higher education, there was a real need to harness their potential in Sussex. Increasingly, students are deciding not to leave Brighton and Hove when they graduate, figuring that it's a pretty good place to live and work, but they need help in setting up their business. Others move here and can't find their way around or access the infrastructure - all of which can make the difference between make or break.

SINC offers free advice to help people develop their business idea. Business incubation, is what director (and Sussex Businessman of the Year last year) Mike Herd calls it. Come to him or the team with an idea, and they'll either show you how to get to the next stage or send you home to think again.

The SINC team offers market research, market sizing, business planning, and subscriptions to excellent workshops under its Knowhow Exchange service. Most importantly, SINC knows its way around the professionals and professional operations who can take your idea to the next step. With academic resources as a back up and those 50 companies on site - most of them new businesses which have grown under SINC's banner - the place provides a focus of activity where people can share ideas, technology and experience.

How much it costs depends on how much you use it; initial consultancy is free and welcome as long as it looks like your idea can grow. "There's nothing that's not appropriate", explains Mike. "We're looking for high growth, million pound ideas which might not be earning anything at all yet". With 30% revenue growth every six months and a handful of floatations in the companies under SINC's wings at the Centre itself, it's worth giving them a call "We will charge sometimes for a consultancy fee" explains Mike, "but in many cases we simply offer support and hope to share in the company's success in whichever way we can." A diamond.

SINC is one of the many partners Sussex Enterprise has teamed up with to encourage businesses both new and established to grow. Sussex Enterprise is the new style Chamber of Commerce and the winner of the Small Business Service franchise for Sussex and provides a subsidised range of business services from mailing lists to business counselling, export development to a free 24 hour tax and legal helpline to anyone who joins. There are no specific criteria you need to meet for joining Sussex Enterprise, but if you're identified by any of their partners as a high growth start up, you could be in for some serious support. It's all about encouraging the right people to get the right help, and if you look for it, it's coming out of Sussex's ears.

The six Enterprise Agencies around Sussex are also partners of Sussex Enterprise, and are the first port of call for small businesses looking for advice on the early needs from writing business plans and accounting to market research. If you've got your wits about you, it's also a good place to do that all important networking thing. Once you've grabbed one of the Sussex Enterprise tentacles, you'll find lots of information on where to go next, from the banks who are helpful to Business Angels, both of which could provide financial support or investment.

Many of the new businesses in Brighton and Hove belong to that strange breed of new media, driven here from London with a dream of working on a laptop on the beach and watching the sun set over the English Channel. To provide them with a reality check and to encourage them to look beyond their browsers to the network they could work with, Wired Sussex was born. A subsidiary of Sussex Enterprise, it was another response to the needs of the mass of university graduates leaving Sussex and Brighton with dollar signs in their eyes and no real desire to leave town. Sarah Turner was one of the brains behind the networking events which helped small businesses to "punch above their weight". For the 400 new media companies currently in Brighton and Hove, she and her colleagues in the Old Steine are a focal point of contact. "One of our major objectives is to help them secure finance, to help them think in the right way," she says, "coaching them to pitch for investment and then to put them in front of real investors in London".

Wired Sussex has an extensive database and it's free to join it. It's a good place to look for employment in new media or its related services with between 25 and 50 jobs advertised at any one time. Finance, ecommerce and legal issues are all featured there too.

For artists, South East Arts, soon to be re-named under the Arts Council banner, is the first point of contact. It gives professional advice to new and established artists across Kent, Surrey and East and West Sussex with information on funding and support. It is also the distributor for the Regional Arts Lottery Programme (RALP), so good to get in with if you're looking for money to make your project work.

There's a long tradition of art playing a big part in Brighton and Hove life and as such, the local authority is very supportive. From the Open House groups who show their work in their own homes during the Festival in May to the informal artists who work out of Fabrica, there's plenty of networks to inspire the artist in his or her garret.

Being a friendly kind of place, Brighton is big on networking. We probably do it in everything we do without calling it something as revoltingly American as "networking" anyway; most of the information in this guide comes from us swapping information at toddler groups or at the newsagent's. Certainly, cold calling is not as cool as meeting potential business partners over breakfast, chatting about what you do, what you'd like to do and who you'd like to do it with. The result is a plethora of breakfast, lunch, cocktails and dinner networking clubs. You won't find them advertised because it's all done by word of mouth of course, but try the women's group SWAN, www.theswangroup.co.uk, 01273 704480, or Business Lunch Club on 01903 871030 for starters; you'll find yourself being invited to all the others once you get on the scene. And we'll be doing something very Juicy when we get our act together, so check the website for details.

The companies listed in this directory are some of the big success stories in Brighton and Hove; Midnight was voted small business consultancy of the Year last year, Internate is the on-line marketing branch of Designate, the fastest growing marketing company in the South East and DMH is so successful with its "holistic approach to its clients' issues" that it's even turned its offices into an art gallery. The rest of the companies featured in this directory have been handpicked - many from the networking groups - to provide you with most of your business needs. They have paid for their space because there's only so much altruism we're capable of, but they all come recommended by people we trust or we've used them ourselves.

09

schools

Choosing the right school is possibly the most important factor for parents or would-be parents moving into or around Brighton and Hove. We've compiled a list of some of the schools in the area which parents have recommended to us. This list and the information we're giving is based purely on the word of parents and children who chose them. It is not meant to be comprehensive, and has nothing to do with Ofsted reports or league tables. This information should be seen as complementary, to be used in conjunction with the official information. The Council (01273 293502) will give you a full list of State schools, and ABC magazine features a considerable number of advertisements for private schools and nurseries. If a particular school is not listed, that's no reflection on the school, it just means that no one recommended it to us. If you feel that we've missed out anywhere, please write in and we'll sort it out next time.

Officially, there is no catchment policy in Brighton and Hove; you choose the school you want and nobody's going to stop you from applying. But as the best schools fill up with the locals, there's going to be precious few places for anyone living outside of the area. But remember that as good as a school is this year, it's only as good as its headteacher, and headteachers move on. The good thing is that there are plenty of schools to choose from in Brighton and Hove both in the public and private sectors.

primaries

Balfour Infants

Balfour Road, Brighton

📞 *01273 500617*

Balfour Juniors

Balfour Road, Brighton

📞 *01273 553521*

Academically, Balfour infants and juniors is second to none in the area, but some Balfour Junior parents who prefer their children to be able to cultivate their artistic leanings, tell us that they have to spend a good deal on extra-curricular activities. But if art and music get pushed out to accommodate the highly structured curriculum, maybe Balfour can get away with it because its parents tend to be able to pay for the after-school art classes at Beacon Arts and the private piano or violin lessons. The clutch of arty types who fall into the Balfour catchment area are also more likely to fill in the gaps at home. But the schools do benefit enormously from parent power, with most local parents taking an extremely active involvement. The combination of their reputation, history and parent involvement means that it's hard to quibble about Balfour's place at the top of the tree.

Cottesmore St Mary's Primary

Upper Drive, Hove

📞 *01273 555811*

The local infant and junior school in Upper Drive is a large-halled, stone building with a rather traditional interpretation of the school curriculum. It is one of the handful of Roman Catholic schools in Brighton and Hove and feeds the gorgeous-looking Cardinal Newman secondary school which sits on the other side of the road (Incidentally, the only reason we haven't featured CN is because we couldn't find anyone who goes there.) Local Catholics get first crack of the

whip if you're into the three R's, a highly moral framework and a rather stern approach to discipline.

Davigdor Infants School

Somerhill Road,

Hove

📞 *01273 731397*

One of the reasons that young families are flocking to the deli and café community of Seven Dials and the borders of Hove is Davigdor and its junior school, Somerhill. The Council policy may be that you don't have to live in the area, but because the school is in such demand, the reality is that you do. It's a small, family environment that doesn't put children off education for life, and the head and teachers really do listen to parents. The kids make up their own rules, and the goldfish sitting in his open-topped bowl in easy reach for nicking in the entrance to the school is proof that they stick to them.

Downs Infants School

Ditchling Road,

Brighton

📞 *01273 500146*

Downs Infants and Junior schools have an artier profile than Balfour, being a little closer to Fiveways. The Infants school is impressive with art covering every wall, and class sizes kept to 30. Its exceptional education in art and music sells the school to the local arty community. The headteacher who used to sit naughty kids outside his door has now gone and has been replaced by the much more sympathetic Miss Kruger whose commitment to the children is shown through her lateral interpretation of the numeracy and literacy hours.

Downs Junior School

Rugby Road,

Brighton

☎ *01273 558422*

Fortunes are changing at Downs Junior with a very active PTA group introducing money and ideas to an eager head. It's an enormous school by primary standards (500 pupils), and that can lead to some disorganisation and more traditional approaches to teaching and discipline. The numeracy and literacy is "coming on", according to one parent, and the playground is being upgraded - largely thanks to the PTA. A new £8,000 climbing frame, an amphitheatre for kids' own plays, African tribal dancing and storytelling which is part of the cultural curriculum, and a plan for rubberised ball areas... All these should improve the school tremendously. For working parents, the Breakfast and After School clubs are handy, and fun for kids with arts and crafts, chess clubs and basketball.

Elm Grove Primary

Elm Grove, Brighton

☎ *01273 708004*

The distinctly academic Elm Grove School used to be one of the most popular primaries in Brighton but now it is in a transitional stage. Former headmistress, Mrs Crossingham, has left and John Lynch, who built an excellent reputation at Standford, took over in January. Many parents have complained that the academic push has been too strong and that the arts, music and PE have dwindled to virtually nothing. The word is that the school has become a victim of its own success; class sizes have grown and both the parents and arts rooms have gone to make way for more pupils. However, a new wing is being built and many are hoping that John Lynch will redress the balance, but only time will tell. The school continues to provide a good range of after school activities from table tennis and drama to art and basketball, some of which are free.

Goldstone Junior

Laburnam Avenue, Hove

☎ *01273 739730*

Situated on the north side of the Old Shoreham Road, Goldstone Junior has an innovative policy which includes music and arts in the numeracy and literacy push. Compared to some of the schools' take on numeracy for six-year-olds (reciting times tables - no really), the sight of children giggling as they lie down on the floor to measure each other is a joy. PHSE (Personal, Health and Social Education) is one of those newfangled subjects parents didn't have in their day, and at Goldstone, role playing, which forms its bottom line, seems to bring out a laudable confidence in its pupils.

Middle Street Primary School

Middle Street, Brighton

📞 *01273 323184*

Right in the heart of old town Brighton and serves a mixed community of media kids and inner city types. It also has a nursery for three to four-year-olds. Right-on and committed staff.

Queen's Park

Park Street, Brighton

📞 *01273 686822*

Queen's Park school has a fantastic location, perched at the bottom of the park and within skipping distance of the park playground. Unlike St Luke's, Queen's Park has a separate nursery and a two-form entry. The school also has a lower intake than the others and so the class sizes are smaller, and since

Queen's Park has become extremely popular, entrance is difficult unless you live very close by. Queen's Park and St Luke's have similar educational philosophies and both work in close partnership with parents. The parent teacher's association is extremely active and their school fairs are always popular. Mrs Scott, the head teacher, has built the school's social and academic reputation, helped by a loyal teaching staff. The school exudes a cosy, close knit environment, which seems to appeal to both parents and children alike.

Rottingdean CE School

Whiteway Lane, Rottingdean

📞 *01273 303109*

Only a five-minute drive from Kemp Town, it has a very good reputation and is high on the league tables.

St Bernadette's RC Primary School

Preston Road, Brighton

📞 *01273 553813*

A highly recommended primary with, unsurprisingly, a heavy Catholic bias (99 per cent of the pupils are Catholic), where the teaching, discipline and ethos comes from the religion. Its policy towards special needs, for example, follows Jesus's model rather than the local education authority's. Academic achievement and social skills are also based on the Christian ideal with a good deal of support from the local parish and parents. Montessori has influenced much of the teaching, a legacy from the former deputy head who trained as a Montessori teacher, so expect a high level of independence from pupils.

St John The Baptist RC Aided Primary

Whitehawk Hill Road, Brighton

📞 *01273 607924*

St John the Baptist will appeal to those who want a traditional Catholic academic education with strong emphasis on discipline and the three Rs. Situated right at the top of Whitehawk Hill Road, it has wonderful views all over Brighton and has vast playing fields. The school has a one-class entry and an admissions policy, which gives preferential treatment to Catholics, but if you're a nice, middle-class, non-Catholic family, you stand a good chance. Acting head Ms King has recently replaced Mr Sullivan so expect some changes.

St Luke's Infants

Queen's Park Rise, Brighton

📞 *01273 699924*

Since becoming head teacher, Nesta Saunders, has transformed St Luke's,

turning it into a happy, child centred place of learning. The recent changes have not gone unnoticed and it is soon to receive a government award for school improvement. Though it is large, with a three-class intake, the focus is firmly on the needs of the 7 and under age group and the school's warm environment reflects this. St Luke's has long enjoyed an excellent reputation for the arts and a trip around the classrooms will give you an insight into the wonderful work that takes place there. Academically, its reputation continues to grow, and each year more and more parents try to find a place for their children. The very active PTA has organised two wonderful Christmas Fairs with the help of the local church who have brought their choir in to sing with the children.

St Luke's Juniors

St Luke's Terrace, Brighton

📞 *01273 675080*

The Junior School, headed by the dedicated Ron Guildford, has improved vastly in the last few years and now enjoys an excellent academic reputation. Recently, Ron Guildford received a letter from David Blunkett congratulating him on the school's success in the league tables. Though the emphasis is increasingly academic, the arts continue to thrive and a professional writer has been working with the children helping them to develop their literary awareness. The PTA has recently been revived which has improved parents and teachers morale. However, there is still more work to be done in that area and the school lacks the warm and communal atmosphere that exists in the infants school. St Lukes provides a range of extra-curricular activities including athletics, football and chess.

Somerhill Junior

Somerhill Road, Hove

📞 *01273 739659*

Davigdor keeps strong ties with its little sister, sharing its huge field for football, baseball and other sports. Kids coming in aged seven join a 'family' made up of one child from each year to help them find their feet. It's a good example of the school's emphasis on pastoral care; the lack of classrooms, with an open-plan space divided off by curtains is another, allowing mixed-age groups to interact well. But on the whole, the feel is traditional, with children taught to write with ink pens. The headteacher is unusually candid in the way she presents children's work to would-be parents, picking up examples as she sees them rather than digging out the scholarly stuff. Good on art and music, with regular concerts.

Stanford Infants

Highcroft Villas, Brighton

📞 *01273 555240*

On the whole, Brighton is big on the arts, and at Stanford the infants make pottery masks in the school kiln and learn about multi-cultural arts within a broader curriculum. Arts include dance and music, and are used in numeracy and literacy hours. The school has had a major overhaul in the past few years; new head teacher, Mrs Wicker, now describes it is a parent-friendly school which encourages children to become confident enough to go on to the next, more formal stage of their education with a love of learning. The ethos of the school is an extremely supportive one, with staff encouraged to take courses, classroom assistants properly trained, and a staff room where teachers are recognised for their achievements.

Stanford Junior

Stanford Road, Brighton

01273 565570

Stanford Junior verges on the hippy with its strong concentration on relationships, but that's fine by us and many people in Hove, Preston Park and Fiveways. Former superhead, John Lynch left last year after creating a happy school in which bullying is just about a thing of the past - a feat of Lynch's which the children recognise and appreciate. He has now gone on to Elm Grove leaving Mrs Robinson as acting head.

As we went to press, we heard about two schools which we didn't have time to review ourselves. *Carlton Hill Primary School in Sussex Street, Kemp Town (01273 604966)* and *St Paul's in St Nicholas Road, Montpelier (01273 721001)*. Unusually for state education at the moment, offer class sizes nearer to the 20 mark rather than the 30+ you get in places like most of the others in Brighton and Hove.

secondaries

Blatchington Mill Secondary

Holmes Avenue, Hove

☎ *01273 736244*

On the north side of the Old Shoreham Road, this is one of the better secondary schools and sixth form colleges, which was awarded performing arts status last year. Its Glenn Miller-style band, The Millstones, plays in the Brighton Festival and tours internationally, winning it enough financial support to build a new theatre. Young musicians at Hangleton Junior and surrounding junior schools are often picked up by Blatchington scouts and encouraged to join the many

ensembles and orchestras at the school. Parents report a strong sense of discipline, effective control of bullying and has an accessible attitude to pupils and staff. The school is also strong in English, IT and drama. Brighton and Hove's mayor, Jenny Langston, is chair of the board of governors.

Dorothy Stringer High School

Loder Road,

Brighton

☎ *01273 557311*

Dorothy Stringer has become the most sought-after secondary school in Brighton, which means that it has become oversubscribed and its boundaries are receding. The school has a sound academic reputation and headmaster, Trevor Allen, leads the school in a disciplined but highly approachable way that appears to be very successful. The school is famed for its music department and Stringer children have sung both with The Brighton Youth Orchestra at Glyndebourne, and at the London Palladium. The sports facilities are excellent and include a swimming pool, tennis courts and large playing fields. Parents appear to have few complaints except that classes are too big as the school increases in popularity - a universal problem with the comprehensive system.

Varndean

Balfour Road,

Brighton

☎ *01273 561281*

Varndean has an excellent reputation for secondary academic education. It shares a site with Dorothy Stringer and the Balfour schools, but gets serious competition from Stringer and has reinvented itself as a college of technology.

sixth form colleges

BHSVIC

205 Dyke Road, Hove

☎ *01273 552200*

Brighton and Hove's sixth form college, where the brainiest kids from here and Lewes vie for places. Cosier and more intimate than some of the halls they may have come from, it boasts excellence as well as happiness among its students.

alternative education

Finally it looks like pluralism in education is to get the seal of government approval, although in politics it's rare to find a solution without some kind of compromise. As they fight to keep the integrity of their educational systems, it may be some time before we can have a real choice in education, but at the moment, Steiner and Montessori are the most likely to get their state funding.

Brighton and Hove Montessori

67 Stanford Avenue, Preston Park

☎ *01273 702485*

For children of two and a half years old to eight. Montessori teaching is purposeful with activities very rooted in the real world; polishing shoes, washing up, cleaning, rather than water and sand play. The idea is that children learn how to be comfortable in their world and grow at their own pace. The teaching follows the individual's interest rather than the other way round, and reading and writing come naturally when the time is right. Keeping your child here to the age of five or six is a good alternative to the Reception classes for four-year-olds. Josephine is every child's favourite teacher, and her reputation over the last 15 years is one of the big pulls to this school. It was the choice of both authors. Plans for an elementary school (six to nine and nine to 12) are already under way.

The Brighton Steiner School

John Howard Home,

Roedean Road, Kemp Town

☎ *01273 386300*

Children work in a disciplined environment but are allowed to learn about the world in an organic and non-competitive way, preserving their natural hunger for knowledge. In addition to academic success, the curriculum is consciously directed towards building social skills, creativity and the awareness of spiritual and moral elements in life. In the Nursery and Kindergarten, imagination and play are emphasised with formal learning starting around age seven. Children stay with the same class teacher from seven to 14, then enter the Upper School, taught solely by specialist subject teachers.

The Dharma School

White House,

Ladies Mile Road, Patcham

📞 *01273 502055*

In a big, old-fashioned school building on the edge of town, children follow the national curriculum in a Buddhist environment. There's a nursery and even the youngest kids learn to meditate in a morning 'puja'. The approach is traditional, with classes organised by age and going through to GCSE, but the feeling of calm is palpable and the kids have an uncommon courtesy to each other and adults.

Lewes New School

Talbot Terrace, Lewes BN7 2DS

📞 *01273 477074*

Felicia McGarry has taken what she considers to be the best of Steiner,

Montessori and progressive education and designed this idealistic vision after years as a teacher in the State sector. The flooding that devastated the school only weeks after it opened means that it would be unfair to give a review of what we saw, but the spirit of Lewes New School is certainly willing.

Stonelands School of Ballet and Theatre Arts

170-172 Church Road, Hove

📞 *01273 770445*

Boys and Girls, aged 6-16

Day and Boarding

If your little darlings are budding thespians then this could be the school for them. Stonelands is a full time vocational school that offers all forms of dance, drama and singing. Class sizes are no bigger than 12 or less but be warned the prices are steep.

private schools

Brighton And Hove High School

Junior School

Radinden Manor Road, Hove

📞 *01273 505004*

Senior School

Montpelier Road, Brighton

📞 *01273 734112*

Placed firmly at the top of the Sussex league tables, Brighton and Hove was one of the first schools in the country to provide high quality education for girls, and early pupils were among the first women in England to go to university. Although it enjoys a brilliant academic reputation, the school also has vibrant art, music and drama departments. Brighton and Hove's academic reputation is famed, but one parent told us that she was impressed by the discouragement of personal competition. Despite this, it is worth pointing out that Brighton and Hove is deeply selective and will only take in girls who are already at the top of their class.

Brighton College

Eastern Road, Brighton

☎ *01273 704201*

If you want a traditional, Christian, fully rounded, private school education that focuses on discipline, high achievement, sports and old-fashioned English public school values, then Brighton College is the place for you. The buildings, dating back to 1848, are beautiful, and the sports facilities are as good as you'd expect from this kind of school. Parents and pupils rave about the music and drama departments. As Brighton is such a cultural pick'n'mix you'll find parents from every background choose Brighton College from the arty to the very rich. The school is co-educational but boys still

outnumber the girls. The school does have an admissions policy and many parents opt for entrance to the senior school preferring their kids' primary experience to be less pressurised. Old Brightonians include Sir Michael Horden, and Peter Mayle.

Mowden

The Droveway, Hove

☎ *01273 503452*

Tucked away in the heart of leafy, upmarket Hove Park, Mowden is a boys private prep school run by Christopher Snell, the third generation of his family to be headmaster. While the fees are not cheap (starting at £2,000plus per term), the school gives boys not just an excellent academic and sporting education, but also confidence and moral awareness via a friendly, family-style approach. To help the boys relax they do yoga in the afternoons. Compared to some of its tougher and more exclusive rivals, Mowden is a haven for those wanting to nurture intelligence, a sense of achievement and humanity among their male offspring.

Newlands School

Eastbourne Road, Seaford

☎ *01323 892334/490000*

📧 *www.newlands-school.com*

An independent day and boarding

school from three to 18 set on a picturesque site in Seaford. The school has excellent sports and recreational facilities and has recently introduced a superb theatre arts programme offering a full range of dance, drama and music lessons enabling children to develop their talents and receive a thorough academic education simultaneously. A fleet of mini-buses transports day children across Sussex. The school does not select pupils but achieves very good academic results and the Gannon Centre on site provides extra tuition and support for children with a range of special needs.

Roedean

Roedean Way, Brighton

☎ *01273 603181*

The famous ivory tower on the hilltop with its own tunnel down to the sea has managed to keep hold of its reputation as top gels' school, while joining the 21st century. Set up by early feminists, it has always been keen to encourage girls to get ahead and provides exceptional facilities to help them get there. An indoor swimming pool, theatre, dance studio, design technology and language labs lead off corridors connecting bedrooms to classrooms and individual studies. The environment inside is cosy while the wind of the outside world hammers against its impenetrable walls. Roedean gels never even need to leave the building, apart from a little community service every week to give them a sense of the real world they were born to rule. Day girls, weekly boarders and full-time boarders come from all over the world, and there are probably more Chinese and African faces here than anywhere in Brighton.

St Aubyns

76 High Street, Rottingdean

☎ *01273 302170*

The children at St Aubyns enjoy the peaceful and relaxing location of Rottingdean village set between the sea and the downs. It is a traditional Christian prep school but has every modern facility imaginable from a computer suite to a performing arts studio with music, art, and extensive sports facilities. Fencing lessons and horse-riding are popular choices. The emphasis on small classes and good behaviour means its pupils are successful academically. The school provides all that you would expect for fees that reach £2,800 for day pupils and £3,765 for boarders, per term. It's recent conversion to co-education and the enthusiasm of the headmaster, Mr Gobat, also contributes to its popularity. Don't be put off by its out of town location, day pupils of all ages commute from Brighton and Hove on the school bus.

St Mary's Hall

Eastern Road, Kemp Town

☎ *01273 505004*

St Mary's Hall in Kemp Town is a Christian, independent, day and boarding school for children of three to 18. The Junior school accepts boys but after the age of eight it focuses solely on girls. St Mary's Hall doesn't have a selection policy, which is unusual in the private sector. The policy of welcoming all abilities attracts parents who like the idea of private education but don't want their offspring to be pressurised. St Mary's prides itself in its caring approach, enjoys a reputation for being a gentle but academic school and the class sizes are very small. As you would expect from an independent school, the music, art, drama and sports facilities are all extensive.

Windlesham School

190 Dyke Road, Hove

☎ *01273 553645*

A homey environment for three to five year olds extending out the back into a warren of classrooms and lawns, swimming pool and sports courts for the older ones, Windelsham is led by Mrs Bennett-Odlum, a shiny happy sporty type the kids flock to. Specialist drama and music teachers coach the boys and girls through impressive school productions, and a choir practices twice a week. An unusually good understanding of alternative forms of education among the teachers means that children from outside poshschoolville are accommodated comfortably, but at £1,200 per term fee for the over six's, scholarships to Brighton College and Hurstpierpoint, Brighton and Hove High and St Mary's are the traditional route out at 11.

nannies and au pairs

The difference between a good nanny and a good au pair is price, professionalism and if you don't work at home, peace of mind. Agencies like Bunnies in Preston Park (01273 505001) have been a consistent source of extremely reliable au pairs, but to avoid employing someone you've never met, ask them to find a girl (or boy) who is already in the area.

Jed's two-year-old is looked after at home and taken to toddler groups by a 22-year-old Slovak girl. "Au pairs are a fantastic option if your house has the space and you can deal with the idea of another person living with you. You've got to put down your boundaries, but when it works well, it's like living with a friend. Your children see them so much and become so comfortable with them that the childminding element is extremely comfortable. There's trust and friendship and although it can be a little disconcerting to find yourself living with a 21-year-old blonde who walks around the house in a G-string, these are sacrifices you've got to make. It's for the good of your kids"

Nick and Cathy work in the film industry which takes them all over the world - often at the last minute. Rachel was the only nanny who wanted to work their odd hours, so the job was hers. "To look back on it now, we were so lucky to find such a genuine, hardworking person who the kids took to so quickly. Nannies are normally a bit more mature than au pairs, and this was very important to us as Rachel is often left to look after them all day by herself. The kids benefit so much as they get undivided attention from her instead of a busy parent on the phone all day."

If nurseries are going to charge an arm and a leg to have your child sticking stars on to paper, you could spend that money on a school, particularly if they accept the three- and four-year-old grants. You could find yourself paying next to nothing for an excellent education at somewhere like Brighton and Hove Montessori School (01273 702485), or The Lewes New School (01273

477074) which uses a modern mix of Montessori and Steiner techniques (see Alternative Education section above).

Juicy Advice: Visit schools which have a specific philosophy such as Montessori, Steiner, The Drive and Lewes New School before you make a decision. Understanding the different options will allow you to make a more informed choice. Ask to sit in on a class and watch the practice rather than listen to the ethos - which could put you off.

nurseries & early childcare

nurseries

With doors opening at 8am and closing around 6pm, with breakfast, lunch and tea provided, day nurseries are a Godsend to thousands of working parents. But there are precious few which you'll find recommended in The Juicy Guide. Children are often palmed off with a weekly diet of convenience food, the kiddy-friendly names of Cowboy Casserole distracting parents from the fact that their children are unlikely to be given any fresh fruit or vegetables all week. Provide a lunchbox yourself, make sure staff will be consistent with potty training and ask about a high turnover of staff.

Blueberry Day Nursery

5 Davigdor Road, Hove

📞 *01273 711112*

A welcoming, happy environment where you know that your kids will have a great time, with a strong emphasis on play and good support for potty training when your child is ready. A big wholesome lunch is provided and they are happy to accept alternatives if your child has any allergies. Lots of information for parents and they will do a day book if you feel at all worried about anything. Blueberry has a full guide of their policies and a parents' guide and handbook. Beware the long waiting lists - it's so popular because it's so good. They take children from 18 months and go through to reception year. They are open from 8am to 6pm, but have a wide range of different sessions that you can chose at different times of the day".

Early Years Day Nursery

41 Dyke Road, Hove

📞 *01273 500151*

Open 8am to 6pm with all-day care or half-day sessions available. The nursery supplies nappies and has a full-time chef who cooks onsite. Paul lives in Hove, works part time at home and sends his daughter there: "Molly went to Early Years from the age of two to four. It's a really

professional organisation, but can cost up to £30 per day. The building and facilities are fantastic and we now understand that there is a considerable waiting list to get a child in there. It's known as the 'American Express' nursery, as employees of Amex get some sort of subsidy from the company. Chris Eubank has also just sent his son there. All in all, we were very pleased with it, but sometimes it felt like dealing with British Telecom - quite a lot of bureaucracy, and there does seem to be quite a high staff turnover of the carers. Though this did not affect us, some kids were getting new carers (mostly female, between 18 and 25) more than once a year. Molly loved it and misses it and her friends - which I suppose is the acid test."

Joyland Nursery

Grantham Road,

Preston Park

📞 *01273 554886*

Open from 8.30am-5.30pm, with a number of different options of sessions. Lunchboxes only. Sharon's three-year-old's school care is split between Joyland Nursery, a term-time only nursery, and St Mary's Church Playgroup. "Joyland has a real family environment (being in a terraced house helps) and the children really feel like they belong. Educationally there is a reading/writing structure, but this is not enforced if the child does not feel ready for it. Learning through play is the key and activities are many and varied. What I also liked was the quiet area, which encouraged my sleepy head son to have a snooze in the afternoon if he felt like it. It also has a big garden and a pet rabbit"

The Orchard Day Nursery

89 Queens Park Road,

Brighton

☎ *01273 622883*

Open 8am-6pm, with morning and afternoon sessions or all-day care available. Kids bring their own lunchboxes, but tea (beans and soup in winter, sandwiches and fruit in summer) is prepared and cooked onsite. Be aware that it has a very long waiting list.

The Play Station

next to St Matthias Church,

Ditchling Road,

north of Fiveways, Brighton

☎ *01273 501300*

Family-run nursery with a happy and stimulating atmosphere: monthly themes as well as cooking, sticking and all the usual messy stuff (membership of the Early Years Development & Childcare Partnership). Mini-bus for after-school pick-ups and outings.

state nurseries

Tarnerland Nursery

St Johns Place, Kemp Town

☎ *01273 607651*

The Royal Spa Nursery

Park Hill, Kemp Town

☎ *01273 607480*

These two are worth a mention for being the only State-funded independent nurseries in the whole of East Sussex. Many of the primary schools have nurseries attached, but these two stand alone. Both The Royal Spa and Tarnerland come highly recommended and have fantastic locations with The Royal Spa nestling next to the playground in Queen's Park and Tarnerland situated just off the Queen's Park Road. The Royal Spa was purpose-built and the huge garden within the park provides a lovely environment for young children.

finding your school

League Tables will only give you a guide, so consider this advice compiled from a number of teachers from alternative to State education. When looking around, check the following - and watch out for sales flannel.

nursery, primary & junior

- What training do the staff have? If Montessori or claiming to be part of another educational system, check they belong to and are inspected by the correct outfits.
- Who inspects them? Are Ofsted reports visible?
- How do the adults interact with children? If very small children, do they talk down to them or ask parents about them when they can answer for themselves? Do they get down to their level?
- How many children in classes? How many trained and experienced staff to look after them?
- Is it colourful and homely inside?
- Is the environment calm or rowdy? If it's full of exuberant kids, check to see it's not disorganised, and that the quieter kids are being cared for. If it's too calm, are the kids happy or constrained?
- What happens in the course of the day? How formal/informal?
- What are the aims of the school? What is its ethos?
- What records are kept on the child?
- What equipment/activities does the school have?
- How much space is there for bigger children, and how safe is it?
- Do children have free or restricted access to each other, to toilets, snacks etc?
- What is the settling in procedure?
- What is the supervision procedure over lunch/playtime?
- What is our gut feeling about the place and the staff?
- Imagine your child there; would he/she be comfortable, safe and happy?
- Do you like the staff? Can you imagine having an open and frank relationship with them if your child goes to this school?

finding your school

- Past results at GCSE and A level. Ask if there's a difference in results between boys and girls.
- Truancy rates - not just from school but from lessons; some children may make the register, but spend their days wandering around the school.
- What's the take up at sixth form?
- Extra curricular activity. Duke of Edinburgh for example. School trips.
- When looking around, look at the displays; are they marked, or are they there to look good?
- Look at textbooks to see how new they are
- Look at exercise books to see how well they've been marked; how long is the comment? What is being rewarded?
- Ask about reward systems.
- Check the pastoral approach. Do year heads rotate so that they can maintain their relationship with the children throughout their schooling, or do they end at the end of each year?
- Staff morale. What's the relationship between staff and head? Do they call each other by their first names? Do the heads go on school trips? How involved are they? What's the turnover of staff?
- Homework - what happens if it isn't done?
- What's the discipline policy? Why would a child by excluded or suspended? How many cases?
- Do they have plans for extension? What will they do with it?
- How active is the parent/teacher association?

shopping

Shoppers come from all over Europe to our fine City to find some of the most
original clothes, gifts, antiques and homeware - and we have listed the very best of
them here. Brighton and Hove is a retail nirvana, a shopping heaven littered with
whatever shops you want selling everything from chocolate to clothes, from fish
furniture to interior design and antiques. Whatever your heart desires, you'll find it
here - and odds on there'll be the perfect café next door too.

As a rough guide, it's worth remembering that the antique shops are mostly
in The Lanes, the junk, retro and kitsch gift shops are to be found in the North
Laine, the luxury interior shops are in Hove and the charity shops are scattered all
over. Kemp Town, Brunswick and Seven Dials each has its own unique ambience
and distinctive shopping community and are well worth visiting. Most of the chains
are in Churchill Square or just outside on the Western Road (Marks and Spencers,
Littlewoods, Gap...). The big high-street fashion names like Jigsaw, Jaeger, Karen
Millen, Bertie, French Connection and Monsoon are in the East Street area behind
Hanningtons.

Churchill Square is worth a visit and has been given three awards, one of
which is from the International Centre of Shopping Centres for its innovative
design and refurbishment.

This is the largest and most comprehensive shopping guide to the city of
Brighton and Hove ever to be put together, and to make it easy for you to get
around it we have created a mini shopping index divided into sections. The sections
and everything in them are in alphabetical. That'll make it easier. If you find
anything that's not listed here, let us know and we'll include it next year.

antiques

Bric-A-Brac

25 Gloucester Road,

North Laine

☎ *01273 697300*

Wonderful hand-crafted retro furniture with casually scattered leopard skin cushions to create that genuine Fifties film-star look.

If you buy one of their chairs and give them some material, they'll cover it for you.

Brighton Architectural Salvage

33/34 Gloucester Road,

North Laine

☎ *01273 681656*

The choice of serious home-decorators looking for original pieces. Period fireplaces, ironmongery, stained glass, and reclaimed flooring.

The Brighton Flea Market

31a Upper St James Street,

Kemp Town

☎ *01273 624006*

Think pink: the flea market exterior screams camp from its mid-Kemp Town location. Prepare to be bewitched by its dazzling selection of stalls ranging from bric-a-brac, second-hand toys, paintings, costume jewellery, bargain velvet curtains and a wide range of antique furniture including beds.

Dermot and Jill Palmer Antiques

7-8 Union Street, The Lanes

☎ *01273 328669*

Something for the professional interior decorator. Three floors of French and English antiques.

Enhancements

1 Cavendish Street, Brighton

☎ *01273 677303*

Affordable antiques and bric-a-brac bargains; wooden laundry rails, tallboys and Victorian wardrobes.

Jezebel

14 Prince Albert Street, The Lanes

☎ *01273 206091*

Decadent shrine to the Art Deco era. Frocks, furniture, and costume jewellery.

Snooper's Paradise

7-8 Kensington Gardens,

North Laine

☎ *01273 602558*

In the heart of the North Laine and spread over two floors, this is heaven on earth for any bargain hunter. A good old-fashioned rummage will be rewarded with unusual antiques and rare retro relics! Tuff Tarts designer clubwear is tucked away in one corner and brings Snooper's Paradise bang-up to date with its fantastic cyber creations.

shopping antiques • arts

arts

Artworker Shops Ltd

27 Kensington Gardens, North Laine

📞 *01273 689822*

Grand Parade, Brighton

📞 *01273 675461*

The Kensington Gardens shop specialises in fine art materials and Grand Parade sells graphic materials.

CJ Graphic's

32 Bond Street, North Laine

📞 *01273 734400*

Bursting with specialist paints, pens, paper and all things arty.

Economy

82 St George's Road, Kemp Town

📞 *01273 682831*

A favourite with Brighton parents, this shop is a dream for children's art stuff. Paper, pens, pipe cleaners, stickers, feathers, scissors, glue, crepe paper and all things to do with handicrafts.

Lawrence TN And Son Ltd

208 Portland Road, Hove

📞 *01273 260266*

The best specialist art shop in town for printmakers and artists. Lawrence also provides a mail order service.

Pen To Paper

4 Sydney Street, North Laine

📞 *01273 676670*

Specialist handmade paper shop which also stocks pens, and sartorially inspired stationery.

auction houses

Raymond P Inman

Fine Art Auctioneers,

35 Temple Street,

Brighton

📞 *01273 774777*

📱 *07769 697747*

bookshops

Borders

Churchill Square Shopping Centre,

Brighton

📞 *01273 731122*

The place to sip coffee, rest your tired toes and browse through the best selection of magazines in Brighton. Borders is big, bold and well stocked with CDs and books. The café stays open late and welcomes book club meetings, live music and author signings. Children's storytime events on Saturdays at 11am.

Brighton Books

18 Kensington Gardens,

North Laine

📞 *01273 693845*

Specialist collection of second-hand books, including first and limited editions. There are extensive sections on art, dance, drama, philosophy, journalism and fiction.

NF Brookes

124 Queen's Road,

Brighton

📞 *01273 323105*

No sign on the door to tell you the name of this place, but look up the address and find a place where chaos reigns. Hundreds upon hundreds of books are stacked in what outwardly appears to be no particular order, but the owner has his system, knows where things are, and more often than not finds what you're looking for and hands it to you in triumph.

City Books

23 Western Road, Hove

📞 *01273 725306*

Brunswick locals voted it the best shop in the area and we can understand why. The brilliant fiction department has lured authors like Louis de Bernier and Iain Banks. They've also got excellent sections on children's books, travel, music, local history, education, science fiction and alternative health.

Colin Page Antiquarian Books

36 Duke Street,

The Lanes

📞 *01273 325954*

Specialist bookshop dealing with antiquarian, architecture, antique and art books.

David's Comic Shop

5 Sydney Street, North Laine

📞 *01273 691012*

If the word of graphic novels and comics is a bit of a mystery come here and... it will probably look even more mysterious. Still, if you're a fan, it's got everything.

The Green Buddha Bookshop

15 Bond Street, North Laine

📞 *01273 324488*

Incense and ambient music permeate the atmosphere in this shrine to relaxation. Specialises in alternative, Eastern philosophy and self-help books.

Kemp Town Bookshop

91 St George's Road, Kemp Town

📞 *01273 682110*

Small but choice selection, with a good children's section and a community notice board. If they do not have what you want they will order it and phone you as soon as it arrives. They also sell cards and wrapping paper.

Out

4 & 7 Dorset Street, North Laine

📞 *01273 623356*

Exclusively gay and lesbian bookshop. Along with magazines and videos there's a wide range of gay literature and art on offer.

Oxfam Books

30 Kensington Gardens, North Laine

📞 *01273 698093*

Quality second-hand bookshop stocking a wide selection of subjects.

The Peace Centre

Gardner Street, North Laine

📞 *01273 620125*

More than just a book shop, this is where you'll buy your cards if you want to ensure that your money goes back to save the planet. If you want to get involved with environmental issues, this is your Brighton portal. There's also e-mail and internet access.

Practical Books

14/14a Western Road, Hove

📞 *01273 734602*

The best place in town to find foreign language books.

Reservoir Frogs (In Hive)

6 Kensington Gardens, North Laine

📞 *01273 687802*

A two-floor comic heaven, with a lot of other stuff - tattoo, fetish, drugs... that whole sub-culture.

Sancho Panza

2 Surrey Street, Brighton

📞 *01273 773054*

One of those jumbling, treasure chest shops. The place to come if you want something culty or kitsch, something from the Sixties (a Thunderbirds annual), the Seventies (David Cassidy's autobiography), or something you never realised you were even looking for.

Sandpiper

34 Kensington Gardens,

North Laine

📞 *01273 605422*

Sandpiper only stocks remainders and returns from shops so you can find some really good bargains. They are particularly good for coffee table editions.

Savery Books

Five Ways, Brighton

📞 *01273 503030*

The two shops are now one. Wide selection of second-hand volumes at good prices.

Sussex Stationers

55 East Street, The Lanes

📞 *01273 328032*

114 St James Street, Kemp Town

📞 *01273 608229*

50 Western Road, Hove

📞 *01273 204700*

A Sussex institution and excellent local stationery chain that also sells popular fiction, non-fiction and children's books.

Two Way Books

54 Gardner Street, North Laine

☎ **01273 687729**

An odd establishment that's frequented by characters straight out of Graham Greene's Brighton Rock. It is packed with collector's comics, paperbacks and genuine Forties, Fifties and Sixties Penguins.

Waterstones

71-74 North Street, Brighton

☎ **01273 206017**

Waterstones is huge - five floors of books on every subject imaginable. It goes without saying there's an extensive collection on everything and anything and you receive expert advice from their knowledgeable staff.

clothes shops

new

Badger for Men

25 Bond Street, North Laine

☎ **01273 722245**

Quality collection of stylish, casual, designer men's clothes and shoes. Stock includes Diesel, Timberland, Rockport and Birkenstock.

Badger for Women

26 Bond Street, North Laine

☎ **01273 325421**

Badger stocks the most fabulous shoes and classic clothes collection for women who prefer the understated look. Designer names include Timberland, Rockport and Dockers.

Brief Encounter

13 Brighton Square, Brighton

☎ **01273 208404**

Tactile collection of sexy knickers, bras, corsets, nighties and swimwear for hedonistic women of the world. Stock includes La Perla, Lejaby, Chantelle and Cotton Club.

Cutie

33 Kensington Gardens, North Laine

☎ **01273 697498**

As the name suggests, an ever so cute collection of new and old T-shirts, frocks and skirts for girls who like the Barbie doll look. The best selection of itsy-bitsy pink and baby blue clingy T-shirts in town. You will also find quaint furry romper suits and a natty collection of animal print beanbags and cushions.

East

25 Kensington Gardens,
North Laine

☎ **01273 622282**

Upmarket shoes and casual wear for men and boys. Stocks Duffer of St George, G Star, Hope and Glory, Desil and Lime House. Also look out for their mini Duffer sweatshirts for cool kids.

East Is East

51 East Street, The Lanes

☎ *01273 776711*

Asian-inspired classic womenswear mainly from northern India. The shimmering dress coats, silk jackets and skirts are cut to flatter and their generous sizing means that most ranges go up to size 18. You can complement this with their gorgeous jewellery range and it's cheap, costing mainly between £3 and £6. Handbags and a limited range of complimentary homeware is also available. A limited range each season ensures that you won't look like every other woman in town.

Glass House

East Street, The Lanes

☎ *01273 326141*

Gorgeous floaty and tailored clothes for women who have (physically and spiritually) outgrown Top Shop. Particularly good for taller women.

Glitzy Tartz

26 Sydney Street,

North Laine

☎ *01273 674477*

Outrageous and ultra-sexy gear for girls who've got it and want to flaunt it. Rubber dresses, plastic-studded corsets and chain mail bikinis ... and those are just some of their more modest items.

Greenwich Village

Bond Street, North Laine

☎ *01273 695451*

Hippy chic paradise. A plethora of stalls stocking everything from saris, kimonos, ponchos, bags and Indian children's frocks. Their collection of Buddhas and glitter parasols are well worth a look.

Igigi

Western Road, Hove

☎ *01273 734160*

Sensual and beautiful clothes, jewellery and accessories that will make you feel like a Queen. Go with a friend and take turns to lounge on the velvet sofa. Zoe buys all the clothes, so ask her or her mum to dress you. It's all part of the service.

Inside Out

34 Upper St James Street, Kemp Town

☎ *01273 674819*

If you veer towards the ethnic but also like to be smart, this is the shop for you. Inside Out stock their own ethnically-inspired collection as well as gorgeous global imports, silver jewellery, scarves and hats.

Long Tall Sally

10 East Street, The Lanes

☎ *01273 731791*

Specialises in stylish solutions for tall women, including a fine selection of

shopping clothes shops

evening frocks and suits.

Magick

1-2 Sydney Street, North Laine

☎ *01273 686568*

If you're in the mood for a little devilish behaviour look no further than Magick. Silky and blazon outfits adorn the hangers. Check out the delectable corsets that come in every hue, the temptress frocks with thigh-high slits, and the divine, horned devil tiaras.

Mambo

37 West Street, Brighton

☎ *01273 323505*

Ultra-cool, urban sportswear for boys and gals. Check out their strident collection of Hawaiian shirts and skateboard gear.

Moist

20 Dukes Lanes, The Lanes

01273 220544

Trendy and casual sportswear for those in the know. Stocks Red Eye, Custard and Animal.

Mother Hemp

22 Gardner Street, North Laine

☎ *01273 818047*

Casual, well-cut unisex clothes, accessories and bags made from Hemp, as well as an eclectic range of Hemp products such as

perfume, shampoo lager, fabric, Frisbees and paper.

Motto

12 Duke Street, The Lanes

☎ *01273 326633*

Upmarket designer collection including Ghost, Nicole Farhi and Ted Baker.

Primart

188 Western Road, Brighton

☎ *01273 205211*

A big and bright emporium of cheap clothes for all ages. Primart's stock is not dissimilar to M&S, but it costs half the price and the kids' collection is fab.

Profile

3, 4 and 25 Dukes Lane, The Lanes

☎ *01273 733561*

Classic but ultra-stylish designer collection of men's and womenswear, including suits, coats, mackintoshes and shoes. Designer range includes Hugo Boss, Armani, Versace, Paul Smith, and Joseph. **Women's wear is at 5 Dukes Lane (**☎ *01273 323275*).

RE-AL

7 Dukes Lane, The Lanes

☎ *01273 325658*

The last word in skateboard chic, selling clothes, trainers, beanies and boards. Stocks Neil and Board Babes.

Route One

3 Bond Street, North Laine

☎ *01273 323633*

Extreme clothes and skateboard gear.

TK Maxx

32-38 North Street, Brighton

☎ *01273 727483*

Two floors of cheap designer gear brought to the masses. Some of the stock lacks élan, but you can still find some ultra-stylish gear in among the more mass-produced lines. Sells clothes, handbags, boots, underwear and accessories.

Urb

40 Middle Street, Brighton

☎ *01273 325336*

Hip sportswear for men and women. Names include Dickies and Addict.

Way Out West

23 Market Street, Brighton

☎ *01273 747462*

Ultra-feminine, but urban womenswear with an emphasis on sex and glamour.

Yamama

92 Trafalgar Street,

North Laine

☎ *01273 689931*

Cheap, stylish - often woolly - clothes that epitomise the Brighton student look.

childrens' clothes, toys & buggies

A Lot Of Gaul

32 Kensington Gardens, North Laine

☎ *01273 621135*

For those lovers of all things French, find Madeline, Tintin, Barbar, The Little Prince and more. Stocks books, toys, T-shirts, dolls, clothes, tapes and videos.

The Animal Shop

12 Bond Street, North Laine

☎ *01273 206836*

Cuddly animals a-go-go: find any creature in the world in this animal paradise that also stocks animal-themed ceramics, stationary, jewellery and umbrellas.

Baby Bargains

2 Warren Way, Woodingdean

☎ *01273 302682*

Selection of new and reconditioned prams, cots, buggies, bouncers and general baby equipment. But be warned - there's little grace here. We tried it and found the after sales service rude and dismissive. There are nicer places to shop.

Blue

20 Church Street, Brighton

☎ *01273 700370*

▤ *www.bluecrafts.co.uk*

shopping children's clothes, toys & buggies

Ceramics, glass necklaces, handmade cards and kiddy clothes including the fleecy Toby Tiger. It's the only outlet in town for the gorgeous Quiver women's label and there's even an art gallery at the back of the shop featuring Jane Arkwright.

Cat And Mouse

17 Sydney Street, North Laine

☎ *01273 600145*

Totally original, stylish and practical designer children's wear and accessories. The baby clothes and the party frocks are both sublime and affordable.

Daisy Daisy

33 North Road, North Laine

☎ *01273 689108*

Extensive selection of second-hand kids' clothes in good condition as well as new toys. It is expensive, but you will find Oililly and Petite Bateau in among The Gap cast-offs. The best selection of wooden toys in town.

Dials

Dyke Road, Seven Dials, Brighton

☎ *01273 771111*

Cute collection of funky American 'stylie' kids' clothes aged from first-born to seven. Find mini Elvis T-shirts, Oshkosh and Levi's, as well as an ever so hip collection of homeware and gifts.

Gymboree

Unit 31 Churchill Square, Brighton

☎ *01273 775123*

Smart, stylish and vibrant American kids' clothes and shoes for babies and up to the age of seven.

Havelock Road Post Office

107 Havelock Road, Preston Park

☎ *01273 552002*

Friendly post office where they sell pre school Orchard toys.

National Schoolwear Centres

40 Blatchington Road, Hove

☎ *01273 739676*

✉ *schoolshop@lineone.net*

✉ *www.n-sc.co.uk*

The only shop in Brighton and Hove which sells generic uniforms for all the different schools. For stripes and some of the posher uniforms, you'll still have to trek up to John Lewis, but for logoed school bags, plimsolls, leotards, swimwear, ballet gear, literacy and numeracy course books and a rash of green and blue skirts, tops and shirts, this is a one-stop shop.

Nursery Stars

☎ *01273 306 240*

Mail order company selling beautiful cringe-free children's music. Over The Moon, featuring traditional nursery rhymes with modern ambient arrangements, is a great chill album both for post-clubbing parents and a soothing bedtime solution for cranky kids.

Pine Secrets

65 East Street, The Lanes

📞 *01273 729271*

The perfect place to shop for a present for just under a fiver. Large selection of Beany babies, little toys, cuddly animals and knick-knacks.

Poppets

50 Blatchington Road, Hove

📞 *01273 770449*

A choice selection of second-hand children's clothes. Take the best stuff that your kids have grown out of and they'll sell them for you and share the profits. A particularly cheap option for leotards and ballet kit.

Rascals

267a Preston Drove, Fiveways

📞 *01273 505504*

Baby and pre-school equipment including three wheeler buggies and hand made furniture, both new and second hand. They also sell washable nappies and organic baby products.

Toby Tiger

15a Montpelier Place, Montpelier

📞 *01273 710610*

Home-spun felt and fleece clothes and toys for small people. The finger puppet show (£29.99) is the kind of quality toy that will last for years which is probably why it's so pricey, and there are enough finger puppets to keep parents amused for hours. Ring before you go; it's only open when Toby himself gives his mum a break.

Toys and Togs

94 Boundary Road, Hove

📞 *01273 880808*

Second hand and seriously cheap goods for babies and toddlers. Bikes, prams, three-wheelers and Little Tike type cars. They also do good second hand bikes for grown ups.

rental

Masquerade

40 Preston Road, Brighton

📞 *01273 673381*

Fancy dress and costumes.

Revamp

11 Sydney Street, North Laine

📞 *01273 623288*

Glam fancy dress.

Walk In Wardrobe

Western Road, Brighton

📞 *01273 775583*

Hire or buy glamorous evening frocks for that once-in-a-lifetime night out.

second-hand & charity

Camden Traders

Bond Street, Brighton

☎ 01273 697464

Retro groovy gear, mainly from the Seventies, but there's also some contemporary stuff - 501s, ponchos, maxi skirts and cocktail frocks.

D & K Rosen

Church Street, Brighton

☎ 01273 326931

If you want a second-hand suit, shoes or shirt, this is the place to come. There's a vast selection to trawl through, but you need to be prepared to put in the time and effort. Make sure you stop to have a chat with owner Mr Rosen - he's a sweetheart and it's one of the genuine Brighton experiences.

The Glamour Chase

34 St James Street, Brighton

☎ 07932 498155

The aptly-named Glamour Chase is the place to find the most sumptuous clothes from the past for next to nothing. Browse through their collection of original Mod gear, Fifties stilettos, Forties frocks, Seventies casual gear, Audrey-inspired little black dresses and fake fur trims. It's only been open a wee while, but has already attracted the attention of "beautiful people" and the BBC. Noel Gallagher and a variety of models and 'It Girls' have become customers.

Ju-Ju

24 Gloucester Road, North Laine

☎ 01273 673161

Young and groovy shop specialising in contemporary, funky gear.

Jump The Gun

32 Gardner Street, North Laine

☎ 01273 626777

The fantastically dressed Vespa in the window gives the game away. Stocks everything for serious 'mad about mods' types, including memorabilia, Fred Perry, Ben Sherman, natty suits and T-shirts.

Marie Curie Cancer Cure Charity Shop

99 St George's Road,
Kemp Town

☎ 01273 673695

Good quality charity shop, with good condition high street names and a great selection of kids' books.

Revisions

3 Pool Valley, Brighton

☎ 01273 207728

Genuine nearly-new designer gear including Gucci, Prada, Chanel, Katherine Hamnet and Galliano. The stock has a high turnover, but it ain't cheap, so take your credit cards.

Starfish

25 Gardener Street, North Laine

☎ *01273 680868*

Eclectic selection of retro clothing, including a great range of leather jackets and loud party wigs.

Strip

82 North Road, Brighton

☎ *01273 571674*

Casual but hip second-hand gear with some new bits and bobs. T-shirts, sweatshirts, hats and fleeces.

Tab

7 Kings Road, Brighton

☎ *01273 821448*

Retro clothing and interiors from the Fifties and Seventies. Tab has a delectable selection of chain belts, A-line frocks, garish psychedelic wallpaper and loud cardigans. For those who want to get really nostalgic, it also sells mint-condition Jackie magazines.

To Be Worn Again

51 Providence Place, Brighton

☎ *01273 624500*

Stocks a state-of-the-art collection of retro clothes mostly from the Seventies.

shoes

Buffalo

33 Duke Street, North Laine

☎ *01273 738866*

Wild, outlandish shoes and trainers for those who like toppling around on five-inch rubber soles, shrieking "Look at me!"

Ghita Schuy

17 St George's Road, Kemp Town

☎ *01273 885275*

Exquisite Moroccan-influenced, hand-made shoes, bags and slippers. Ghita has now introduced a lovely children's range of delectable silk slippers and the rich and famous are already sending in their orders, so it won't be long before Madge pops in for a matching pair for Lourdes and Rocco.

Jones

20-21 East Street, The Lanes

☎ *01273 32874*

80 Church Road, Hove

☎ *01273 733016*

Classic and contemporary shoes for both sexes.

Pullingers

9 Bond Street, North Laine

☎ *01273 725476*

and

5 George Street, Kemp Town

☎ *01273 670187*

Old-fashioned store selling good quality classic shoes and boots. If you have big feet they stock women's size

shopping second-hand • shoes • DIY

nines. They've got the best selection of Dr Martens in town, including a big range for those fashion conscious kids.

Vegetarian Shoes

12 Gardner Street, North Laine

☎ *01273 691913*

Like the name suggests they sells shoes and boots for people who don't want to wear leather. The stock ranges in style, the shoes look like leather and they do a fine range of stilettos and mules.

DIY

B&Q

Pavilion Retail Park,

Lewes Road, Brighton

☎ *01273 679926*

43-61 Brighton Road,

Shoreham by Sea

☎ *01273 463423*

National superstore so you should know what to expect...

Brewers

49 New England Street,

Brighton

☎ *01273 570243*

Brewers exceptionally knowledgeable staff and fantastic stock make it the decorators' paint shop. Not only do they sell Fired Earth, John Oliver and Farrow and Ball, but if you find a paint range that you like they will order it for you.

Dockerills

3abc Church Road, Brighton

☎ *01273 607434.*

Ironmonger with good old fashioned service.

Fired Earth

15c Prince Albert Street,

The Lanes

☎ *01273 719977*

Women-led team who buy the best slate tiles and slates in town. All the tiles are on display but, beware, this is no cheap decorator's shop; expect to spend serious money on quality stuff.

Harvest Forestry/ Organic Matters

1 New England Street, Brighton

☎ *01273 689725*

Mediterranean pigment-based paints ideal for decorative effects. And while you're there, there's the bath bombs, the crafts, the organic veggies (with home delivery if you order over £25) and the best Christmas trees in town. Everything is organic or at least farmed in sustainable soil.

Homebase

Holmebush Farm Retail Park,

Upper Shoreham Road

☎ *01273 871403*

Old Shoreham Road, Hove

☎ *01273 729637*

Nationwide DIY superstore.

Inside Out

34 Upper St James Street,

Kemp Town

📞 *01273 674819*

As well as clothes, they also stock their own Regency-inspired paint collection.

MacDougall Rose

12 Richmond Parade,

Brighton

📞 *01273 606482*

Do not be fooled by MacDougall Rose's appearance of being only for professionals, they welcome all and sundry. Dulux specialists and the staff are knowledgeable and friendly.

Paint Magic

31 Western Road, Hove

📞 *01273 747980*

Jocasta Innes' shop stocking her own paint range as well as John Oliver and Fired Earth. There's a gorgeous selection of mosaics and they run courses in decorative paint effects and furniture making. If that's not enough, they also sell handmade kitchens to die for.

Sutton's Furnishings

56 Church Road, Hove

📞 *01273 723728*

A beautiful paint range, including Designers Guild, Zoffany's and Osbourne and Little.

Wickes

Davidgor Road, Hove

📞 *01273 207766*

Aisles and aisles of just about everything you'll ever need if you're doing up your house or decorating the Christmas tree.

fabric shops

The Fabric Warehouse

42 George Street, Kemp Town

📞 *01273 620744*

Fantastic selection of unusual and discount fabrics sold at very reasonable prices including an excellent curtain material selection.

Fabric Wear

Gardner Street, North Laine

Implausibly cheap saris, sheer cottons, silks, zips, needles and curtain material.

Saffron

21 Bond Street, North Laine

📞 *01273 694919*

Specialises in silk and cotton handweaves from southern India, as well as stocking a wonderful selection of coloured cottons and ethnic cushions.

Southern Handicrafts

20 Kensington Gardens, North Laine

📞 *01273 681901*

Southern Handicrafts is the shop for

serious dressmakers. Wide selection of doll-making equipment, handicrafts, embroidery, silks and the best selection of fake fur in town.

flowers & garden

Bonsai KO

45 Sydney Street, North Laine

☎ *01273 621743*

A wide selection of Bonsai sold by a man who knows an extraordinary amount about his subject.

Botanica

47 Gardner Street, North Laine

☎ *01273 686377*

Designer florists selling beautiful and exotic blooms.

Gunn's

13-14 Sydney Street, North Laine

6 Castle Square, Brighton

Western Kiosk, Churchill Square

☎ *01273 683038 (use the same number for all three shops)*

Family-run business with a fantastic range of exotic flowers and blossoms. A firm favourite with Brightonians, this is the cheapest and 'juiciest' florist in town.

Flowers By Best

42a Ship Street, The Lanes

☎ *01273 205040*

Stylish and unusual flowers and also specialises in hand-tied bouquets.

food & drink
(including organics)

butchers

Archers Organic Butchers

128 Islingword Street, Hanover

☎ *01273 603234*

The place where Hanover folk buy their organic meat and it's all delicious.

Choice Cuts Organic Butcher's

95 Preston Drove, Preston Park

☎ *01273 381616*

Organic meat, eggs, homemade chutneys and some vegetables.

Brampton's Butcher's

114 St George's Road, Kemp Town

☎ *01273 682611*

A family-run, old-fashioned butchers, selling high quality and free range meat. People travel from all over town to buy their meat and poultry here.

delis & specialist foods

Appetites Delicatessen

68 Dyke Road, Hove

☎ *01273 323266*

Specialises in tasty vegetarian stuff, juices, cheeses and all things yummy.

Cantors Of Hove

20 Richardson Road, Hove

☎ *01273 723669*

Tiny little shop selling a fine selection of rye bread, bagels and salt beef.

The Cheese Shop

17 Kensington Gardens, North Laine

📞 *01273 601129*

The place to shop if you are mad about cheese, it has the finest selection in town. As well it might, really.

The Cherry Tree

107 St James Street, Kemp Town

📞 *01273 698684*

Quality Turkish style delicatessen that stocks sumptuous culinary ingredients such as strings of dried chillies, giant garlic bulbs, fresh olives, olive oil, exotic cheeses, cured meats, sandwiches, fresh herbs and a whole array of dried and tinned quality Mediterranean produce.

Choice Cuts Deli

94a Preston Drove, Fiveways

📞 *01273 381616*

Owned by those nice people next door at Choice Cuts Butchers, this deli is full of the organic goods that you'd expect from such a right on establishment.

Choccywoccydoodah

27 Middle Street, Brighton

📞 *01273 381999*

Pure chocolate heaven: beautiful and sometimes positively abstract

chocolates and special occasion chocolate cakes made to order. Look in the window, gaze at the sheer beauty of the cakes and prepare to be amazed.

Deb's Deli

4 Gardner Street, North Laine

📞 *01273 604925*

Classic English and continental sarnies and ingredients as well as a choice selection of meat and vegetarian pies and quiches.

Embrotap

10 Church Road, Hove

📞 *01273 733246*

Chinese supermarket that sells the most extensive soy sauce range in Brighton as well as Japanese, Indian and Thai food.

Golchin Food Store

132 Western Road, Hove

📞 *01273 324514*

Small but tasty selection of continental and vegetarian food. Buy your feta and halloumi from huge cheese buckets.

Le Gourmet

159 Dyke Road, Seven Dials

📞 *01273 778437*

Quality European deli which mainly sells French and Italian fare. The cheeses, meats, and fresh pasta are particularly delicious, as is their freshly made takeaway food.

Infinity Foods

25 North Road, North Laine

📞 *01273 603563*

A mini vegetarian food market that sells the widest and most delicious health food range in Brighton. Their selection includes fresh organic produce, Japanese soups, gluten-free and dairy-free products, fresh bread and homeopathic remedies.

The Italian Shop

91/94 Dyke Road, Hove

📞 *01273 326147*

Genuine Italian bread, olives, cheese, pasta and Mediterranean goodies. Everything in this shop is mouth-watering and the staff are lovely.

The Kemp Town Delicatessen

108 St George's Road, Kemp Town

📞 *01273 603411*

Continental delicacies, fresh bread, croissants, hot coffee, delicious sandwiches and a choice range of meats and cheeses.

Lanes Deli and Pasta Shop

128 Meeting House Lane, The Lanes

📞 *01273 723522*

Specialises in fresh pasta plus the usual deli stuff and organic wines. The sauces and pasta are delicious but, be warned, the prices are steep.

Montezuma's Chocolates

15 Duke Street, The Lanes

📞 *01273 324979*

Positively gourmet organic chocolate store. Savour such delights as the dark chocolate truffles, cocoa powder, cooking chocolate, or order a children's hamper filled with wickedly delicious mixed choccy buttons.

Organic Matters

1 New England Street, North Laine

📞 *01273 689725*

The organic part of Harvest Forestry (see DIY section above) with home delivery of fruit & veg boxes over £25.

Protos Fruit And Veg

St Georges Road, Kemp Town

📞 *01273 681518*

Open seven days a week, Protos has a tasty selection of fruit and vegetables and sells plants and flowers. It also stocks a choice range of organic and dried health food.

Ryelight Chinese Supermarket

48 Preston Street, Montpelier

📞 *01273 734954*

Sells everything you need to cook the perfect Chinese.

Sensational Sausages

57a George Road, Hove

☎ *01273 723200*

Selling a tasty and extraordinary range of sausages, as well as a wide range of deli fare. Try the roasted houmous, it's particularly delicious.

Spaghetti Junction

60 Preston Street, Montpelier

☎ *01273 737082*

Tasty deli-type stuff with an emphasis on yummy sandwiches.

Sunny Foods

76 Beaconsfield Road, Preston Park

☎ *01273 507829*

A small, but well very stocked health food store selling a delicious range of organic, health and natural products.

Taj Mahal

21a/b Bedford Place, Brunswick

☎ *01273 325027*

The place to shop for Asian and Oriental food. Taj Majah's exotic fresh produce section is second to none as is their amazing selection of olives, feta cheeses and hallal meat.

Yum Yums

22-23 Sydney Street, North Laine

☎ *01273 606777*

Oriental food store that stocks fresh and dried ingredients and the things you need to cook them in. The noodle bar upstairs is always worth a visit and it's cheap.

drink

Brighton Malt House

North Road, Brighton

For whisky connoisseurs. Ring the bell - and it's only open at weekends.

Butlers Wine Celler

247 Queen's Park Road, Brighton

☎ *01273 698724*

Henry Butler sells speciality wines for connoisseurs. His partner,Richard Piggott runs:

winesforbrighton

9-12 Middle Street, Brighton

☎ *01273 206073/698724*

✉ *info@winesforbrighton.co.uk*

Interesting and eclectic wine cases delivered for free to your home or office. And together under the winesforbrighton label, they run a wine course which dispels some of the myths of wine snobbery with informal and interactiveclasses for people who swallow.

Grapevine Organics

39 Carlisle Street, North Laine

☎ *01273 705028*

Kevin Trott specialises in delicious organic wines and champagnes. Buy by the box and expect delivery within 24 hours.

Latin Spirits And Beers

PO Box 3092, Littlehampton BN16 ITW

📞 *01903 856223*

Supplying funky spirits from Lajita Mescal to 47 different kinds of tequila, as well as vodka laced with ingredients such as Siberian ginseng and black samson root. Although they are based in Littlehampton they will deliver to your door.

Le Grand Fromage/ L'Esprit Du Vin

8 -10 East Street, Shoreham

📞 *01273 440337*

L'Esprit Du Vin has a fabulous selection of fine wines (including organic), while Le Grand Fromage stocks unusual and quality cheeses.

Royal Wines

57 Queens Road,

Brighton

📞 *01273 779935*

Complete with bar stools and pool tables to aid your wine tasting and buying.

Southovers Wines

Southover Street,

Hanover

📞 *01273 600402*

Known for it obscure wine collection, this is the John Peel of wine shops. It stocks 300 different types of beer and ale from around the world.

fishmongers

Fish At The Square

St George's Road, Kemp Town

📞 *01273 680808*

As well as supplying wonderful and often unusual fresh fish, they also sell delicious homemade fish cakes and Thai fish curry.

Kevin's

17 Richardson Road, Hove

📞 *01273 738779*

Fresh, high quality fish served by the charming Kevin who is always ready with a smile. You can order in advance.

Kings Arches Fish Shop

Kings Road Arches, Brighton

As recommended by Rick Stein, buy freshly caught local fish at a tiny window next to the Fishing Museum on the beach.

Shoreham Fish Market

Shoreham Lagoon

Buy the widest selection of the local fisherman's catch including lobster, crab and bream.

organic delivery

Archers Organic Butchers

128 Islingword Street,

Hanover

📞 *01273 603234*

See Butchers' section above.

Beans and Things

☎ *01273 477774*

Organic deliveries to your door if you can be bothered to hassle them about the brochure you ordered three months ago. Once you're on their books, though, we hear they're great.

b.right.on Food Co

☎ *01273 705606*

Home-cooked organic meals delivered to your door. Miranda and Pete will deliver Goan vegetable caldine (£3.99 per 500g), wild salmon teryaki and fragrant rice with a wasabi/soy dressing (£4.50 per 450g) or Thai fishcakes (£2.50 per 250g) and a host of other vegan, vegetarian and fishy delights. They also sell the largest range of Mexican, Peruvian and Spanish chillis in Brighton.

Choice Cuts For Organic Meat

95 Preston Drove,

Preston Park

☎ *01273 381616*

See Butchers' section above.

Kudos Foods

☎ *01323 811118*

🖥 *www.kudosfoods.co.uk*

Home delivered food from the farms and fields around Ripe. Ask Avril to supply everything you need (except the waiters, of course) for a supper party; for example lentil, bacon and tomato soup, basque chicken followed by three chocolate terrine for four comes to £28.85. She'll deliver it to your door the night before. Also useful for busy parents with nutrition on your mind with not time to get to Sainsbury's.

Magpie Organic Delivery

☎ *01273 621222*

From the people who collect your recyclable waste.

The Organic Oasis

☎ *01444 459596*

Choice Cuts is owned by Organic Oasis, a French-style, organic deli and butcher's in South Street, Haywards Heath. It does a fantastic assortment of ready-made food, and if you join its Sussex Good Food Club (£20 a year) it will deliver to your door. For example, a spicy parsnip and apple soup (£1) with organic French bread (£1) followed by chicken tagine with apricots soaked in white wine and almonds, broccoli and a huge green salad (£3.50) and local sheep cheese and grapes (£2) came without an additive in sight and at £7.50 a head was a real bargain. Give them 48 hour's notice and they can do anything: a vegan dinner party for 50 came with five courses, each inspired by a different country and cost £1800.

Harvest Forestry

Organic Matters,

1 New England Street, Brighton

☎ *01273 689725*

A bizarre-looking establishment where the roof is graced by Taj Mahal domes. Sells organic produce, home decorations, Mediterranean plants and the best Christmas trees.

Home Grown Organics

☎ *01903 879 541*

An organic gardener who can transform your window boxes, garden or allotment, providing you with your own scrummy home-grown goodies, herbs and flowers.

Middle Farm

Firle (on the A26 to Eastbourne)

☎ *01323 811411*

Not just a kids' playground, Middle Farm sells a huge range of organic products including dozens of different ciders and English wines (01323 811324). The farm shop sells at least 70 brands of cheeses, all of which can be tasted, as well as organic meat and additive-free meat.

Old Spot Farm

Piltdown, Nr Uckfield

☎ *01825 722894*

Set up by farmer Ray Gould back in 1979 to supply organic, extensively farmed meat to his own children, the farm is now more of a shop with Ray selling free-range, additive-free, organic chickens, beef and pork from half a dozen local farms. They also make their own sausages and cure and smoke bacon.

The Organic Baby Co

54 Meads Street, Eastbourne

☎ *01323 411515*

Delivery and pick up service for parents who worry about what's filling those landfills.

Ridgeview Estate Winery Ltd

Fragbarrow Lane, Ditchling Common

☎ *01444 258039*

Almost organic Champagne (ie not officially classed as such, but near as damn it), and certainly worth a taste.

interiors & exteriors

Acme Art

41 Gloucester Road, North Laine

☎ *01273 601639*

Ever felt that what your lounge was lacking was a particularly odd sculpture? Then Acme is the answer to your dreams.

Ananda

24 Bond Street, North Laine

☎ *01273 725307*

Exquisite, quality Asian imports from Indonesia and India. Extremely tasteful selection of coffee tables throws, rugs, lamps and tribal textiles.

Aquatech

23 New Road, Brighton

📞 *01273 607766*

Better known as The Fish Furniture shop, Aquatech sells coffee table fish tanks, long, thin fish tanks, fish furniture and well, all things fishy, but at a price.

Decorative Arts/
Arts & Crafts Home

28 Gloucester Road,

North Laine

📞 *01273 676486*

Two highly original interior stores sit side by side. Shop stocks handcrafted furniture from Morocco, Thailand and Nepal, and showcases new work from local artists. The neighbouring art and crafts shop specialises in creating replica handcrafted furniture and William Morris wallpaper from the historic art and crafts movement.

Bazar

58 Church Road, Hove

📞 *01273 737121* and

32 London Road Brighton

📞 *01273 628435*

Vases, candleholders and some chintz, but they specialise in metalwork and you'll find some great items among the kitsch.

Blackout

53 Kensington Place,

North Laine

📞 *01273 671471*

The favourite shop of Brightonians. Be dazzled and amazed by their extraordinary array of exotic and global trinkets. Find Chinoserie, Mexican candles, jewellery, plastic tablecloths, Chairman Mao wrapping paper, hats, clothes and loads of other perfectly inessential items.

Blue-Bell

28 Kensington Gardens,

North Laine

📞 *01273 699456*

Stylish and hip solutions for the urban gardener in a town made up of patios. Selection includes wild watering cans, designer gardening books and post-modern planters.

Boudoir

13 New Road,

Brighton

📞 *01273 710818*

Decadence and design all within spitting distance of the Pavilion's Regency hedonism.

The glittering Puss In Boot boots, antiques and fake fur cushions in the window only tell half the tale; tell them what you're looking for and they'll scout out the most eclectic gifts for you.

Brighton Pottery Workshop

94 Trafalgar Street, North Laine

☎ *01273 601641*

Peasant-style urbanware pottery in the style of traditional ceramics made in Brighton in the18th century. The pots come in vibrant blues and greens. Resident potter, Peter Stocker, is more than happy for you to come and watch him work while he crafts you a masterpiece.

Brunswick Interiors

27 Western Road, Hove

☎ *01273 206982*

Specialises in re-upholstery. Stocks a designer range of tables, natural flooring, blinds and curtain materials. Offers full interior design service.

Caz Systems

18-19 Church Street, Brighton

☎ *01273 326471*

Ultra-modern state-of-the-art lighting specialists and contemporary kitchen and bathroom accessories. Look out for their French glasses and funky toasters. This is the place to buy that Smeg fridge.

Chairmaker

54 Western Road, Hove

☎ *01273 777810*

🖥 *www.chairmaker.co.uk*

Elegant contemporary and classic bespoke furniture. Designed on the premises and made from beech. Each piece is an individual work of art.

Cissymo

25 Church Street, Brighton

☎ *01273 205060*

and

38 Sydney Street, North Laine

☎ *01273 607777*

Among other delightful items, Cissymo also sells starfish loo seats, fabulous key rings, oriental kitsch space savers and some very tasty jewellery and they have just opened a second shop in Sydney Street.

Crofts Independent

39 St James Street, Kemp Town

☎ *01273 687811*

Fantastic selection of Spanish stuff, from good earthenware - the pots, pans and paella dishes - to a wide range of tacky Spanish imports.

Domus

2 Union Street, The Lanes

☎ *01273 737356*

Stocks the best in contemporary design, stylish kitchenware, plates, luggage and lights.

Elephant

1 Duke Street, The Lanes

133 Ship Street, Brighton

☎ *01273 731318*

(both shops have the same number)

The newly refurbished Elephant shop in Duke Street now boasts five floors of gorgeous colonial-style and modern furniture, upholstery fabrics, sofas, vases, beds, blinds, curtains and state-of-the-art lighting. The Ship Street branch sells sumptuous futons, cards and gifts.

Em-Space

20 Sydney Street, North Laine

📞 *01273 683400*

Contemporary cards and a few choice gift items. View the work of local artists and photographers in the small gallery space at the back of the shop.

End Of The Line

4 St James Street, Kemp Town

Extremely cheap cards, gifts and strange ornaments. Lots of the stuff is tacky, but you'll find some real bargains if you search long enough.

England At Home

22 and 32 Ship Street, The Lanes

📞 *01273 205544/738270*

Pure Elle Decoration. Number 32 sells modern, sharply styled kitchenware while number 22 stocks contemporary furniture and homeware.

Evolution

42 Bond Street, North Laine

📞 *01273 205379*

89 Western Road, Hove

📞 *01273 727123*

Perfect for cheap, fun presents. Find everything from mugs to kitsch handbags and wooden mobiles from South America in their eclectic range.

Farnsworth

55-56 East Street, The Lanes

📞 *01273 321218*

The kind of place you might walk past without a glance, but if you did you'd be missing out on their great range of contemporary kitchenware, children's toys and smart country wear clothes.

The Floor

32 Gloucester Road, North Laine

📞 *01273 602894*

Mediterranean and designer tiles and flooring, supplying the more unusual and exotic flooring needs. Stocks Fired Earth, rubber tiles, lino and a wide range of real wood floors. After sales service is still poor.

Fossil 2000

3 Kensington Place, North Laine

📞 *01273 622000*

Vast selection of A-grade crystals and massive amenites. Plates and bowls carved from 360million-year-old marble containing fossils fly out of the shop, as do trilobites (first vertebrate and definitely our ancestor). Coprolite (that's dinosaur dung) is as popular as ever with the kids. Prices start at 20p.

Gaff

66 Trafalgar Street, North Laine

☎ *01273 819202*

Exquisite contemporary rugs inspired by modern art. Choose from a brilliant array of vibrant designs or work with Gaff to design your own unique carpet.

Hocus Pocus

38 Gardner Street, North Laine

☎ *01273 572202*

Sells all things related to witchcraft, the occult, and mysticism. If you want to delve into the black arts then this is the shop for you.

In The Frame

Bond Street, North Laine

☎ *01273 724829*

Framing service and good selection of modern art.

Linorf Interiors

49 St James Street,

Kemp Town

☎ *01273 691936*

Tasteful range of post-modern-inspired interiors and homeware, including hand-blown glasses, tables, frames and designer beds, as well as a beautiful range of jewellery and handbags by Derberg/Kern. Soon

they will be stocking fitted designer kitchens by Da Da.

Malarkey

34 Bond Street, North Laine

☎ *01273 722339*

Malarkey is the place to go if you don't want to settle for a mediocre card to go with that unusual gift.

Nona Samini Boutique

3/20 Brunswick Square, Hove

☎ *01273 206639*

Still unpacking the boxes when we went to press, Nona Samini could only promise us a lifestyle store set in her own home which, she says, is inspired by rustic Italy. Italian soaps, romantic antique chandeliers, paintings, cushions, throws and an excuse to nose around someone's private house are among the reasons to shop this side of Hove.

The Old Postcard Shop

38 Beaconsfield Road,

Preston Park

☎ *01273 600035*

Go on. Guess.

Orientasia

9 East Street, The Lanes

☎ *01273 748698*

Undoubtedly the best selection around of genuine oriental carpets, rugs, kilms and fantastic cushions.

Oxfam Fair Trade

146a North Street, Brighton

📞 *01273 326364*

Beautiful selection of cards, throws, tableware, mugs and plates made by fair trade workers from around the world.

Penny Lane Gallery

35 Upper St James Street, Kemp Town

📞 *01273 686869*

Extraordinary Beatles memorabilia shop that sells everything from Yellow Submarine blow-up chairs, to vintage records, posters, original prints and Fab Four mugs and cups.

Pussy

3a Kensington Gardens,
North Laine

📞 *01273 604861*

Pussy stocks goods that create a sexually charged atmosphere. Purr over the ever so chic keyrings, books, bags and other carefully selected items for the home.

Pyramid

9a Kensington Gardens, North Laine

📞 *01273 607791*

A happening selection of retro chrome fans, funky lighting and lava lamps.

Rapid Eye Movement

23 Gardner Street, North Laine

📞 *01273 694323*

The place to shop for wild lights on strings in the shape of ducks, Marilyn Monroe and Taz of Tazmania. Also find smart shot glasses, table lamps that you can display your photos in and sonic watches.

Risby-Butler

42 Church Road, Hove

📞 *01273 749933*

A well-groomed Dalmatian greets you sweetly as does her equally charming owner. Delectable sofas, a sumptuous selection of fabrics, translucent muted glass lamps and more. Expect to find Corbusier, Timney Fowler, Noguchi and Mackintosh. Also provides interior design, curtain making and upholstery services. And there's even an art gallery upstairs (see City Art).

Rin Tin Tin

34 North Road, North Laine

📞 *01273 672424*

The ultimate shop to buy Forties, Fifties and Sixties memorabilia. Stock includes furniture, kitsch plates, old lights, toys and ornaments.

Roost

26 Kensington Gardens,
North Laine

📞 *01273 625223*

Modern collection of synthetic items for the home, including tables, bins, chairs and jugs.

shopping make up etc

SF Cody Emporium

186 Western Road, Brighton

☎ *01273 328207*

Brightly-coloured, mass-produced, cheap and sometimes stylish gifts and home accessories.

The Sofa And Futon Shop

11 Gardner Street,
North Laine

☎ *01273 677017*

Competitively priced and beautifully crafted handmade sofas and futons. Choose from an exotic selection of fabrics.

Sutton's Furnishings

56 Church Road, Hove

☎ *01273 723728*

Posh designer fabrics, wallpaper, furniture coverings, sofas, lights, groovy handles. Stock includes Designer's Guild, Osbourne and Little and John Oliver.

Tsena

6 Bond Street, North Laine

☎ *01273 328402*

Cute handmade ceramics, cards, funky mirrors and photo frames.

Tucan

29 Bond Street,
North Laine

☎ *01273 326351*

Specialising in all things South American. Find riotous colourful furniture, musical instruments, clothes, pottery, mirrors, toys and jewellery.

V2000

39 Gardner Street, North Laine

☎ *01273 603800*

Beaded curtains, feather boas, bags, balls and things that are stylish just because they are so kitsch.

Vanilla

23 Ship Street, Brighton

☎ *01273 725538*

Contemporary home-ware furnishings that come in natural earthy fabrics. The Prickly Pear handbags are divine, as are the ultra hip Loge chairs, which are aptly sub-titled, arm chairs for pop stars to watch TV in.

Wallace McFarlane

14 St George's Road, Kemp Town

☎ *01273 297088*

Candles, cards, frames, posh soaps and many other unusual and stylish gifts served by helpful and courteous staff.

Winfalcon

28 Ship Street, The Lanes

☎ *01273 72890997*

One-stop mystical shop in the heart of The Lanes with enough Tarot cards, crystals, fairy cards and witchcraft to get your life working properly again. Also a healing centre, this is where you'll be able to track down almost anyone on the alternative network. The crystals and pendulums are at kiddy-eye level and the staff are so chilled that they're happy to let them touch everything.

Yashar Bish

96 Gloucester Road, North Laine

☎ *01273 671900*

Formerly called Anatolia, this is an Aladdin's cave of antiques, rugs and earthenware all the way from Turkey. The recent split in partnership of the owners means less of the pots and more of the eclectic Oriental handmade carpets from Turkey, embroidered textiles from Uzbekistan and Turkmenistan, ornate backgammon sets and coloured glass lights. The smell of the East is enough to remind you of the authenticity.

make up, smelly stuff, aromatherapy & pampering

Bay House Aromatics

88 St George's Road,
Kemp Town

☎ *01273 601109*

Great essential oil suppliers at reasonable prices. They can source every oil, list every ingredient in their products and are fantastically helpful.

Lush

41 East Street, Brighton

☎ *01273 774700*

Presentation is everything in this shop where blocks of giant soaps lie in enticing hues of blue and green. The herbal face masks, bath bombs and vast range of regenerative treatments are all made to look as edible as is humanely possible. Rumour has it that in New York, Mayor Giulliano refused to allow Lush to open in Times Square because it would make the streets too smelly.

Mac

6 Dukes Lane, The Lanes

☎ *01273 720026*

The star's favourite make-up store is now in Brighton. The vast lipstick range shimmers and beckons you to try each and every colour. Delightful staff offer make-up consultations redeemed against sales, and compared to other posh cosmetic companies, Mac is cheap, so go on, indulge yourself.

The Nail Studio

1 Brunswick Road,
Brighton

☎ *01273 327274*

Delightful women will attach false nails to your stubby ones. Booking is essential, but no manicures.

Neal's Yard

Kensington Gardens, North Laine

☎ *01273 6014464*

You know the stock: medicinal herbs, alternative health books, aromatherapy oils and the cheapest echinacae in town.

Pecsniff's

45-46 Meeting House Lane, The Lanes

☎ *01273 723292*

Specialist aromatherapy shop selling soothing and effective blends of essential oils.

www.vitaltouch.com

▤ *www.vitaltouch.com*

OK, OK, so they're not exactly based in Brighton or Hove, but they're our mates, and it's our book and their products are so gorgeous that you need to know about them. Katie Whitehouse is a natural therapist who has been teaching and practicing aromatherapy massage and reflexology for years. Her range of ready to wear and bespoke aromatherapy products includes pregnancy, labour and post natal kits, Deep Action inspiration gels and any number of delicious massage oils. Wrapped and schlapped to your door, they make great gifts.

markets

BHASVIC College Car Boot Sale

Open Sat 8am; Sun 9am

Free for all selling toys, children's clothes, second-hand home accessories and junk.

Brighton Station Sunday Market

Open Sun 6am-12pm

Brighton's very own Portobello Road. Get up early, stroll around the stalls and check out the variety of junk, CDs, records, bikes, books, old clothes and retro furniture.

North Laine Junk Market

Upper Gardner Street,
Brighton
Open Sat 10am-2pm

Old junk, clothes, records and tat, but there are real antique bargains to be found so it's always worth a look.

The Open Market

London Road
Open Mon 7am-1pm; Tue-Thur 7am-5pm; Fri 7am-6pm

Cheap, permanent market selling fruit and vegetables, plastic toys, sweets, meat, fish and a continental food stall.

Upper Gardner Street

North Laine
Open Sat 10am-2pm

Mostly junk, clothes and records, but some gems can be found lurking if you search long and hard enough.

opticians

Brompton's

32 Gardner Street,

North Laine

📞 *01273 697711*

The sublimest selection of sunglasses and specs in Brighton. Only stockists in town of Booth and Bruce.

Peter Menington

22 Kensington Gardens,

North Laine

📞 *01273 620987*

Wide selection of designer eyewear including Cutler & Gross and DNKY.

photographic shops

Jessop's

125 Queen's Road,

Brighton

📞 *01273 321492*

and

154 Western Road, Brighton

📞 *01273 693500*

Across the board film, camera and professional developing service

Monolab

10 Upper Market Street, Hove

📞 *01273 731116*

Offers black and white printing and development service.

record shops

Bang

16 Bond Street, North Laine

📞 *01273 220380*

Listening facilities in this friendly outlet for drum'n'bass, techno and hip hop. Good on tickets - and there's a big noticeboard outside which is always up to date. They'll order anything you can't find in the shop.

The Borderline

Gardner Street, North Laine

Colourful and eclectic, Borderline is ideal for thirtysomethings who don't feel ready for Phil Collins just yet. Sells everything from world to drum'n'bass to funk. Not dangerous, but happening enough to make you feel in touch.

The Classical Longplayer

31 Duke Street, Brighton

📞 *01273 329534*

📧 *classicallongplayer@hotmail.com*

As the title suggests, this is the home of everything classical. The shop has been providing works from Beethoven and Brahms to Schubert and Tchaikovsky to Brighton's symphony fans for the last fifteen years.

Dance 2 Dance

129 Western Road, Hove

📞 *01273 220023*

A dance shop - no really, it is - selling house, drum'n'bass and trance and all manner of DJ equipment from decks to record boxes. And they've got decks so you can listen before you buy.

Electrodisc

111 Gloucester Road,

North Laine

☎ *01273 676509*

Fantastic facilities - a lounge complete with seating, magazines and in-house DJs make this super-trendy shop cool, but not imposing.

Happy Vibes Records (HVR)

52 Gardner Street,

North Laine

☎ *01273 699904*

If you want to know what's going down in the world of breakbeat and funk, this is your first stop. There's a downstairs listening room and they're very good on tickets.

Klik Klik Whirly Beep Beep

91 Trafalgar Street,

North Laine

☎ *01273 622940*

Sample trance, techno and nu-energy records from the privacy of a listening booth, or chose something from its range of clubwear. This is also the place to visit to find the word on the street or discover where old Space Invader's machines retire to.

The Record Album

8 Terminus Road, Brighton

☎ *01273 323853*

Apparently, the oldest record shop in England and, as you'd imagine, a million miles from the megastore ideal. They specialise in deleted records, soundtracks, rarities and that sort of thing.

Recordland

40 Trafalgar Street,

North Laine

☎ *01273 672512*

Maybe the best jazz record shop in town - from be-bop to easy, it's all here.

Rounder Records

19 Brighton Square,

The Lanes

☎ *01273 325440*

Right in the middle of The Lanes, Rounder is very straight, very sensible but very useful. Also good for tickets.

Urban Records

24 Gardner Street,

North Laine

☎ *01273 620567*

A vinyl-only shop - so a home for the purist and DJs. The place if you're into serious house and garage.

supermarkets

ASDA

Brighton Marina Village

☎ *01273 606611*

1 Crowhurst Road, Hollingbury

01273 541166

Both now open 24 hours a day.

Co-Op

(Some are open from 7am-10pm and
8am-8pm on Sundays)

London Road and
Baker Street

📞 *01273 606722 (department store)*

76-82 Blatchington Road, Hove

📞 *01273 73394*

124 Dyke Road, Hove

📞 *01273 206553*

56-57 Lewes Road, Brighton

📞 *01273 684610*

Nevill Road, Hove

📞 *01273 205481*

33-39 Old London Road,
Patcham

📞 *01273 552001*

269 Preston Drove, Brighton

📞 *01273 562315*

3-5 West Way, Hangleton

📞 *01273 732741*

Whitehawk Road, Brighton

📞 *01273 682763*

Sainsbury's

93 Lewes Road, Brighton

📞 *01273 674201*

1-4 London Road, Brighton

📞 *01273 685461*

Old Shoreham Road, Brighton

📞 *01273 439257*

Home delivery on the Net

📧 *www.sainsburystoyou.co.uk*

Somerfield

119 London Road, Brighton

📞 *01273 601521*

Tesco

Upper Shoreham Road, Shoreham
(Holmebush Centre)

📞 *01273 367600*

Boundary Road, Portslade

📞 *01273 367500*

Tesco Metro, Dyke Road, Brighton

📞 *01273 369400*

Waitrose

130-131 Western Road, Hove

📞 *01273 326549*

tobacconists

Burkitts

117 Church Road, Hove

📞 *01273 731351*

Old-fashioned tobacconist that has
been run by the same family since
1873. Sells Havana cigars, pipes,
tobacco in jars, and more often than
not you will spot Brighton thesps
buying their baccy here. Great gifts for
smokers.

Taylor's

19 Bond Street,
North Laine

📞 *01273 606110*

Sells a wide range of fresh tobacco
including chocolate flavour. It
specialises in Havana cigars, lighters

and everything a lady or gentlemen might require.

cannot be categorised

Brighton Bead Shop

21 Sydney Street,
North Laine
01273 675077

Crammed full of intricately designed beads and innovative ideas for their uses, it's a one-stop shop for experienced designers and novices keen to have a go.

Burchell's

103 Gloucester Road,
North Laine
01273 69820

Religious artefacts and icons.

Cash Converters

50 St James Road,
Kemp Town
01273 691414

Almost a modern day pawn shop. Take in your bike, sofa, wheelbarrow or stereo and they will give you cash.

M&D Hawkins Antique Arms & Armour

27 Meeting house Lane,
The Lanes
v01273 321357

Extraordinary historical collection of armour and weapons for those of a military inclination.

Movie Mania

12 George Street, Hove
01273 622388

The place to go for old movie memorabilia - posters, still, books and mags.

Sin Bin

George Street,
Kemp Town

Formerly Manaia in North Road, the Sin Bin is a friendly little place to get your tattoos, piercings, handcuff and whips.

Revolucion

31 Sydney Street,
North Laine
01273 626349

Anything Mexican - from chilli sauces to Mescal to voodoo masks. If it's Mexican, it's here.

The Video Box

107 St George's Road,
Kemp Town
01273 670469

Reflecting the cultural needs of discerning local residents, the Kemp Town Video Box stocks the best art house cinema collection in town.

Also at: *122 Elm Grove, Brighton (01273 623313); 64 Goldstone Villas, Hove (01273 821469); 1 Surrey Street, Brighton (01273 823455); 69 Western Road, Hove (01273 204325).*

Videostar

125 Western Road, Montpelier

📞 *01273 776335*

These charming men know their films so well that they can look at you for less than 30 seconds and reckon on the perfect choice. Go on, test them out…

Also at: *253d Ditchling Road (01273 507055); 229 Queen's Park Road (01273 623464); 60 St James Street (01273 690935); 2 The Broadway (01273 621771).*

time out

arts & film

arts to see

Burstow Gallery

Brighton College,

Eastern Road,

Kemp Town

📞 *01273 704229*

Kathe Kollowitz' German Expressionism was the exhibition of the bleaker months this year in this rather more popular use of Brighton's most famous public school.

Fabrica

Holy Trinity Church,

40 Duke Street, Brighton

📞 *01273 778646*

Art installations housed in a beautiful old church in the heart of Brighton's shopping area. A fantastic place to relax in if the shopping gets too much.

Gallery 73

St James Street,

Kemp Town

📞 *01273 674788*

Collages, embroidered textiles, woodcuts and touchy feely art in the heart of Kemp Town.

Gardner Arts Centre

University of Sussex, Falmer

📞 *01273 685447*

Outside the theatre is a large space often given over to massive sculptures, installations and conceptual art for theatre goers to enjoy. Rachel Whitread was one of the exhibitors as we went to press.

Phoenix Arts

10-14 Waterloo Place, Brighton

📞 *01273 603700*

📧 *www.slab-o-concrete.demon.co.uk/exhibitions.htm*

Artist/charity/collective/co-op in an enormous Sixties building to the east of St Peter's Church in Waterloo Place. Workshops for adults and children open days dotted throughout the year, plus exhibitions in the rooms that used to be home to huge mainframe computers in the Seventies

Preston Manor

Preston Drove

📞 *01273 290900*

Edwardian home of the Stanford

family who once owned the whole area around Preston Park. It dates from the 1600s, but most of the furniture and fittings are more Upstairs Downstairs with mangles and smoothing irons, tin baths, as well as a butler's pantry. Check out the eccentric pets' cemetery in the walled gardens.

Royal Pavilion

Pavilion Gardens, Brighton

📞 *01273 290900*

Possibly the most sumptuous, ostentatious and hedonistic piece of architecture in the UK. Originally the holiday home for the Prince Regent, it became the place for aristocratic hangers-on and the Prince's arty entourage to spend their spare time in. Make sure you get a guided tour through the fabulously over-the-top palace for a feast of gossip and information. Kids love the stuffed swans in the kitchen's baking tins and Queen Victoria's princess-and-the-pea bed and expect to bump into The Beast or Aladdin around every corner. Storytelling and art sessions for kids during half-term.

The University of Brighton Gallery

Grand Parade, Brighton

📞 *01273 643012*

Originates, shows and tours an eclectic range of international and national art as well as local and student work from its parent, The University of Brighton. It features wide-ranging exhibitions, including multi-media and art installation pieces, but the highlight of the year has to be the graduate shows in June where you can pick up some real steals from the big names of the future. Some exhibitions also tour.

White Gallery

86-87 Western Road, Hove

📞 *01273 774870*

📧 *www.thewhitegallery.co.uk*

An absolute must for art lovers, with a loan scheme subsidised by South East Arts to allow your money to go directly to the artist while you take your time paying the gallery interest free. Look out for established painters such as Paula Rego, Picasso and Lucian Freud, as well as emerging young artists. A recent group show entitled 'The Men's Room' explored issues around masculinity and included prints, paintings and men's jewellery.

cinemas

Brighton Cinemateque

Media Centre, 9-12 Middle Street, Brighton

📞 *01273 384300*

Showing everything that you won't

find in any other cinema, from Russian films to early silent movies and digital shorts. Only open a few nights a week, so ring for details or pick up their brochure around town.

The Duke Of York's Picture House

Preston Circus, Brighton

📞 *01273 602503/626261*

Brighton's most popular art house is on Viaduct Road at the edge of the Fiveways and Preston Park communities and within walking distance of the student quarter behind the London Road. It's a proper carrot cake independent with all that implies. 'One-night only' showings are its speciality, so make sure you paste its calendar of events on your front door to avoid missing such favourites as Brighton Rock, The Italian Job or an Almodovar retrospective. The Brighton Jewish Film Festival is on here in November with some screenings at the Cinemateque.

Gardner Arts Centre

University of Sussex, Falmer

📞 *01273 685447*

Arts films and seasons - similar to the sort of things you'd find at the Duke Of York's but with more of a student slant. Basically, if it's got subtitles and lacks a coherent narrative, it's in.

Odeon

Kingswest, West Street, Brighton

📞 *0870 5050007*

A big, old-fashioned, multi-screen cinema that boasts a built-in Haagen Dazs café, so at least if the film's rubbish, you can enjoy the ice-cream. Just remember to add 15 minutes to your timing - the ice-cream queue can take its time.

UGC Marina

Marina Village, Brighton

📞 *0541 555145*

A mega-screen multiplex showing all the latest blockbusters. The main joy here is that it shows films at a remarkably civilised time; most evenings the main show doesn't start until 9pm. A UGC card allows you to see an unlimited number of films for £9.99 a month. The downside is that to qualify, you have to commit to a year's worth of visits.

comedy

Funky Hippos @ The Beach

Kings Road Arches, Brighton

📞 *01273 722272*

Stand-up comedy in a relaxed environment, held on a Tuesday night at the moment, though by the time you read this that will probably have changed. A bite to eat, some drinks, a few laughs and then a bit of the old disco boogie. What more could you want from one night?

The Hanbury Arms

83 St Georges Street, Kemp Town

📞 *01273 605789, 550000*

Kemp Town Crack is a new comedy night. They've tried to put less mainstream evenings and events on at The Hanbury to compliment the mystique and the almost seedy vibe of the place.

The Krater Comedy Club @ Komedia

44-47 Gardner Street, Brighton

📞 *box office: 01273 647100*

The best smallish comedy/ performance art venue in town. A lot of acts try out their shows here before going up to Edinburgh - and the successful ones come back. The Krater Comedy Club, a stand-up fest, is on Saturday and Sunday nights. Watch out for the monthly News Revue.

live performance

Akademia

14 Manchester Street, Brighton

📞 *01273 622633*

Forms part of the University of Brighton's Student Union, Akademia only open to students and their guests during term time. Thursday night is the exception when it hosts a comedy club. A venue throughout the Festival and open for rep companies during the holidays.

The Brighton Centre

Kings Road, Brighton

📞 *01273 290131*

Demonstrating that what's good for graduation ceremonies and conferences is not always good for gigs, the Brighton Centre squats on the seafront in all its Seventies concrete glory. Poor bar service will frustrate the seasoned music fan, but in its defence the existence of the Brighton Centre does mean that Brighton attracts the big-name bands that other South Coast towns can't accommodate. Indie kids, mainstreamers and middle-aged couples alike will find enough to please them from Primal Scream and Macy Gray to the shamanistic Holiday On Ice, Xotica. Only in Brighton...

The Brighton Dome

Box office, 29 New Road,

Brighton

📞 *01273 709709*

Currently being refurbished, the Dome (rather confusingly encompassing the Dome auditorium, Corn Exchange and Pavilion Theatre) is due to reopen towards the end of 2001. Its Thirties Art Deco interior will be restored and revitalised, concealing within it enough high-tech equipment to support a mix of high art, pop concerts and conference money-earners. The Dome promises big-name dance, opera and drama, and concerts covering everything from classical to pop. The intimate Pavilion Theatre runs a lively programme of music and cabaret, while the lofty Corn Exchange stages everything from The Afro Cuban All Stars and Nitin Sawhney to Siobhan Davies Dance Company and Unicorn Children's Theatre.

Brighton Little Theatre Company

Studio Theatre, 9 Clarence Gardens, Brighton (opposite Pavilion)

📞 *box office: 01273 205000*

Amateur repertory company staging some 11 productions a year, running the full gamut of the theatrical genre with Sir Donald Sinden its founding president. Catch its annual outdoor performance at Lewes Castle.

Concorde II

Madeira Drive, Kemp Town

📞 *01273 606460*

This is where you will find yourself if you want to see the up-and-coming bands of the moment. An excellent booking policy and a bar almost as long as the walk home along the seafront make the Concorde II

currently the best venue in Brighton for live music. Best known as the home of the Big Beat Boutique, all kinds of acts also play here from Badly Drawn Boy to Asian Dub Foundation, Public Enemy and Kathryn Williams.

Free Butt

25-26 Albion Street, Brighton

📞 *01273 603974*

If having the band playing in your face and sweat running down the walls is what you're looking for then the Free Butt is for you. Essentially a pub venue, the Free Butt is a loud and beery place where you're likely to see esoterically named bands that will test your eardrums and your hardened gig-goer's credentials to the limit.

Gardner Arts

Lewes Road, Falmer

📞 *01273 685861*

Sussex University-based arty theatre with a strong emphasis on the avant-garde. Kids' pantos here tend to be particularly worth a visit. Its new venture into kids' drama and interactive theatre is a must for everyone under the age of 10.

Komedia

44-47 Gardner Street, Brighton

📞 *box office: 01273 647100*

Komedia was set up in 1994 to bring European-based visual and physical theatre to Brighton. Specialising in fringe productions, the Komedia is the place to go for comedy, performance theatre or kids' drama.

The Lift

11-12 Queens Road,

Brighton

📞 *01273 779411*

Above the Pig In Paradise pub in the centre of town, The Lift has a well earned reputation for putting on eclectic nights of left-field music ranging from the sublime to the ridiculous and back again - often on the same night. Entry is usually fairly cheap, so don't worry if you haven't heard of the names on the bill. This is what gig-going should be like: you may be shocked, you may be appalled, you may be awed, but you will be entertained.

The New Venture Theatre

Bedford Place, Brighton

📞 *01273 746118*

🖥 *www.newventure.org.uk*

This training ground of new writing and directing allows Brighton and Hove to witness some breathtaking new theatre and, natch, a few duds along the way. Check out Kes during the festival and their HotBed production of A Tale of Two Todgers by New Venture regular Brian Behan. The food there is top notch too.

The Old Market

11a Upper Market Street, Hove

📞 *01273 736222*

Newly restored Romanesque forum in an old marketplace where the performance space is geared towards opera and acoustically-correct theatre. Local theatre groups, opera companies and chamber orchestras line up to appear and there's also a pub open to non-theatre-goers. If there were more bands on maybe it could capitalise on its excellent acoustics, location and size and give the Concorde II a real run for its money. Alas, you won't find yourself here very often if you're looking for indie or rock gigs. If you do go though, put up with the somewhat inadequate bar and enjoy the civilised atmosphere and the fact that - unlike in many other venues - you'll probably be able to hear the vocals properly. Courtney Pine was a recent guest here.

Pressure Point

33 Richmond Place,

North Laine

📞 *01273 235082*

Traditional indie venue above the pub. The walls are black, the floors are sticky after years of beer abuse... you know the sort of place. A good venue, one of the stalwarts. If it's a guitar band you want, this is the place to look.

The Sallis Benney

Grand Parade,

Brighton

☎ *01273 643010*

The University of Brighton's own theatre, it's rarely open to the public except during the month-long Festival in May when the likes of Perrier award winning Jazzers, The Higginbottom/Mayne Quartet do their thing to a roaring crowd. Also look out for summer-term student shows.

Theatre Royal

New Road, Brighton

☎ *box office: 01273 328488*

The Theatre Royal first opened its doors back in 1774 and still maintains its reputation as Brighton's luvvie establishment, thanks to the procession of grand, theatrical names who have passed through its doors from Marlene Dietrich to Sir Lawrence Olivier and Helena Bonham Carter. It has recently taken over by the Ambassador Theatre Group who want to create even more of a West End by the sea. Alan Ayckbourn, Joe Orton, Moscow City Ballet and English Touring Opera have already visited this year and Willy Russell's Blood Brothers will be showing over an extended summer run.

museums

Remember to take local ID to most of these museums and you'll get in at reduced price.

Booth Museum of Natural History

194 Dyke Road, Brighton

☎ *01273 292777*

The Booth is full of insects, beasties and all manner of things to do with natural history, but what it's renowned for is being home to more stuffed birds than there are in a stuffed bird shop. A spooky old place to hang around.

Brighton Fishing Museum

201 Kings Road Arches, Brighton

☎ *01273 723064*

This museum keeps the spirit of this one-time fishing village alive. See The Season chapter for information on its activities during the festival.

Brighton Museum and Art Gallery

Church Street, Brighton

☎ *01273 290900*

With some of the best artwork outside of the capital.

Brighton Sea Life Centre

Marine Parade, Madeira Drive,

Brighton

☎ *01273 609361*

The perfect place to take anyone from little Johnny to Granny on a rainy day.

Creatively designed, it's a joy on the eye and is filled with more fish than there are stars in the sky. The rays can be fed and stroked, the seahorses are beautifully displayed in magnified glass and the shark tunnel is a treat for anyone scared of the misunderstood little loves.

The Engineerium

Nevill Road, Hove

☎ *01273 559583*

This small boy's dream of a museum is set in a beautifully restored Victorian station, housing an impressive collection of steam engines, from small toys right up to a 10-metre-high beam engine. Exhibits include the Giant's Toolbox, a superb interactive exhibit explaining all the major principles of mechanical engineering, plus the giant has thoughtfully left belongings around the building for younger kids to spot! The staff are knowledgeable and very helpful. The first Sunday of each month has engines in steam, including the huge beam engine – fun for kids of all ages.

Sussex Toy & Model Museum

52/55 Trafalgar Street, Brighton

☎ *01273 749494*

Toys and er, models. As we went to press, this little treasure trove was about to be re-opened after two years

of festering in a leaky, cash starved state of disrepair. Happily, the toys and models are none the worse for it.

brighton storytellers

Brighton Storytellers are a mixed bag of folk who tell and perform stories of all kinds. During the winter they usually book a programme of well-known and gifted narrators. Stories told can be traditional or modern, comforting or scary, or bizarre. Stories and performances are held on the 1st Sunday in the month from September to May, currently upstairs at Puccini's, opposite Brighton Town Hall. Bigger venues are booked during the Brighton Festival. Performances cost £3-£5, depending on venue & teller.

arts to do

workshops

Brighton is mad about drumming, and there are few events more stirring than the sight and sound of the Carnival Collective leading a procession of drummers and dancers through town to the beach for the symbolic Burning of the Clocks ceremony to mark the end of the year. Throughout the Festival, there are plenty of music, arts and dance workshops. After last year's Festival, when Zap trained most of the kids in Brighton to beat their own drums, adults might want to sign up to keep ahead of the pack.

BA Spurr
☎ *01273 884226*

Art workshops for adults.

Bucarr Ndow
☎ *01273 232629*

Master drummer teaching Djembe drumming. .

Fern Keita
☎ *01273 607238*

African drumming workshops for women.

New Holistic Health Centre
Beaconsfield Villas, Brighton
☎ *01273 696295*

Offers a myriad of workshops.

Peter Evans
☎ *01273 733773*

Singing teacher.

Salsa (Cuban-style)
Sussex Arts Club, Ship Street, Brighton
☎ *01273 727371*

Salsa workshops. Leo - also from Cuba - teaches Salsa brilliantly at different venues. The wonderful Philippa King also teaches on the Thursday night sessions at the Arts Club. Contact Leo at *leocubano@hotmail.com*

kids' activities

Brighton and Hove is a haven for kids. The Council has spent a fortune on sandpits and playgrounds on the seafront, the Summer Fun in the Park programme provides free storytelling, and you can find African drumming and face-painting every day in different parks throughout the summer holiday. But things don't stop at the end of the summer hols, and there's an imaginative programme of art clubs and pre-school sessions at the libraries and museums in Brighton and Hove at around £3 per child. For example, Acting and telling nursery stories at Preston Manor, seaweed and sand play at the Booth Museum, astronomical observation of Jupiter and Saturn at Foredown Tower and food sculpting at Hove Museum were just some of the sessions which went on in February this year. Check with each venue to find out what's on - especially during the school holidays.

See the Museums section in the Arts & Film chapter for a more detailed description of the museums.

Booth Museum of Natural History

194 Dyke Road, Brighton

☎ *01273 292777*

Brighton Museum

Church Street, Brighton

☎ *01273 292797*

Brighton Pavilion

Pavilion Buildings,

Brighton

☎ *01273 290900*

Foredown Tower

Foredown Road, Portslade

☎ *01273 292092*

See Days Out chapter

Hove Museum and Art Gallery

19 New Church Road, Hove

☎ *01273 290200*

Preston Manor

Preston Drove, Preston Park

☎ *01273 292770*

kids' activities introduction

Brighton Central library

Vantage Point

New England Street, Preston Circus

☎ *main number: 01273 290800*

☎ *children's lending, music and reference library: 01273 296957*

Stuck in what used to be the DVLC, this is a far cry from the days when it was part of the Brighton Museum. Still, it's only a stop gap until the Council get the go-ahead to start building the Jubilee Project which will amalgamate the Prince Regent swimming pool and children's music playhouse.

Hove Library

182-186 Church Road,

Hove

☎ *01273 290700*

regular dates

Borders Bookshop

Churchill Square Shopping Centre,

Brighton

☎ *01273 731122*

Special children's storytime events on weekend mornings - readings complete with balloons, music and refreshments. The café's a refuge for the parents. The place to sip coffee, rest your tired toes and browse through the best stocked magazine section in Brighton while the kids sit cross legged and listen to what Harry Potter did next.

The Duke of York's Picture House

Preston Circus, Brighton

☎ *01273 602503/626261*

Junior Dukes, the cinema's kids club, opens its doors on Saturdays at 11am for competitions before the film. Birthday boys and girls even get to start the film in the projection room. Bigger kids can be left, while (if you've got any sense) you go and sit in a café and relax.

Kids@Komedia

44-47 Gardner Street, Brighton

☎ *box office enquiries: 01273 647100*

On Saturday and Sunday mornings, the arty Komedia puts on kids' shows. Take them to the Junior Dukes Film Club on Saturday and the Komedia on Sunday, and they'll look after you when you're old.

indoor activities

Badgers Mini Tennis

Church Place, Kemp Town

☎ *01273 671622*

Coaching for four years and up at Manor Gym in the winter and Badgers Tennis Club in the summer.

Brighton and Hove Gymnastics Club

St Agnes Church, Hove,

☎ *01273 776209*

Older kids must book regular sessions.

Candy Castle

Enterprise Point, Melbourne Street,

Brighton

📞 *01273 276060*

Bouncy gyms and ball ponds.

Glazed Expressions

31 North Road, Brighton

📞 *01273 628952*

Another painting studio for would be artists, and a treat for a quiet afternoon with even the littlest of kids. The studio fee is £4, and you can stay as long as you like. The items start at £3 (tiles, little ornaments, little bowls etc) The firing and glazing is done by the pros, and you collect 24-48 hours later. They also do kids parties for a minimum of six children where the birthday child gets a piggy bank which their mates have painted for them.

Grand Ocean Hotel

Saltdean

📞 *01273 302291*

A grand old swimming pool which is almost always empty. The ballpond is only open to residents but you can hire it for children's parties. Open 8-12noon, 1-8pm. £2.10 and £1.25. Under fives free.

King Alfred Leisure Centre

See leisure centres

Paint Pots

39 Trafalgar Street, Brighton

📞 *01273 833643*

Paint your own pottery for a two hour studio fee (£3 for kids) plus the raw material for a variety of prices (a cereal bowl costs £5). The idea is for the kids to paint it while you have a cup of tea. Owner, Vicky Rawlinson, bakes and glazes the pottery and you collect a couple of days later.

Sealife Centre

Marine Parade, Brighton

📞 *01273 604233*

The ballpond here is free and open for kiddy parties and coffee hungry parents. The Sealife Centre itself is an expensive but worthwhile treat.

The Triangle Pool

See swimming pools in Sports chapter.

Wacky Warehouse

The Saltdean Tavern,

Saltdean Park Road, Saltdean

📞 *01273 302863*

More bouncy gyms and ball ponds. (It's attached to a pub - and they let you take drinks in).

music, arts, dance & martial arts

Beacon Arts

Knoyle Hall, Knoyle Road, Brighton

📞 *01273 557124*

Tap, ballet, jazz and drama classes. Jo Alderson runs art workshops for kids here and at Balfour Infants School.

Children's Music Playhouse

The Bowling Green, Preston Park

📞 *01273 554455*

Jackie Chase and her band of musicians are still campaigning for a council run community centre which offers music and arts for all children. The Council is promising a place in the Jubilee Centre which will also house the Prince Regent swimming pool and the children's library, but building is still a way off. Ring for details about their piano, guitar, drum and singing lessons as well as music and movement classes. Also practical science, drama, French and music theory.

Dance Art Studio

📞 *01273 556313*

Principal Lynda Forster is everything you would expect a ballet teacher to be - small, neat, dressed in black and devoted to her 'gels'. Real grown up ballet for little girls.

Doris Isaacs School of Dance

📞 *01273 680066*

Traditional, but relaxed teaching of ballet, jazz, tap and modern.

Helen O'Grady Drama

📞 *01273 881440*

Maggie Jemmett is a very motivating and positive lady and children are drawn to her like a magnet.

Hove Dance Centre

📞 *01273 733937*

Lots of dance classes including an afternoon disco for littlies.

Ittaikan Aikido Club

Dorset Gardens, Brighton

📞 *01273 696383*

paulb@beel.fsnet.co.uk

Paul Bonett (3rd Dan) and Brian Stacey (4th Dan) take a special juniors version of the Aikido class on Sunday afternoons from 4.30 to 6pm.

Phoenix Arts

10-14 Waterloo Place, Brighton

📞 *01273 603700*

Activities for kids include Colourbox, a six-part course for 7 to 11-year-olds in design, collage and drawing.

Stagecoach Theatre Schools

📞 *01273 747072*

Ring Kate Bennett more formal but fun approach to drama, singing and dance for 4 to 16-year-olds

Wendy Whatling

📞 *01273 549633*

kids' activities music, arts dance & martial arts

Wendy Whatling teaches all ages dance of all types from jazz to tap to ballet. Wendy choreographed the highly acclaimed tribute to Hillsborough "Their Scarves Were Red" at the Gardner Arts Centre earlier this year."

Yoga for kids

For 5 to 9-year-olds and 9 to 12-year-olds at Natural Bodies (see Health chapter for details) and at Balfour Infants for 8 to 14-year-olds.

outdoor activities

Brighton Pier

Madeira Drive,

Brighton

☎ 01273 609361

Amusement arcades, dolphin derbies, simulators and rides to scare the hardiest and sweeten the littlest.

Stanmer Park

Lewes Road,

Brighton

The garden at the disused Stanmer House is a natural activity centre for kids, with wooden swings hanging from the cedars and fallen tree trunks sculpted into badgers (or are they moles?) for kids to scramble over. The dairy farm always seems to have calves in the barns, and the duck pond, cafe and vast open spaces are a winner with kids all year round. Plans are being

discussed for the currently disused Stanmer House to include an art gallery, apartments and a centre for disabled children.

Pells Outdoor Swimming Pool

The Pells, Lewes

☎ 01273 472334

Saltdean Lido

Saltdean Park Road, Saltdean

☎ 01273 305155

Opened in the 1930s by Johnny Weismuller, this is a good, proper lido just like they should be.

parent and baby/toddler groups

Brighton and Hove Gymnastics Club

St Agnes Church, Hove

☎ 01273 776209

Children's Music Playhouse

The Bowling Pavilion, Preston Park

☎ 01273 554455

Singing and music groups for the under fives.

Fiddlesticks Music

Stanford Avenue and

Southover Street

Brighton

☎ 01273 882951

Kemp Town Toddler Group

The Krypt, St George's Church,

St George's Street,

Kemp Town

There's a drop in on Tuesdays and Thursday from 10am.

Little Dippers

67 Upper Gloucester Road,

Brighton

☎ 01273 328275

Remember the babies swimming underwater on the opening title sequence of Tomorrow's World and the British Gas ad? Lauren Heston encouraged them to use the breathing reflex babies rely on in the watery womb, and can do the same with yours. Her half hour classes are only for babies of 12 months and under.

Mini Music

Portland Road, Hove

☎ 01273 327509

Mosaic

Community Base,

13 Queen's Road,

Brighton

☎ 01273 234017

Cultural activities for children of mixed and ethnic races. Every third Sunday, a bring a dish social invites older children and their families, but at the moment, it's only the under

fives who get to take advantage of the 9.30-11.30 soft room play every Tuesdays. Members only - although membership is free for black and mixed parentage.

Rum a Tum Tum

Hanover Community Centre,

Southover Street, Brighton

☎ 01273 710896

Steiner Parent and Toddler Group

Whitehawk Road, Brighton

☎ 01273 386300

Breadmaking, singing and a calm, creative environment for the under threes. Steiner also has regular bazaars, fetes and creative workshops. Highly recommended for kids of all ages and all educational choices.

Tumble Tots

Various venues in Brighton,

Hove, Hassocks, Cuckfield,

and Worthing.

☎ 01273 723511 for details.

Twinkle Twinkle

☎ 01273 272501 for details.

Whitehawk Toy Library

Whitehawk Road,

Brighton

☎ 01273 296924

Lends toys and has indoor activity days during school holidays.

Wam - The Parent Network

📞 *01444 230043*

📧 *EA_ALLAN@Compuserve.com*

Enables parents to make friends with other parents and it is split into local groups. Events include children's activities, coffee mornings and playschemes.

playgrounds

Blaker's Park

Tiny little park between Preston Drove and Stanford Avenue with Council tennis courts and a young children's playground.

Hollingbury Park

Playground for younger and older kids (but beware the hideous teenagers coming out of Varndean and Stringer for a fag behind the slide at 3.15). Tennis courts and wide open space for a good run around.

Hove Park

Hove Park is a delight for buggy pushing dog walkers, with circular paths, playgrounds, squirrels and a sweet café complete with veranda, even if the owner doesn't like kids running around.

Preston Park

Large space with cycle tracks, bowling green, tennis courts and young children's playground. Two cafes.

Queen's Park

Kiddy dream of a park with pirate ship and café with mini milks and homemade cakes. Parents take picnics and make friends with their kids' friends' mums and dads. Duck pond and tennis courts too.

St Ann's Well

Tree lined and packed with squirrels with a sweet little well in the middle. Two playgrounds for toddler and bigger kids.

Seafront Playground at the Ellipse

Brand new playground which was still being built when we went to press.

children's parties

The **Sea Life Centre**, **Bowlplex**, **Monkey Puzzle** and all the sports centres organise their own. Bowlplex is particularly well organised. Sea Life is educational and suitable for kids up to 8 and for not much more than £6 provides the usual junk food that kids love, a must-have beanie baby type toy gift. More than 10 kids and they throw in a free cake. Most places will work with you to organise what you want; an art teacher at the **Beacon Arts** was willing to do art work to a theme, arrange songs and a little show with the kids while parents got the tea.

The Magic Rabbit (☎ *01273 206562*) is a big favourite as a visiting show, appealing to adults with his dry sense of humour while the kids go gooey over the rabbit. **Mr Pineapple Head** (☎ *01273 473913*) is a clown for young kids and **Dandelion Puppets** (☎ *01273 857482*) provides lovely nature stories in a Punch and Judy style.

sport

sport to do

bowls & balls

Bowlplex

The Marina

☎ 01273 818180

Brighton Bears Basketball Club

Gemini House,

136-140 Old Shoreham Road, Hove

☎ 01273 778520

Brighton & Hove Gymnastics Club

St Agnes Church, Goldstone Lane, Hove

☎ 01273 776209

Brighton Rugby Football Club

Waterhall Playing Fields, Mill Road, Brighton

☎ 01273 562729

cricket

Sussex County Cricket Club

The County Ground, Eaton Road, Hove

☎ 01273 827100

If you want to get involved in village cricket and want advice on how to contact your local team, the Sussex Cricket Board at the County Ground will be able to help you out.

football

To find out about playing the local leagues, phone the Sussex County Football Association on **01903 753547**.

Hove & Kingsway Bowling Club

The Beach, Kingsway, Hove

☎ 01273 734386

Hove Rugby Football Club

Park View Road, Hove

☎ 01273 505103

golf

There are six golf clubs in the Brighton & Hove area which are all listed below, but if you need any further assistance, or you want to know about clubs in the county, contact the East Sussex County Golf Union on *01273 589791*.

Brighton and Hove Golf Club

Dyke Road, Brighton

📞 *01273 556482*

Dyke Golf Club

Dyke Road, Brighton

📞 *01273 857296*

East Brighton Golf Club

Roedean Road, Brighton

📞 *01273 604838*

Hollingbury Park Golf Club

Ditchling Road, Brighton

📞 *01273 552010*

Waterhall Golf Club

Mill Road, Brighton

📞 *01273 508658*

West Hove Golf Club

Church Farm, Hove

📞 *01273 419738*

gyms

Alive

25-27 Castle Street,

Brighton

📞 *01273 739606*

Fitness and natural health centre with gym, sauna, sunbed and an extensive range of classes, including yoga, aerobics, dance, flamenco, salsa and tango. Virtually every complimentary therapy is also on offer: aromatherapy, massage, shiatsu, homeopathy and cranial therapy. You can attend as a non-member, but it also offers very flexible membership deals.

Brighton Health and Racquet Club

Village Way,

Falmer

📞 *01273 667800*

Enormous and supposedly the best gym in town. It's a bit of a drive for anyone who doesn't live on campus at the University of Sussex, but with its top-of-the-range tennis and squash courts, gym and swimming pool, it's probably worth it. There are crèche facilities, children's swimming lessons and kiddie yoga on offer while you work out.

Cheetah Gym

King Alfred Leisure Centre,

Kingsway, Hove

📞 *01273 206644*

Claims to be the most comprehensive weight-training facility in the south. It's a favourite among Hove's gay men and also has a ladies-only section. There's no crèche, but next door at the King Alfred Leisure Centre they have and they'll take your little ones.

David Lloyd Centre

The Marina, Brighton

☎ *01273 666400*

Well-equipped gym where you can pump your inner thighs while looking out to sea. The swimming pool is enormous and often empty and kids are welcome at most times of the day (Mon-Fri 9am-12.30pm and 1.30pm-8pm). The café, which maybe isn't the best café in town (unless you think paying over the odds for a ham sandwich a good deal), also has a seaview and is a perfect place to watch the sunset. There's a crèche, as well as its own expanding nursery school.

Dragon's Health and Leisure Club

St Heliers Avenue, Hove

☎ *01273 724211*

Said to be a favourite among young singles (isn't that what gyms are for?), the swimming pool and beauty therapies attract a less iron-pumping crowd off-peak. Crèche facilities, ballet classes for members' kids, resident osteopath and sports massage mark it out.

Riptide Gym

150 Kings Road,

Brighton

☎ *01273 725444*

Situated on the seafront between the piers at the bottom of West Street. No

pool, but spinning classes (aerobics on a bike) and crewing classes (aerobics on a rowing machine) are a speciality. In the summer, the windows open on to a seaview, and give the rest of us a chance to watch those glistening bodies take shape.

Shape Health Studios

38 Devonshire Place,

Kemp Town

☎ *01273 234500*

Possibly the cheapest and sweetest gym in town with a swimming pool just big enough to fit four naked grannies in (we didn't try - it's just a guess). Actually the neo-classical statues are the only naked bodies allowed in since the naked single-sex days were replaced by costumes-only split sex days. There's a sauna, steam room and enough equipment to satisfy those who are looking for somewhere to spend a quiet hour, and at £25 per month, it's top value. (Also at Fonthill Road, Hove, 01273 232300.)

skates & reins

Sussex Ice Rink

Queens Square,

Brighton

☎ *01273 324677*

(see Seaside chapter for details on where to hire roller blades, skates and skateboards.)

Horse Riding

Southdown Riding School

Race Hill, Brighton

☎ *01273 679299*

Rottingdean Riding School

Chailey Avenue,

Rottingdean

☎ *01273 302155*

leisure centres

King Alfred Leisure Centre

Kingsway, Hove

☎ *01273 290290*

A flume-filled swimming pool with all the usual.

Moulsecoomb Community Sports Centre

Moulsecoomb Way, Brighton

☎ *01273 622266*

Portslade Sports Centre

Portslade Community College,

Chalky Road, Portslade

☎ *01273 411100*

Southwick Leisure Centre

Old Barn Way, Southwick

☎ *01273 263200*

Stanley Deason

Wilsons Avenue, Brighton

☎ *01273 694281*

University Of Sussex

Sports Service, Falmer

☎ *01273 678228*

Withdean Sports Complex

Tongdean Lane,

Withdean, Brighton

☎ *01273 542100*

swimming pools

Prince Regent

Church Street,

Brighton

☎ *01273 685692*

A swimming pool in the middle of town where there's a free crèche Tuesday and Thursday mornings. That means you can get a stress-free swim.

Pells outdoor swimming pool

The Pells,

North Street, Lewes

☎ *01273 472334*

An outdoor lido with plenty of room for lounging.

Saltdean Lido

Saltdean Park Road, Saltdean

☎ *01273 305155*

Opened in the 1930s by Johnny Weismuller, this is a good, proper lido just like they should be. It's open from the end of May to the end of September.

Lewes Leisure Centre Swimming Pool

Mountfield Road, Lewes

☎ 01273 486000

Swim while looking out over the Downs.

Surrenden Pool

☎ 01273 504858

On weekends, you can hire the pool for your own personal use at £43 per hour on Saturday and £46 on Sunday. Not such an extravagance if you share it with up to 30 mates.

The Triangle swimming pool

Burgess Hill

☎ 01444 876000

Flumes and waves worth travelling the distance for.

tennis and other things with raquets

Council courts are in just about every park in Brighton and Hove. You can't pre-book, but most of the courts have clubs attached. The best bet is to turn up and someone will either kick you off or collect payment. The city is very pro-active in promoting tennis to budding young Henmans and even has its own tennis development officer at the Council. Call Nicky Salmon: **01273 292570** for a list of clubs attached to the Council courts.

Badgers Tennis Club

Church Place,

Kemp Town

☎ 01273 671622

Four tennis courts in a hidden little corner of Kemp Town. Membership is £120 pa or £275 for a family of four plus a joining fee of between £10 and £50. Kids can learn to play mini-tennis from 4 years old, with indoor coaching up the road at the Manor Gym. Members can take guests in for a fiver per session up to 6 times a year.

Brighton Health and Racquet Club

See Gyms section at the start of this chapter.

Brighton Squash Club

Tongdean Lane,

Brighton

☎ 01273 383071

Dragons Health Club

See Gyms section at the start of this chapter.

Grasshoppers

The Drive, Hove

☎ 01273 330130

Pavilion and Avenue Lawn Tennis Club

19 The Droveway, Hove

☎ 01273 506087

Preston Lawn Tennis & Croquet Club

Preston Drove, Brighton

📞 *01273 505731*

Sussex County Croquet Club

Victoria Road, Southwick

📞 *01273 591874*

Sussex County Lawn Tennis Club

Kingston Lane, Southwick

📞 *01273 593644*

Withdean Sports Complex

Tongdean Lane

📞 *01273 542100*

Pay and play at these Council-run indoor courts.

stag & hen parties

(well, it's a kind of a sport)

Red 7 Leisure

Paston Place, Brighton

📞 *01273 671177*

One of the very few things we haven't personally tried, so be it on your own head...

sport to see

a bit of a flutter

Brighton Racecourse

📞 *01273 603580*

From April, flat racing kicks off three days a week at The Racecourse normally on Wednesday or Friday afternoons. If you've got kids, make sure you get to the Amateur Race Days where you can flutter on the Arab stallions on Sundays while the kids bounce on the bouncy castle.

the dogs

Coral Greyhound Track

Nevill Road, Hove

📞 *01273 204601*

cricket

Sussex County Cricket Club

The County Ground, Eaton Road, Hove

📞 *01273 827100*

The home of cricket. When the weather's fine and you've got a bit of time on your hands, is there a finer way to spend an afternoon? This year, the season runs from 18 April and finishes on 10 September with a match against Gloucester.

football

Brighton & Hove Albion Football Club

Withdean Stadium,

Tongdean Lane,

Withdean, Brighton

admin offices: 5th floor,

118 Queens Road, Brighton

📞 *01273 778855*

ticket office: 5 Queens Road, Brighton

📞 *01273 776992*

There ain't no stopping The Seagulls. Depending on when you're reading this, they'll either be lording it at the top of Division Three or having a sharp taste of nosebleed reality in Division Two. Still tenants in their own town, Brighton and Hove FC are doing well in the Withdean Stadium and there's still a plan to develop a proper ground out Falmer way, but there's a lot of forms still to be signed. In the meantime, if you want to get tickets the best thing to do is phone the ticket office.

sport sport to see

time out

health & beauty

You've had a tough day at the office and the trains weren't working - there was a track on the line or something - and you were stuck at Burgess Hill for an hour and the kids aren't well and they're screaming and not doing what you want and there was a queue a mile long in the supermarket and there was nowhere to park and it's raining and... and... and... what about me? Relax. Take the weight off your feet and have a look here. There'll be something to soothe those muscles and ease your soul. If it's gyms and swimming pools and all that strenuous stuff you're looking for, see the Sport chapter.

spas, tanks & salons

Beauty Business

65 Western Road, Hove

☎ *01273 822476*

Spot the limos parked outside on a Saturday as the essential start to a hen party weekend. Expect all the usual treatments: massage, manicures, aromatherapy, hair-styling and all-over body indulgence.

Bristol Gardens Health Spa

Bristol Gardens, Kemp Town

☎ *01273 698904*

Naturist's dream spa with four floors of naked folk happy to dispense with their modesty in return for a no-

looking policy. Mixed singles during the week and couples at weekends after 6pm.

The Flotation Tank

Crescent Clinic, 37 Vernon Terrace,

Seven Dials

☎ *01273 202221*

Back to the womb in an hour of salty, trippy, deep relaxation therapy.

The Pink Pamper

74 St James Street, Kemp Town

☎ *01273 608060*

Mixed beauty salon where men are made to feel more than welcome. Pink Pamper offers hair-styling, beauty, manicures, massage, tanning, nail extensions, aromatherapy and much, much more.

Saks Beauty Salon

David Lloyd Centre, The Marina

☎ *01273 666426*

Try the Sensory Heaven aromatherapy massage and facial for two hours of total bliss. Everything for the serious hedonist, including stand-up and lie-down sunbeds.

The Treatment Rooms

15 New Road, Brighton

☎ *01273 738886*

Blissful facials without the usual hard sell of lotions and potions afterwards. By the summer, they should have moved into next door to Pinocchio's restaurant giving even more space for some serious pampering.

healthcare

acupuncture

Dolphin House Clinic

14 New Road, Brighton

☎ *01273 324790*

Elaine Gibbons

☎ *01273 562676*

Specialises in pregnancy.

Steve Guthrie

(Also at Dolphin House)

Dyke Road Natural Therapy Centre,

274 Dyke Road, Brighton

☎ *01273 561844*

Janine McKerron

☎ *0802 693929*

Anne Marie Urbanowicz & Thomas Sydenham

The Crescent Clinic,

☎ *37 Vernon Terrace, Seven Dials*

01273 202221

The Waytefield Clinic

37 Preston Drove, Preston Park

☎ *01273 550727*

Good holistic clinic with diverse range of therapies, run by physical therapist Margaret King.

clairvoyant & healers

Ruth Farber Nathan

☎ *01273 305664*

✉ *ruthfarbernathan@aol.com*

Discreet and spookily accurate with a celebrity clientele.

Sally Roberts

Holistic Health Clinic,

53 Beaconsfield Road, Preston Circus

☎ *01273 696295*

Intuitive healing.

reflexology

Yael Jury

☎ *01273 390151*

Home visits.

chinese medicine

Chinese Medicine Centre

122 St James Street,

Kemp Town

☎ *01273 699852*

chiropractors

Brighton Chiropractic Clinic

34 Brunswick Square, Hove

☎ *01273 733469*

Helle Henrikson

Lewes

☎ *01273 483327*

alternative health clinics

Dolphin House Children's Clinic

14 New Road, Brighton

☎ *01273 324790*

Dolphin House is a registered charity and has a sliding scale of donations, providing homeopaths, acupuncturists, nutritionists, auric healing, osteopathy and herbal treatments. The same practitioners also run an adult clinic at normal prices.

homeopathy

For general advice and orders, call *Helios Pharmacy on 01892 537254*. For consultations contact the following:

Kate Diamontopolou

Preston Park

☎ *01273 563787*

Expert in vaccinations.

Sahani Gonzales

☎ *01273 689194*

Jan Mathew

Fiveways

☎ *01273 388857*

Pemma Sanders

Kemp Town

☎ *01273 699775*

holistic massage

Michelle Guilford

☎ *01273 690793*

Debi Jakeman

☎ *01273 724554*

Philippa King

The Clinic, 69 Gordon Road,

Preston Park

☎ *01273 232629*

Magda Reising

☎ *01273 735071*

Reiki master.

Ruth Smith

☎ *02173 699470*

Sharon Williams

☎ *07720 190722*

Will also do home visits.

Janice Wolsey

☎ 01273 711799

📱 07976 432104

📧 UKHandsOn@aol.com

Will also do home visits.

nutrition

Vicky Lader

☎ 01273 772420

Weight loss and nutrition counseling

Caroline Warren

☎ 0410 864588

Food intolerance testing

osteopathy

including cranial osteopathy

Rex Brangwyn

98 The Drive, Hove

☎ 01273 775559

Cranial therapy - brilliant for kids.

Aaras Patel

Dyke Road Natural Therapy Centre,

274 Dyke Road, Brighton

☎ 01273 561844

Aaras moved from Deryn Bell's old practice in Preston Park when Deryn moved to Devon last year. She specialises in cranial paediatric and structural osteopathy and is particularly good with children.

Liz Pegg

The Crescent Clinic,

37 Vernon Terrace, Brighton

☎ 01273 202221

rebirthing

Pat Bennaceur

☎ 01273 720853

yoga & meditation

Alive

25-27 Castle Street, Brighton

☎ 01273 739606

Hatha yoga on Monday 8.15(pm), Wednesday 6pm, Thursday 11.15am, Sunday 9.30pm.

Brighton Buddhist Centre

17 Titchbourne Street, North Laine

☎ 01273 772090

Drop-in and courses in yoga and meditation.

Brighton Natural Health Centre

27 Regent Street, North Laine

☎ 01273 600010

Evolution Arts and Natural Health Centre

2 Sillwood Terrace, Brighton

☎ 01273 729803

Kemp Town Crypt Community Centre

St George's Road, Kemp Town

Astanga-based yoga, beginners and general level, Thursdays 6pm-7.30pm

Natural Bodies

18 Bond Street, Brighton

📞 *01273 677949*

Look out for Liz Warrington's Iyengar classes (01273 504692) for adults and kids.

Phoenix Community Centre

7 Phoenix Place, Brighton

📞 *01273 602965*

Osho's Kundalini Meditation every Tuesdays at 7pm, with monthly meditation Sundays. Osho meditations are physical and cathartic for people who think of shopping lists every time they try to meditate. Kundalini is for the end of the day and is peaceful and deeply relaxing.

Southover Community Centre Yoga

📞 *Southover Street, Hanover*

Monday nights (7.30pm) drop in for Iyengar. No phone number available.

pregnancy & birth

active birth classes

Karel Ironside

365 Ditchling Road, Preston Park

📞 *01273 277309*

midwifery

Wisewoman

📞 *01273 276288*

waterbirths

Active Birth Centre

📞 *020 7482 5554*

Order your birthing pool and they'll deliver and collect.

dentists

East Sussex Health Authority will provide you with a full list of dentists (01273 485300). Those listed here have been recommended by local residents; this is not meant to be a selective service, but a helpful word-of-mouth guide.

Note: East Sussex Health Authority has not seen or endorsed this guide.

Fiveways Dental Practice

288 Ditchling Road, Brighton

📞 *01273 504923*

Chris Gull

01273 690696

Hove Court Dental Centre

2 New Church Road, Hove

📞 *01273 770377*

Holistic dental practice using chiropractic dentistry, homeopathy and cranial osteopathy.

Martin Kean

The Avenue Dental Surgery,
37 Stanford Avenue, Brighton

📞 *01273 554082*

Paddy Naylor

32 Brunswick Place, Hove

📞 *01273 732607*

Child-friendly dentist.

DM Shepherd

38 Surrenden Road, Preston Park

📞 *01273 501909*

Peter Smith

📞 *01273 711999*

Designer dentistry.

J Wood

38 Montpelier Road, Brighton

📞 *01273 733901*

Sue Wood

4/5 North Street Quadrant, Brighton

(by the Clock Tower)

📞 *01273 325132*

Mr Woods

47 Montefiore Road, Hove

📞 *01273 732485*

doctors

East Sussex Health Authority will provide you with a full list of dentists (01273 485300). Local residents have recommended those listed here; this is not meant to be a selective service, but a helpful word-of-mouth guide.

Note: East Sussex Health Authority has not seen or endorsed this guide.

Dr Adam

4 The Old Steine, Brighton

📞 *01273 685588*

Dr Alice Butler

138 Beaconsfield Villas, Brighton

📞 *01273 552212*

Dr Gray

Park Crescent, 1A Lewes Road,

Brighton

📞 *01273 603531*

Dermot Kelleher

100 Beaconsfield Villas, Brighton

📞 *01273 555999*

Dr Sacks

Montpelier Surgery, 2 Victoria Road,

Brighton

📞 *01273 328950*

Former paediatrician.

health & beauty

dentists • doctors

time out

days out & pub walks

days out & pub walks a bit of culture

Looking for that perfect Sunday pub lunch with a cobweb clearing walk? Something to do with the kids during the holidays that's a bit more interesting than the latest episode of The Tweenies? Something to do on a miserable Thursday? Have you ever seen the world through a camera obscura?

Foot and Mouth has devastated much of the rural tourist industry and Sussex has been hit hard. Check with some of the farms before you set off on your day out to see if they're still open.

a bit of culture

Anne of Cleves House Museum

52 Southover Street,

Lewes

☎ *01273 474610*

Bentley Wildfowl and Motor Museum

Halland, Nr Lewes

☎ *01825 840573*

Bateman's

Burwash, nr Tunbridge Wells

☎ *01435 882302*

Rudyard Kipling's home after he left Rottingdean in 1902 until 1936. Corn grinding on Saturdays in the water-driven turbines.

Battle Abbey and 1066 Battle of Hastings Battlefield

Battle

☎ *01424 773792*

Guided tour through one of history's bloodiest moments, and abbey ruins. Children's play area.

The Body Shop Tour

Watersmead,

Littlehampton

☎ *0800 0960809*

Chartwell

Westerham, Kent

☎ *01732 868381*

Winston Churchill's home for more than 40 years.

Glenda Clarke, Tourist Board Guide

📞 & 📠 *01273 888596*

📧 *glendaclarke@cwctv.net*

Glenda Clarke knows the secrets of Brighton more than most and leads her walks through some of the city's more interesting history. "Spooky Brighton Ghost Walk" First Saturday every month of the year, 8pm from Visitor Information Centre, Bartholomew Square. "Legends of the Lanes" "Rich and Famous - and infamous!" A more interesting walk of fame than the Marina's version promises "Quadrophenia" relives May '64. Mods and Rockers rule, OK. Follow the films progess through the streets and alleys. Jimmy's back!

Fishbourne Roman Palace

Salthill Road, Fishbourne

Nr Chichester

📞 *01243 785859*

Foredown Tower Countryside Centre

Foredown Road, Hove

📞 *01273 292092*

Home to a fascinating Camera Obscura - but remember you need a nice day for it to work properly. Open Thursday, Friday, Saturday, Sunday.

Glynde Place

Glynde

📞 *01273 858224*

16th century house in lovely little village near Lewes. Lunch at the Trevor Arms

Kipling Gardens

Rottingdean

Nothing to do with exceedingly good cakes, but he of "The Jungle Book" and "If" fame. Rudyard lived here 1897-1902. Visitors can summon his spirit in the wild garden or by playing croquet on the gorgeous lawns.

Lewes Castle and Barbican House Museum

169 High Street,

Lewes

📞 *01273 486290*

Michelham Priory

Upper Dicker, Hailsham

📞 *01323 844224*

Gorgeous Tudor mansion and medieval priory with moat.

Regency Town House

Brunswick Square,

Hove

📞 *01273 206306*

Grade 1 listed building and heritage centre which transports its visitors into the heart of urban 1820's life in Hove. It maybe beautiful and interesting and all that, but not particularly kiddy friendly.

days out & pub walks a bit of culture

Wakehurst Place

nr Haywards Heath

☎ *01444 894066.*

Country estate of the world-famous Kew Gardens and home to the new 80 million pound Millennium Seed Bank project which aims to save thousands of endangered plant species from extinction.

It features an interactive exhibition to explain the project and the chance to look into the laboratories and see the scientists at work. Wakehurst also has 180 acres of formal botanical gardens and woodland, the Elizabethan mansion, a gift shop, and restaurant.

West Blatchington Windmill

North of Holmes Ave,

Hove

Last open to millers in 1897, this lovely old windmill is almost in full working order with much of the original bits and bobs still there.

Take the kids to see what life was like in a rural milling town (such as Hove?) and then treat them to tea in the barn.

for kids

Ashdown Forest

🖥 *www.ashdownforest.co.uk*

Reputedly the place which inspired AA Milne's Pooh sticks episode.

Bockets Farm

Leatherhead

☎ *01372 363764*

Working farm with cows, pigs, sheep, water buffalos and llamas, lambing, tractor rides and play area. At Christmas, it's the best Santa's grotto around. A great half way house to meet up with mates from London.

Borde Hill

Haywards Heath

☎ *01444 450326.*

Two hundred acres of parkland, bluebell woods and pirates adventure play area, walks, lake and wood.

Butlins

☎ *01243 820202*

OK, OK. But your kids are not going to have the same snobbish pre-conceptions as you have when they see Noddyland and the dome covered flumes and sub-tropical swimming pool. A family ticket at Bognor is £16.50 for the day (10am-8pm). You can stay at the resort for more and do the Red Coat thing after the kids have gone to bed, or stay in some lovely little B&B in Arundel and come back the next day. The Jublilee Guest House (01243 863016) is bang opposite Butlins for weekend visitors who can't get onto the resort itself. Think of your kids and tell your mates it's the new Disneyland.

Chessington World of Adventures

Chessington Park,

Chessington

☎ *01372 727227*

Fun for all the family as long as you can afford the themepark price of £19.50 for adults and a staggering £15.50 for the 4-13's. It's only open from April to October but kids love Cartoonland and Dragon Falls.

Devils Dyke

☎ *01273 886200*

Get there on the heritage open top bus from Brightonif you don't fancy the drive.

Drusillas Zoo Park

Alfriston (on the A26)

☎ *01323 870234*

Fantastic small animal zoo with creative workshops, train, and huge picnic area with play apparatus for bigger kids and playbarn for toddlers.

Herstmonceux Science Centre

Herstmonceux, nr Eastbourne

☎ *01323 832731*

Originally the home of the Royal Greenwich Observatory, this is just the job for budding scientists

Llama Trekking

Walk with llamas. Picnic lunches are

provided in the summer.

☎ *01273 835656* for details.

Middle Farm

Firle (on the A26)

☎ *01323 811411*

£1 entry fee to see small animals, and to watch the milking of the Jersey herd at 3.30pm. Kids wooden play area. Tea shop, cider barn, organic food store and craft shop with picnic tables outside. The Apple Festival in mid October has live music, hot mulled cider, a fairground, horse and cart races, toffee apple dunking and all things British and attracts about 3,500 people. (See also Organics)

Paradise Park

Avis Road, Newhaven

☎ *01273 512123*

Garden centre with botanic gardens and water gardens as well a fossil collection, dinosaur exhibition and rides for the kids. Café.

Rye Heritage Centre

Strand Quay, Rye

☎ *01797 226696*

Ghosts and smugglers in Rye's walking, talking tour of the history of gorgeous old Rye.

Wish Tower Puppet Museum

Martello Tower,

73 Edward's Parade

Eastbourne

☎ *01323 410440*

Puppets from east and west, present and past.

pub walks

The Anchor Inn at Barcombe

☎ *01273 4000414*

If you fancy a good walk to and from your pub lunch, park at the carpark on right hand side of the A275 just before Barcombe, and follow the river to the pub, crossing over at the only possible place. On a summer's day, it's heaven; in winter, it's muddy but serene 40 minute walk. Boat rides and ice creams at the pub's kiosk, and good food at the pub wait you. And it's child and dog friendly.

The Anchor Inn at Hartfield

☎ *01892 770424*

The Bell Inn at Burwash

☎ *01435 882304*

The Bear at Burwash

☎ *01435 882540*

The Elstead Inn

Elstead

☎ *01730 813662*

Real ale, ossabucco and home-made rhubarb ice cream worth the hour's drive.

Firle Place

Firle

(off the A27 on the way to

Eastbourne)

A beautiful old house, full of history. You know the deal. Right in the courtyard there's a cute little tea rooms where you can get your smoked salmon sandwiches and teas. Perfect after a walk on the Downs.

The Giant's Rest at Wilmington

☎ *01323 870207*

Half Moon

Ditchling Road,

Plumpton

☎ *01273 890253*

Walkers retreat and Sunday lunch favourite, but arrive before 12.30 if you want to eat before 2pm. The bar is always packed, hiking boots piled outside the door, and if you're late, you'll have to suffer the blaring TV and billiards crowd in the annex.

The garden is paradise for children, and possibly the best in the area. If its raining, the smoke's too much and the bar is full, it's only a five minute drive to The Jolly Sportsman at East Chiltington, but the kids won't thank you.

Hungry Monk

Polegate

📞 *01323 482178*

Gorgeous old thatched pub with beams, roaring fires and the business for a full on romantic evening with your true love. Set in the middle of a picturesque Sussex village, it's also a good bet for a Sunday lunch and walk. Said the be the originator of the very first Banoffee Pie

The Jolly Sportsman

Chapel Lane,

East Chiltington

📞 *01273 890400*

Reinvented recently as an ever so posh, rustic restaurant. The Venetian blinds, log fires, candlelit tables (for lunch and dinner) and Modern European food (John Dory, scallops in garlic and parsley) make the vibe distinctly adult, and a perfect place to treat yourself for a smart lunch in the country.

A few locals still huddle the bar, while the *Guardian* and *Telegraph* readers (and writers) laze over the papers and ponder whether to go for the 2 course for £15.85 or the 3 course for £19.85. The garden is a haven for kids, but you won't find any nuggets on the menu. The chef will do half portions of anything you want from the main menu though - including pasta and sausages.

Littlington Tea Gardens

Littlington, East Sussex

Established over a 100 years ago, the tea gardens are the perfect place to go after a stroll in Seven Sisters Park. Enjoy a delicious English tea in the midst of a host of gorgeous flowers. Littlington cream tea: tea, two scones, cream, jam and butter (£4). Savoury tasties including sandwiches are also on offer. Honey roast ham salad (£5). Baked potato with Greek yoghurt and fresh herbs (£4.50) and they have a licence, try the Don Darius at £8 a bottle.

The Mermaid Inn at Rye

📞 *01797 223065*

Gorgeous ancient pub with good food and four posters in five of the 31 bedrooms (@ £75pp). A pricey treat for a romantic weekend away.

The New Inn at Winchelsea

📞 *01797 226252*

The Ram Inn at Firle

📞 *01273 858222*

Classic cars and open tops crowd the car park in this otherwise sleepy village on Sunday lunchtimes and misty evenings when the food is hot, the music is live, and the fires roar. It's recently been taken over by the landlord's offspring, and is now hopping with parents and their kids on a weekend. Something to do with the piles of toys in the family room, the large spaces, the toddler loo seats and the promise of a children's playground in the garden perhaps? For a weekend walk, follow signs from the pub to Firle Beacon, and make sure you've got your kite. If it's too windy for the top of the hill, follow the mass of ramblers around the back of the village.

The Rose and Crown at Mayfield

☎ 01435 872200

The Sandrock Inn at Ditchling

☎ 01273 842777

A warm welcome from Val and Vern in a lovely village pub. There's a bizarre Tex Mex theme inside, but people do eat the strangest things in villages.

The Shepherd and Dog at Faulking

☎ 01273 857382

Lovely old pub with little poo sticks stream running through the garden which is perched on the back of Devil's Dyke. A lane next to the garden leads up onto the top of the Dyke and affords some breathtaking views of the area. Book if you want a table for a weekend lunch. But parents beware they will not let kids into the bar even to buy a packet of crisps, so if you are a family don't go in winter!

The Smuggler's Inn at Alfriston

6 Market Cross,
Waterloo Square
☎ 01323 870241

Sussex Ox

Milton Street,
Alfreston
☎ 01323 870840

Great for kids with fantastic adventure playground. Perfect for a huge lunch before a walk to the Long Man of Wilmington.

Tiger Inn at East Dean

☎ 01323 423209

A long summer afternoon treat: lunch at the Tiger Inn, then visit the Seven Sisters Sheep Farm before walking through the woods and down the wiggly path to the beach.

The Trevor Arms

The Street, Glynde
☎ 01273 858208

Dogs, hiking boots and green wellies are littered around this delightful proper country pub. The food is good too - Sunday roasts are hearty and no nonsense.

The White Horse
at Ditchling

☎ *01273 842006*

walks in and around
brighton & hove

The walks listed here are recommended for being particularly buggy/kiddie, disabled, old folk and dog friendly.

Brighton Racecourse

Warren Road, Brighton

The race track runs across the top of East Brighton Park, and really, there is no better sight than watching the horses being exercised in the early morning mists against the backdrop of the English Channel. The air's beautiful and fresh - it's the perfect way to start a day.

East Brighton Park

Wilson Avenue, Kemp Town

On the edge of Brighton with options for long walks over to Ovingdean and Rottingdean Windmill. Unlike other parks in B&H, it can be a bit unpoopscooped, and the playground area is one of the shabbiest, but The Friends of Sheepcote Valley are doing a fantastic job in replanting and protection. It's the best wild space in town and the variety of bird life is a joy. The Pavilion Café, with its clock stuck at 4.15, is almost always closed,

except for the summer months when the local campsite uses it for its breakfast.

Hollingbury Golf Course

Ditchling Road,

Brighton

Keep to the edges, dodge the golf balls and head to the woods overlooking Wild Park. The permanent breeze makes it the perfect walk on hot summer days.

Hove Park

off Old Shoreham Road,

Hove

Circular, large, and filled with squirrels. Children's playground, café with Victorian balcony, bowling green and miniature railway.

St Ann's Well Gardens

Sommerhill Road, Hove

Small but perfectly formed little park in the middle of Hove with a scented garden for the blind, enormous playground for kids of all ages, and squirrels and conkers everywhere. Café, toilets and a relaxed community spirit.

The Upper Lodges

(first right off the road to Ditchling from A27)

A myriad of forest walks linking up with Stanmer Park below.

Stanmer Park

(just behind the Brighton

by-pass A27, near Falmer)

Picturesque village turned park with café, toilets, plenty of open space for running around, tree climbing, picnicking, kite flying and cycling. Dairy farm (with calves all year round), duck pond and woods.

Sussex Downs

Endless circular walks with grass paths.

The Undercliff

The severe weather conditions this year have almost destroyed one of Brighton's favourite treats with part of the cliff above the undercliff collapsing unexpectedly over Christmas.

The Undercliff walk which leads from Asda at the Marina to Rottingdean and beyond normally takes walkers, joggers and cyclists past some of the best and sandiest beaches in town; let's hope the Council can make it safe in time for summer.

Wild Park

(off the Lewes Road, just past

Moulsecoomb)

Shortish circular walk unless you're going to climb the steep hill up to Hollingbury Golf Course, but stacked with rabbits.

Withdean Park

(off London Road, past Preston Park)

Not much more than a glorified dog exercise area, except for its collection of lilac trees. Surrounded by rabbit and squirrel filled woods.

the mini
juicy guide to lewes

A gaggle of Lewes residents have given us their juiciest tips and within our mini guide, you'll find restaurants, neighbourhoods, schools and a couple of pubs. If there are any other pubs in Lewes you know of, or if you feel anything vital has been left out... let us know.

The ancient town of Lewes lies about five miles outside Brighton and snuggles around the river Ouse. On the outside Lewes seems a picturesque, old-fashioned kind of a town, an impression backed up by the medieval buildings and the Georgian architecture. But looks can be deceptive and a dark past lurks behind this respectable veneer. First populated by the Saxons, Lewes has had a turbulent history and one of its most bloody episodes is remembered today. In a bloody Protestant purge, Elizabeth I's sister, Queen Mary, had 17 martyrs burnt to death in the High Street. Lewes has never forgotten it and on November 5th, at the famous Lewes fireworks display, an effigy of the Pope burns at the top of the pyre in memory of those Protestant martyrs. Dozens of local bonfire societies march through the town dressed in ancient garb, bonfires are lit and there is a pervasive atmosphere of witchcraft and paganism which thousands flock to witness.

The town contains many sites of historical interest including Lewes Castle, which is of Norman origin, the Anne of Cleaves House and the Folk Museum. These days, Lewes is exceedingly popular and many people relocate here attracted by the gentler pace and the good schools both in the private and public sector. It is also famous for its antiques and huge auction rooms that lie between the school hill and the station.

Southover is the oldest part of town and is made up of old cottages and large family houses with gardens. Houses in the very popular Southover High Street will cost you anything between £300,000-£700,000. Another wannabe area is the more suburban Wallands, where you will find large Edwardian, semi-detached, houses and cottages. The most expensive houses around are near Grange gardens, and cost around £700,000. The other most popular streets are The Avenue and Prince Edward Road which again will cost you anywhere between £500,000-£700,000. Bear in mind that houses go as fast as they come up and all the estate agents have long waiting lists. The Cliffe area attracts the more arty types, the houses are smaller but the community atmosphere is strong particularly since the floods of October 2000. Not surprisingly, house prices in the flooded areas are in a state of flux.

pubs

The Rainbow

179 High Street, Lewes

📞 01273 472170.

Well not quite a pub since it's a Zel outpost with the flavour of Brighton beamed down the A27 for the more avant-garde folk of Lewes. Expect the DJs, the crowd and the good food that you've come to know and love in Zel-land. The roof terrace has a treat of a view of the castle and the rest of this sweet little town.

The Snowdop Inn

South Street, Lewes

📞 01273 471018

Wonderfully eccentric hippy haven decorated in vibrant purple and blues. The girls' loos are Barbie pink and they have a great selection of odd sculptures that may have been salvaged from skips. It's worth a visit just to listen to their eclectic record collection, which ranges from Blue Note jazz to early Janis Joplin. Perfect for a Sunday lunchtime jaunt, they stock some organic beer and kids are welcomed with open arms. Expect great comfort-style vegetarian food at weekends and an extensive selection of scrummy home-made pizza.

restaurants

asian

The Dilraj

12 Fisher Street, Lewes

📞 01273 479279

Well-regarded Indian restaurant sporting a very blue version of Indian decor. The food is wonderful, particularly the Peshwari Chicken (£7.25) and Prawn Sagwalla, (£4.90).

Pailin

19-20 Station Road, Lewes

📞 01273 473906

Delicious Thai food served in full oriental style. Small but popular restaurant that becomes very busy at weekends but you can easily find a

table without booking in the week.
Try a mixed starter of satay, tempura,
spring roll, and one ton dumpling is
£7.50 or hot and sour fisherman's
soup, with lemon grass and mixed
seafood (£7.00).

The Panda Garden

162 High Street, Lewes

☎ *01273 473235*

Chinese food fans love it and swear it
is the most authentic in town which
means it is 'the' place to get a takeaway. The most popular dishes are:
Crisp aromatic duck (£8.50 a quarter)
King Prawns, stir fried with ginger
and spring onion (£6.50).

Shanaz Indian Cuisine

83 High Street, Lewes

☎ *01273 488028*

Sumptuous Indian restaurant
decorated in a spicy red. Many out of
towners trek here for a weekend treat
so book early. Chicken Jalfreshi
(£5.95) (Saag Paneer. (£3.95).

italian

Ask

186 High Street,

Lewes

☎ *01273 479330*

Part of the national chain so expect
generic Italian pizza and pasta fare.
Probably Lewes' most popular
restaurant. Pizzas go for around £6-7.

Tortellinis

197 High Street, Lewes

☎ *01273 487766*

Delicious traditional Italian food
served in cosy surroundings. Try the
Carciofini, a mixed green salad with
Parmesan and artichoke hearts
(£3.95) or the Tagliatelle Paradiso,
served with mushroom, aubergines,
spinach, tomato, and cream sauce
(£6.25). The appalling acoustics
forbid the chance of an intimate
dinner but they're apparently
attempting to sort it out.

upmarket

Circa

145 High Street, Lewes

☎ *01273 4717777*

Conran influenced minimalist
interiors with crisp white table clothes
and reasonably priced tasty dishes.
Expect modern British with a twist of
fusion. Circa is the hippest restaurant
ever to hit Lewes. Wood roasted pear
with a blue cheese and chilli
complimented by a rocket and walnut
salad (£5.75) Pan-fried red mullet
with char grilled fennel and red
chicory with an orange and coriander
sauce. (£13.75). The wine list is a mix
of New World and European and they
are soon introducing an organic range.

Shelley's Hotel

The High Street, Lewes

juicy lewes restaurants: asian • italian • upmarket

☏ *01273 472361*

Posh French nosh served in cavernous surroundings which means that though the food is scrumptious the ambience is more than lacking. Steamed cannon of lamb on Pommes Anna with lemon and coriander jus. (£16.50). Delice of brille topped with tarragon mouse on buttered leeks with a moules and saffron sauce. (£16.50). Be warned that everyone can hear every word. Probably not the place to have a domestic.

schools

Lewes New School

Talbot Terrace, Lewes

☏ *01273 477074*

Felicia McGarry has taken what she considers to be the best of Steiner, Montessori and progressive education and designed this idealistic vision after years in the State sector. The flooding that devastated the school only weeks after it opened means that it would be unfair to give a review of what we saw, but the spirit of Lewes New School is certainly willing.

Lewes Old Grammar School

7 King Henry's Road,

Lewes

☏ *01273 473246*

Independent school for ages between 5-18. Many love it, but locally the

word is that the boys thrive more than the girls.

Priory Comprehensive

Mountfield Road, Lewes

☏ *01273 476231*

Huge sprawling school near the swimming pool with excellent facilities and a happy, inclusive environment. The Priory is known for its progressive outlook, though some say the large classes make bullying difficult to deal with effectively.

Southover C of E Primary School

Potters Lane, Lewes

☏ *01273 473015*

Southover is known locally as the best private school in town except you don't have to pay fees.

St Pancras, Catholic Primary

De Monfort Road, Lewes

☏ *01273473017*

An old fashioned but cosy school that places a strong emphasis on the three 'R's As there are only five classes in the whole school, the classes are integrated with mixed age groups.

the word on the street

This chapter contains the kind of vital information you need to survive whether you've just moved to the area or have lived in Brighton for years. We've compiled a list of everyone you need to make your life run smoothly, with names and numbers gathered from local folk and our own address books. It's a motley list that will grow over the years, but everyone here has been tried and tested. The feedback from the first edition also confirms that we're right about our plumbers, decorators and even our dogwalkers.

We refused all advertising, bribes and freebies to compile this list, but Brighton and Hove are awash with local magazines that will give you more advertising-led information. While we can't recommend anything we haven't tried, these magazines do seem to provide a good service. Make sure you pick a copy of ABC magazine for information about child-friendly Sussex; The Latest for clubbing and listings; The Insight or Wave for alternative stuff; The Source for students and teen info; and G Scene and Impact for gay and lesbian Brighton and Hove. All these magazines can all be found scattered around advertisers' cafes, shops and schools, so it won't be long before you come across a copy.

allotments

If vegetables are your thing, there are 2350 allotments plots in Brighton, Hove, Portslade and Rottingdean which you can rent for £22.60 a year. Several are badly underused, and the Council is keen to encourage a new breed of gardeners to take the Sussex air either on their own or as part of a community. The plots come in two sizes: 125 or 250 square metres. Call the allotments officer at the Council on *01273 292225* for more details.

car mechanics

Mac Electric
Bates Road, Brighton

📞 *01273 555941*

Super friendly. Was recommended by someone who said "They listen to you as if you really know what you are talking about when describing the little foibles of your car and never ever roll their eyes as if to say 'Oh no not another hopeless woman driver'.

Blundells garage for Peugeots
☎ 01273 821818

Dave'n'Pauls
☎ 01273 420107
Citroen experts behind Tates on the Old Shoreham Road.

Jeff Emery
Rock Place, Kemp Town
☎ 01273 690491

J and J Elmes
Arundel Road, Kemp Town
☎ 01273 607926

John Micklan - The Jaguar Man
☎ 01273 607808

12a Hollingdean Road, Brighton
Word has it that people bring their Jags to this unassuming little garage off the Vogue Gyratory from all over the country.

Mark Bayley
2 Cambridge Grove, Hove
☎ 01273 327609
Apparently 30% of Brighton and

Hove's taxis use this guy, so he must be doing something right.

dog walkers

Dial a Pet
☎ 01273 679377

It's a Dog's Life
☎ 01273 720863

Canine Creche
☎ 01293 782754
Rosemary Corbett
(looks after dogs all over Sussex)

hairdressers

Mark @ Saks
David Lloyd Fitness Centre
at The Marina
☎ 01273 666426
Top notch stylist who owns the franchise for the national Saks chain. By the time this book hits the shelves he will have opened his second Saks in Ship Street. See Saks in Health and Beauty chapter.

James Clifton
📱 077333 06639
John Frieda trained, in-home hairdressing.

Gary @ Stage One
Bond Street,
Brighton
☎ 01273 733633

Drag queen by night, hairdresser by day.

Barnets

15 St George's Place, London Road

📞 01273 676862

You can't go wrong with a hair shop called Barnets.

Venus Hair Design

61 Old Steine, Brighton

📞 01273 775322

Sparrows

100 Trafalgar Street, North Laine

📞 01273 622321

Traditional barber with shave, hot towel and the works.

house stuff

It's worth giving Brighton College of Technology a call if you're looking for an extra pair of hands. There's a noticeboard in the Students Union where you can advertise your job to suitably proficient students, and the college picks up the insurance. Phone *01273 667788*.

builders

Ian Ross

📞 01273 888657

Tony James

📞 01273 390153

📱 07802 609937

carpenters

Matt Myles

📱 07967 823727

domestic appliance engineers

Chris Baker

📞 01273 513557

dishwashers, washing machines, tumble driers etc

electrical supplies

Etheridges

Arundel Street,

Kemp Town

📞 01273 603783

Cheap bits for your washing machine.

painters & decorators

Mike Webber

📞 01273 604468

Interiors and exteriors, Mike specialises in paint effects.

Jason Dean

📞 01273 235901

📱 07867 675721

Painter and decorator

John Garrett

📱 07970 073145

Perfectionist painter and decorator

plasterers

John Roberts

📱 01273 889220

plumbers

Colin The Plumber

☎ *01273 671617*

Also heating engineer.

Malcolm Parkes

☎ *01273 700074*

📱 *07715 491696*

tilers

Ty Craker

☎ *01273 626919*

13

useful information

Brighton & Hove Council

☎ *01273 290000*

cashpoints

(other than main banks and building societies)

Barclays:
• Royal Sussex Hospital outside building

Link machine:
• outside main post office, Ship Street

Nat West:
• next to Mothercare on Upper Mall, Churchill Square
• BP garage on Ditchling Road
• Shell garage on Preston Road
• Q8 garage on A23/A27 roundabout

chemists (late)

Ashtons

98 Dyke Road, Seven Dials

☎ *01273 325020*

9am-10pm.

Westons

6 Coombe Terrace, Brighton

☎ *01273 605354*

9am-10pm.

citizen's advice

Citizen's Advice

☎ *01273 772277*

synagogues

Middle Street Synagogue

Middle Street, Brighton

☎ *01273 888855*

The oldest and most splendid of synagogues in the area. It's an Orthodox working shul but open to the general public on the first Sunday of every month from March to November. During the May festival, it's open every Sunday. Its sister synagogue is in New Church Road, Hove.

Hove Hebrew Congregation

Holland Road, Hove

☎ *01273 732035*

Brighton and Hove New Synagogue

Palmeira Avenue, Hove

☎ *01273 735343*

Reform synagogue.

Brighton and Hove Progressive Synagogue

6 Lansdowne Road, Hove

📞 01273 737223

Rabbi Elizabeth Tikvah Sarah has recently taken over from the truly progressive Paul Glantz who went out of his way to welcome mixed families into the Jewish community. The religion school is open to children of members of the shul.

churches

St Bartholomews Church

Ann Street, Brighton

📞 01273 685142

C of E Grade 1 listed building which, say the children of Brighton, is the real Noah's arc upside down.

St Paul's

West Street,

Brighton

📞 01273 739639

Astonishingly laid back local church which is packed to the gills every Christmas as families come to show their kids what church-going should be like.

St Peter's

York Place, Brighton

📞 01273 682960

Austere Parish church with proper job choir in frilly collars and awesome organ. C of E.

mosques

Brighton Islamic Society Mosque

150 Dyke Rd, Brighton

📞 01273 506472

buddist

Brighton Buddhist Centre

17 Titchbourne St, North Laine

📞 01273 772090

county court

County Court, William Street, Brighton

📞 01273 674421

drugs advice

drugs advice and infomation service

📞 01273 321000

emergency utilities

emergency gas, electricity & water

central number: 📞 0800 7838866

family planning

Family Planning Clinic

📞 01273 242091

gay brighton

The Gay switchboard on *01273 204050* is there for counselling and advice, and also helps find rooms in gay-friendly accommodation. There are also some specifically gay hotels/B&Bs

in the Accommodation chapter.

Brash (youth community scheme)

📞 01273 293632

Brighton Lesbian And Gay Switchboard

📞 01273 204050

Brighton Relate

📞 01273 697997

hospitals

These are the only hospitals with A&E facilities:

Royal Sussex

Eastern Road, Kemp Town

📞 01273 696955

Southlands

Upper Shoreham Road, Shoreham

📞 01273 455622

Victoria

Nevill Road, Lewes

📞 01273 474153

For health and dental care for registered NHS patients: 📞 0800 665544

mags & rags

clubbing

G-Scene and *Impact* are both predominantly gay mags. *The Source* is Newsquest's student rag, packed with clubs and pubs and listings for anyone who has the energy to wade through its migraine-inducing design. *The Latest* is a monthly magazine with listings and features.

news

The Argus, the only daily newspaper serving East and West Sussex, comes out twice a day. The Property to let supplement is published on Mondays; Property to buy on Wednesdays; business with Sitsvac on Tuesday; more jobs on Thursday; and cars for sale on Friday. Saturday carries weekend and sports supplements.

Brighton and Hove News is free from the Council and is delivered each month

Friday Ad is the Loot of the South East and comes out every Friday.

The Insight (formerly New Insight) is probably the best of the local reads. It's monthly and free from restaurants, pubs and cafes around town. It does take ads, but their reviews, unlike most in this city, don't seem to be from deep in the pocket of their advertisers.

The Leader is the freebie published by

Argus and distributed to every home on Fridays. It is particularly good on cars for sale.

Latest Homes is The Latest's weekly property mag and has features on celebrity homes and lifestyle as well as ads for houses and flats for sale and rent. It's free and you can pick it up from supermarkets, newsagents etc.

Limited Edition is the glossy freebie from publisher, Newsquest.

other

ABC is the kiddie guide to Sussex and comes out three times a year in cafes in and around Brighton and Hove. ☏ *01273 542257*.

Wave is the alternative magazine for Sussex with features and news on what's happening in holistic B&H. Again, it's free and available from shops and cafes which advertise in its pages.

Brighton and Hove Life is a glossy bi-monthly which is about as OK! as it gets in this part of Sussex. Available from newsagents.

police stations

For all non-emergencies, call **Sussex Police** on **0845 6070999**. This is a central number that deals with the whole of Sussex. (Obviously, if things are a little more urgent, you should call 999).

Lost property ☏ *01273 665510*
The front desk at Brighton Police Station (John Street, Kemp Town) is open 24-hours.

post

The post depot on North Road has a late collection at 8pm.

radio stations

Southern FM - 103FM
Surf - 107FM
Radio 4A - 106.6FM

tourist information

10 Bartholomew Square, Brighton
☏ *01273 292599*
Open Monday to Friday 9am-5pm; Saturday 10am-5pm; Sunday 10am-4pm.

24-help lines

Animal welfare
☏ *0870 555 5999*
Environment Agency
☏ *0800 807060*
Childline
☏ *80800 1111*
Samaritans
☏ *0845 7909090*

Sussex Police

☎ *0845 6070999*

websites

📧 *www.thisisbrighton.co.uk* is The Argus' website and part of the massive fish4 online shopping emporium for everything from a car to a new home.

📧 *www.brighton.co.uk* for listings and events. The tourism section is controlled by the Council's city marketing division, so you can also try www.brighton-hove.gov.org and you'll come across the same information.

📧 *www.hanovernet.co.uk* and 📧 *www.kemptown.org* are both community websites for the respective areas

📧 *www.zelnet.com* is the website for the Connective, Zel's guide to Brighton from the thinking pub-goer's point of view.

📧 *www.scip.org.uk* the Sussex Community Internet Project aims to train anyone and everyone to use the internet. And it's all free.

📧 *www.seelife.brighton.co.uk* Seelife Online Magazine Arts and culture magazine news, infos, reviews

📧 *www.community.brighton.co.uk* Community Brighton lists of community organisations, links to local community sites

📧 *www.escis.org.uk* East Sussex Community Information Service huge database of community information from support groups to dentists

📧 *www.millersroad.co.uk* unpleasant glimpses from the fetid underbelly of post-student life

📧 *www.virtualfestival.org.uk* Brighton & Hove Virtual Festival. A showcase for what local people are doing with new technology in arts, education and business.

And, of course:

📧 *www.juicyguides.co.uk* for reviews and views on the ever changing scene in Brighton and Hove. Plus our City Art exhibition of local artists.

14

index a-z

index

index